"This volume by Dr. Buttrick is certainly a good book. Indeed it is one of the best books on prayer that have appeared in many years . . . It includes in its span practically every aspect of prayer. The thought is deep-going. The organization of the material is excellent. The style is fresh and vivid. The author describes himself modestly as 'only a journeyman preacher.' Would that we had more as competent."

Angus Dun, *Christian Century*

ABOUT THE AUTHOR:

George Arthur Buttrick, Preacher Emeritus to the University and Plummer Professor Emeritus of Christian Morals at Harvard University, is Harry Emerson Fosdick Visiting Professor, Union Theological Seminary. Before going to Harvard in 1955, Dr. Buttrick was for twenty-eight years pastor of Madison Avenue Presbyterian Church.

Born and educated in England, Dr. Buttrick has spent his active ministry entirely in America. He is in wide demand as a speaker and guest preacher all over the world. He is recognized as one of the most influential religious writers of this generation.

Dr. Buttrick served as editor-in-chief of the Editorial Board of The Interpreter's Bible, a twelve-volume comprehensive commentary of the Bible. His other books include *Faith and Education; So We Believe, So We Pray;* and *Sermons Preached in a University Church.*

~

Prayer is the very sword of the Saints. . . . .
        —FRANCIS THOMPSON

~

God answers sharp and sudden on some prayers,
And thrusts the thing we have prayed for in our face,
A gauntlet with a gift in't.
        —ELIZABETH BARRETT BROWNING

PRAYER

GEORGE ARTHUR BUTTRICK

ABINGDON   NASHVILLE

PRAYER

A FESTIVAL BOOK

Copyright © 1942 by Whitmore & Stone; renewal 1970 by George A. Buttrick

Published by Pillar Books for Abingdon

Festival edition published April, 1977

ISBN: 0-687-33361

Printed in the United States of America

To

THE OFFICERS, MEMBERS, AND CONGREGATION
OF THE
MADISON AVENUE PRESBYTERIAN CHURCH
NEW YORK CITY

A PATIENT AND VENTUROUS FOLK
QUICK IN VISION
IN LOVE GENEROUS
FAITHFUL IN PRAYER

"I thank my God upon every remembrance of you, always in every prayer of mine for you all making request with joy, for your fellowship in the gospel, from the first day until now; being confident of this very thing, that he which hath begun a good work in you, will perform it until the day of Jesus Christ: even as it is meet for me to think this of you all, because I have you in my heart. . . . ."—Philippians 1:3-7

FOREWORD

THIS BOOK BEGAN in a conviction of the central crea-
tiveness of prayer, and in a silent protest against yielding it to an unexamined concept of natural law. I said,
only to myself at first, "To argue that man makes natural law his servant, as when he causes water to flow
uphill, and that surely God can do as much in answer to
prayer, is no solution of the problem. For thus God is
exiled among his waterpipes and switchboards. He is no
longer Friend and Father: he is only Mechanic. Such a
faith is not the mending, but the menace, of religion. It
is no gain to find a bright rebuttal—and lose God.
What *is* the real answer?" I knew my incompetence for
the task, being only a journeyman preacher, and know
it better now that the book is written. But I believe I
have found the beginnings of a trail that will lead prayer
out of the killing shadow of the *false totalitarianism* of
the scientific theory of the world.

From that ferment of mind the book gradually
evolved. Where to begin? Not in a study of primitive
prayer—that realm of vague fact, dubious deduction,
and uncertain value—but in a preliminary study of our
world's need, and in a focal study of the prayer life of
Jesus. Thus came Part One. There naturally followed an
attempt to quiet the original ferment, and this venture,
Part Two, was called "Prayer and the World." Then another silent comment could not be dismissed: "But the
thrust of prayer into the world would be worthless, or
dangerous, without the leaven of prayer in personality."
So began another year or two of reading, this time in

7

the psychology of prayer. Many books yielded treasure; yet they seemed, in most instances, more concerned with psychology than with prayer. Therefore Part Three was titled "Prayer and Personality." That done, the book still gave no peace. The pesky voice said, "Books on prayer easily evaporate in theory. Suppose for a moment that you have found some answers: how shall they be made serviceable? People wish and need to know *how* to pray, in private devotion and in corporate worship." Thence came Part Four on "A Way of Prayer."

The field is vast? Of that fact I have been acutely aware. But the fact itself calls for a book of omnibus character to trace the field and lead to more intensive study. The task is exacting and I may fail? That fact also has been no stranger. But if it is a necessary task, someone must begin. I have both yearned and been reluctant to print these pages. Friends have chaffed in kindness, "They never will see print until someone steals the manuscript and takes it to the publishers by airplane." But here is the book, for what it is worth. It has been written during four summers, in a place remote from theological libraries. That handicap may have been fruitful: the book may be less an echo and more a voice.

The material of three series of lectures is incorporated, but the book was projected and begun before the lectures were written. The book is not a *reprise* of lectures: the lectures were cut from the substance of the book. But the friendships which the lectures granted have been a prime encouragement. THE MINISTERS' WEEK LECTURES, given in January, 1938, under the auspices of the Candler School of Theology of Emory University, Georgia, involved Chapters II, V, VII, and a combined early draft of XVII and XVIII. Dr. Lavens Thomas II was particularly kind; and faculty and students by their welcome, questions, and comment gave the lectures a better grace than they could really claim. The AYER LECTURES were given in March, 1940, under the Ayer Lectureship at the Colgate-Rochester Divinity School in Rochester, New York. They involved Chapters X, XI, XII, and XIV. The

President, Dr. Albert W. Beaven, agreed graciously on a choice of topic, and by penetrating remark enriched what the lectures tried to say. The COLE LECTURES, given under the sponsorship of the School of Religion of Vanderbilt University at Nashville, Tennessee, in April, 1941, involved Chapters IV, V and VI combined in shortened form, XI, XII, XIII, and XIV. The President of the University, Dr. Oliver C. Carmichael, showed keen interest and hospitality; and the Dean of the School of Religion, Dr. John Keith Benton, was in very truth both stimulus and cheer. Without these friends named, and many unnamed, these pages could hardly have been written.

As with earlier books, my capable secretary, Miss Elizabeth M. Eliot, has typed many pages both in rough draft and final form. My wife, Agnes Gardner Buttrick, has prepared the Index, corrected proof, and, as always, held up my hands, mind, and spirit. Miss Alice J. G. Perkins read with me in the French the valuable book, unfortunately not available in translation, by Fernand Ménégoz, *Le problème de la prière*. My colleagues in daily work, Dr. Philip Cowell Jones, the Rev. George Cooper Hood, and the Rev. John Underwood Stephens, have been colleagues in thought and friendship; and the last named has given considerable time to items of research. Miss Ethel E. King, Miss Susan Clark Lobenstine, and my sons, John A. Buttrick, G. Robert Buttrick, and David G. Buttrick, have helped in the tedious task of verifying references. The officers and people of the church to which this book is dedicated have left me debtor, both in mind and heart, by their devotion. The Notes show how large is my obligation to many authors. I have often wished that a note of reference could take voice, to tell the sincere depth of my gratitude. Many creditors are, I fear, unmentioned: this acknowledgment is poor. But the thankfulness is large—beyond the compass of words. The dubieties in this book are mine: the verities have said to me often: "Other men labored, and ye are entered into their labor."

Our world, as I write, is under grievous threats which are symptoms of worse threats. There is the threat of

armed aggression. But that itself is a sign of disease—
the multitudinous unrest of poverty-stricken masses,
robbed of their rightful security by former wars and by
an economic system which is breaking under its own
strains, who turn in tragic ignorance to the cruel demagogue and the false lure of conquest. Even that unrest is
symptomatic: the sign of spiritual debility. Our obsessed
exploitation of the planet's resources, our scramble for
gain, and latterly our scientific skepticism have left us
blind toward God. Because we acknowledge no Ultimate Sanction, no bond with the "Ideal Companion,"
the bonds of community are also broken: we feel no
kinship with our fellow man. We may break the threat
of armed aggression, but we shall gain thereby only a
little respite unless the vaster threat of world-wide insecurity is also laid. To break even that far-flung menace
would be in vain, supposing it were possible, without a
revival of faith. That revival is the deepest need. It will
not come by tongue-lashings from politicians or preachers, nor by organizations, nor by new additions to our
embarrassing store of facts. All of these are little pip-
ings in the dark. Revival of faith can never come *from
us*. It must come *from God,* in us and through us. It
must come by prayer; and, indirectly, by testimony to
prayer's light and power. We see now that Augustine,
writing his *De Civitate Dei* when the Goths under
Alaric had already sacked Rome, was a true servant of
his age. That violence also was the sign of moral weakness and spiritual decay. Those who pray are the real
light-bearers in any age. Perhaps by these pages some
may be added to their bright company.

G. A. B.

*Sequanota Club
Charlevoix, Michigan
August 25, 1941*

CONTENTS

PART FOUR

A WAY OF PRAYER

PART ONE

JESUS AND PRAYER

Chapter I

"THIS GREAT ROUNDABOUT, THE WORLD"

PRAYER, WHICH WILLIAM JAMES described as "intercourse with an Ideal Companion,"[1] is either the primary fact or the worst delusion. If God is not, "and the life of man, solitary, poore, nasty, brutish, and short,"[2] prayer is the veriest self-deceit. If God is, yet is known only in vague rumor and dark coercion, prayer is whimpering folly: it were nobler to die. But if God is in some deep and eternal sense like Jesus, friendship with Him is our first concern, worthiest art, best resource, and sublimest joy. Such prayer could brood over our modern disorder, as the Spirit once brooded over the void, to summon a new world. Prayer would not then dispel the Mystery: worship requires Mystery. God would still live in the "dark backward and abysm of time" and in the bright forward and height of eternity: He would still be as far beyond our devious thought as He is beyond our eyes. But the Mystery then would be a gracious Mystery, inviting and needing the friendship of our humanity, granting us light for life here and "authentic tidings" of life hereafter.

Perhaps prayer in our time is the key-city of an irrepressible conflict. Perhaps our scientific agnosticism knows, though dimly, that if prayer can be riddled by argument or captured by scoffing the whole realm of religion will fall. Perhaps the badly shaken forces of religion also know, though dimly, that if prayer is renewed the prevalent skepticism must bow. Fernand Ménégoz has recently suggested that prayer *is* thus crucial:

The problem of prayer! It has been a long time coming. But here it is, all at once, in very starkness. And, like a flash in the night, it throws into vivid relief the nature of the struggle, full of paradox and danger, in which religious thought is today involved. The problem of prayer: that is the critical issue. There the most desperate conflicts between the friends and foes of religion are being fought and will be fought. And the attitude which theology takes toward this issue will determine in large degree the future of Christianity in the world.[3]

If prayer fails, scientific skepticism may lead us back to "chaos and old Night." If prayer stands, our nihilistic concepts of "natural law" must reel back defeated. In the key-city of prayer two irreconcilable world-views are locked in epochal strife. Perhaps the impatience of skepticism with prayer is due, not to any outmodedness in prayer, but to skepticism's own deep misgiving, like that of the tyrant in the Browning poem:

> Do you see? just my vengeance complete,
> The man sprang to his feet,
> Stood erect, caught at God's skirts, and prayed!
> —So, *I* was afraid![4]

Religion must be quick to realize that prayer *is* the key-city—the real focus of man's present unrest. For prayer is the heart of religion. "Prayer is the very sword of the Saints."[5]

I

We turn, therefore, to our modern world. There is little choice. Books and men may covet immortality, but every man is prisoner of his date. Our age is clamorous and sharp: kaleidoscopic, shaken, disillusioned, newly questing, it gives us scant rest. We cannot now discuss prayer in general; for, though we may strive to set the issue *sub specie aeternitatis,* the attempt must begin at some point in history. For us it begins at our point in history, in an age that is not patterned, but divergent—turbulent in event and unlike in mind.

The popularity of Dr. Link's *The Return to Religion*[6] was not altogether due to its content. Like most books of instant favor, it blends truth and half-truth. Its blithe commandeering of religion as a somewhat desirable ally of the normal mind, a nostrum for psychological health, as though God were made for man, is shallow. So is its apparent assumption that extraversion is per se better than introversion—Martha being sound, while Mary is sick. Yet its homespun verities, offered with the imprimatur of applied psychology, are like a sea wind. It merited its welcome. But, with all respect, the *éclat* was considerably due to the book's timeliness. It took the tide at the turn. There is a rhythm in all nature. Belief also is strangely seasonal. There is a "return to religion." The tide has turned. Soon it may flow. We may be at the onset of a new age of faith, a sunrise era in man's pilgrimage.

II

The story of the prodigal is not local, but agelong and age-wide. When famine comes, with only husks for food, self-will thinks of home. Our generation is in "a land of sand and thorns." Our knowledge has reached an impasse; our skill is suicidal. Is there a homeland? We look for help beyond ourselves.

Knowledge has reached an impasse. Astronomy can doubtless discover more millions of worlds in more incredible reaches of space, other midge-breeds of stars in other Atlantics of the void, but to what purpose? The word of Pascal remains: a man is still nobler than the planet which crushes him, for the man knows his fate. Suns and moons apparently know nothing: man's mind under God invests them with their splendor. All their spectra and their orbits are in him. When astronomy reveals aeonian space and time, the astronomer cannot be small. Perhaps mankind's adventure is less than a wisp of smoke from a limitless smoldering, a tiny vagary of whirling electrons and the mammoth skies. Perhaps: but we need not believe it until rocks rush to build a Taj Mahal, and an ink bottle writes a Bible. Many words of

life astronomy has given, and from its book more light
will break, but *the* Word will not be found through a
telescope.

Psychology likewise threatens disappointment after
quickening almost millennial hopes. A doctor—whose
name, well known, shall not be hinted, lest our sophisti-
cates should tear him limb from limb—was sufficiently
open-minded and hopeful to refer one hundred cases to
psychiatrists. His careful judgment is that twenty were
perhaps improved, twenty were worse, and sixty apparently unchanged. He does not offer the appraisal as a
scientific verdict. He would agree that psychology has
given us new revealings and a new technique, with more
good in store. Even so, his experience is significant. It
confirms a gathering doubt. It seems to show that our
modern cult of psychiatry is token of failure in religion
rather than of success in psychiatry. What use in untan-
gling the threads of a raveled mind unless some new
pattern is offered for the reweaving? The new pattern,
to be better than a mere expedient, must imply a basic
faith in man and his world. What faith? What power to
make the faith effective? No study of the mind in its
own chamber can heal the mind. The mind does not live
merely in its own chamber. It cannot be healed merely
within itself. As well might we try to cure tuberculosis
within the lungs without benefit of air and sun. Hereinafter we shall discuss the psychology of prayer and
gratefully own the guidance which psychology has given
and can give. But let it now be written, without cap-
tiousness but without cavil: psychology is limited in
power—if only by its self-ordained limits.

As for natural science, its railroad tracks now confront an ocean. It must take ship or plane with only
stars to guide. For its ponderable world has melted into
imponderable "energies," its solid substance has evapo-
rated into a space-time void, its predictables of cause-
and-effect have surrendered to the unpredictable
"quanta," and its very laws are found to be infected by
the mind. This latter fact, in all this revolution, is the
heaviest blow. Science cannot get rid of the observer,
and the observer cannot get rid of his creaturehood.

The science which sometimes poked fun at an "anthropomorphic God" is now found guilty of an anthropomorphic science! "Thus the whirligig of time brings in his revenges."[7] In any event, what can be thought of a science whose frequent proposal has been that mind is the unwanted child of matter? The proposal makes nonsense of scientific theory, for if all thought is dust, scientific thought is dust. Its theories then are not true: they are but eddies of sand. Men can be trusted to repudiate a creed which makes all creeds confusion. Acceptance would spell insane death, and men are still governed by some mysterious will to live. This denouement of natural science is momentous. It may mark not only the end of a chapter, but the end of an age, in human learning. Materialism in its present form seems doomed. Quantitative study yields place to a philosophy of space-time; and philosophy, by the impelling of the will to live, may soon yield to an empowering and creative faith.

III

As man's knowledge has reached an impasse, his skill has become suicidal. The evidence throngs and clamors. Dr. Alexis Carrel makes articulate a widespread vague misgiving when he roundly declares, in his *Man the Unknown*,[8] that a modern city is an almost fatal environment for the human organism. In cities men swarm, but in none of the fulfilled plan of a beehive. They swarm, and by swarming are deceived into thinking that they can live on one another by their wits. No man can live save by the faithful bounty of field and sky, and there is little field or sky in our modern Babylons. Steam-heated apartments, sex-heated novels, brick chasms filled with gasoline fumes, the tension of a moving belt in factories, the grotesque disparities of wealth and poverty, the uncertainty of toil, the shadow of hunger, the frenzied pleasures, and the fratricidal strife—these are unfair odds for the spirit of man.

For further proof of skills become suicidal, if any proof were needed, witness the perversion of science.

The scientist is not to blame, except by default. He prefers the solitariness of research to the scramble of the world. His coveting is not for gold or power. But he reveals secrets of fabulous gold and power, and men abuse what he reveals. He is in some measure guilty by default, for no man is permitted to be merely a scientist. He is first a man, not exempt from terms of manhood. Thus the president of a national convention of scientists[9] recently warned his hearers that they can no longer neglect their task as citizens. Well might he cry, "Danger!" The danger is almost doom. The scientist and his research are under imminent threat from the very weapons he has given. He must leave his test tubes: there is a crashing on his laboratory door. His gases could have been an anesthesia, his bacteria a healing serum, his electricity a light and warmth. All this he himself had hoped, being a man of truth. But, *perversely,* his gases are also poisonous fumes, his bacteria the pollution of wells, his electricity a leaping death. What shall be done with man's perversity? It leaves theoretical science, however noble, under threat of death from applied science. Man's prowess, boasted to the skies, is the sword of Saul. If there is no help beyond science, science itself is lost.

War is the nadir of our modern helplessness and shame. There was never such world-wide admission that war is a crime, never such world-wide yearning for peace, and never such diabolical war and rehearsal for war. Every nation protests its will for concord, and almost every nation makes staggering outlays for armaments. The will is sincere. A few leaders may covet the "glory" of battle and conquest, a few profiteers may plot their blood-bought gains, and occasionally the mass of men may desperately choose war because it seems more tolerable than hopeless poverty; but most people are sane most of the time, and no sane man craves airplane bombings or poison gas. A few years ago a magazine article contended that men fight because "they like to fight."[10] The dictum seemed final, but was only childish. By the same argument men steal because they like to steal. But there are more honest men than thieves, and more peaceable folk than fighters. The hand can be clenched into a fist, but it is better fitted for craftsmanship and the friendly handclasp. The will to concord is sincere, yet by some perversity we fight. If we complain that we cannot save ourselves from profiteers, dictators, and political bunglers, we only make backdoor confession that we cannot save ourselves from ourselves; for these enemies rise from our ranks and thrive on conditions to which we consent.

Our knowledge has reached an impasse; our skill is suicidal. Famine has overtaken us in the far country. We have tried to play our own Providence. We have forgotten our creaturehood. Boasting our wit and prowess we are like the fly on the chariot wheel, crying, "See how fast I make it go!" "Drunk with sight of power" we have loosed "wild tongues," and life has broken in violence and desolation. We are not the creators of the world, nor can we bend it to our selfish will. We have no magic to change the hour of sunrise or to make private greed issue in public good.

> For still the world prevail'd, and its dread laugh,
> Which scarce the firm philosopher can scorn.[11]

We do not ordain this human pilgrimage: "It is he that hath made us, and not we ourselves."[12]

IV

There is no joy in drawing this indictment, except such as comes from facing facts, but it underscores our need of more than human help. The persistent questions remain concerning prayer. "How can I, praying in America, change life for a friend in Asia?" "And"— sharper question—"assuming such power, have I any right secretly to change his life?" There are other questions induced by the new science and psychology. "What use to pray in a world of law? Snowflakes have angles of crystallization of sixty degrees and one hundred twenty degrees, and praying cannot change them. Thoughts also seem to have angles of crystallization. How can my pious mumblings avail in a fixed scheme? Is there

> A breath that fleets beyond this iron world,
> And touches Him that made it?"[13]

There are questions of personal emotion and apparent failure: "How can I feel God near? Why are my prayers, however unselfish, still ignored or denied?" These questions remain. New knowledge has given them a deeper thrust. We shall not evade them. But they are now in a healthier climate. Yesterday we were not really eager for answer: we preferred the argument. We were proud of our skill, and sure that we could make or manipulate our own bright answer. But today,

> as on a darkling plain
> Swept with confused alarms of struggle and flight,
> Where ignorant armies clash by night,[14]

the questions must be answered; or, rather, answered or unanswered, we must pray. Thus prayer, "on this great roundabout, the world,"[15] is once again not a moot topic: it is an issue of life and death.

V

In Willa Cather's *Death Comes for the Archbishop* there is an account, tender with "the still, sad music of humanity," of why the Ácoma Indians in Colorado chose to live on mesas. The rock gave *safety*. The plains, with Apaches on the south and Navajos on the north, were the scene of a periodic man hunt; but the mesa was accessible only by a narrow rock-staircase which a few men could defend against a host. Thus, "these Indians, born in fear and dying by violence for generations, had at last taken this leap away from the earth, and on the rock had found the hope of all suffering and tormented creatures—safety."[16] The rock was more than safety: it was *sustenance and beauty*. When rain fell, its deep crevices were natural cisterns. Often it had secret springs by which the plain was made fertile. Sometimes the Ácoma, by great labor, would carry soil to the mesa, where the coolness of the rock would keep the soil unparched. Thus barrenness broke into a splendor of flowers. The rock served a subtler but deeper need than safety or even sustenance: the sand was forever blown in new eddies, the clouds forever drifted, but *the rock stood*. Earth and sky were in ceaseless change, but the mesa was fixed in the midst of fleeting time: "The Ácomas, who must share the universal human yearning for something permanent, enduring, without shadow of change,—they had their idea in substance. They actually lived upon their Rock; were born upon it and died upon it."[17]

Our generation, with pride shattered and body bruised, longs for sanctuary, for fruitfulness, for an abiding Home. Prayer is the true Mesa. Why gibe at prayer as an "escape"? The gibe foolishly assumes that we are self-sufficient. In a world where microbes are stronger than man, where sorrow waits, death stalks with violence, and an aroused conscience is a Cave of Furies, to pretend that we need no refuge is only a pretense. The critic who prates about "escape" does not make his bed in the street on a stormy night. Who could gibe at prayer when prayer covets fruitfulness? If only our arid chaos could be made a garden! Contemplate a modern battlefield: it is as wide as a wide country: sleeping babes are among the combatants, and must be murdered as they sleep. Consider the bizarre contrasts of our time: our technical gain and social loss, Radio City and the East Side slums, a transcontinental plane and a Harlem race riot, the precision of a factory assembly line and the unruliness of a sit-down strike. The conviction deepens that this chaos is beyond our human wit. Is there some Mind on which all men may draw? Does that Mind, shaping history, give each praying man his secret orders, thus saving human planning from its own cleverness? If from this Primal Source man could be given "a clean heart" and "a right spirit," could he not grow flowers even on a rock? None could deny that we crave the permanent. Contests held to determine which hymns are most popular are not always edifying, but it is significant that the hymn of first choice is almost always "Abide with Me."

> Abide with me: fast falls the eventide;
> The darkness deepens; Lord, with me abide!
> When other helpers fail, and comforts flee,
> Help of the helpless, O abide with me.
>
> Swift to its close ebbs out life's little day;
> Earth's joys grow dim, its glories pass away;
> Change and decay in all around I see;
> O Thou who changest not, abide with me![18]

This is the agelong prayer. Our age, perhaps more homeless than any age, offers the prayer more poignantly from deeper need. This book will plead that prayer is a rock staircase to an inviolable sanctuary, a courage to win fruitfulness from sand, and a home, even amid earth's changes, in the Eternity of God. The key-city, this mesa of prayer, must stand in the crucial struggle. The nihilism which assaults it must be gainsaid. Then, perchance, our modern autocracies can be undermined in love, our modern democracies saved from license, and a Theocracy raised in the earth. Then

> The bird of dawning singeth all night long: . . . .
> So hallow'd and so gracious is the time.[19]

Chapter II

JESUS AND PRAYER

A CERTAIN MAN was an honest seeker. In a magazine article he has told his fruitless search for faith. Fundamentalism, so called, he could not accept: it strained the mind's integrity. He could not believe, for instance, in the literal inerrancy of Genesis. Modernism, so called, he tried and found wanting: its Biblical criticism, social programs, and new theologies left him still athirst. He became disillusioned with present-day religion. Nor was he alone: he found that many felt forlorn. One of them, a man of insight, reported a dream: "I thought," said this friend, "that I saw you standing on a hilltop, and we, a great host of us, were crowded around waiting eagerly for what you might say. We could see your lips framing the word, but no sound came. . . . We tried to help you by calling out the word your lips were shaping; but we also were dumb! and that word was . . . ."[1] What was it? There is a missing word. In lack of it our modern world does not make sense. Our psychology becomes psycho-mechanics, a tinkering with wires and fixtures without any main contact. Our order of trade is so competitive that advertising is almost mendacious, so ramshackle that millions cannot find work, so shaken by internal strains that picketing is normal and wars are recurrent, so grotesquely unfair that the few are rich while the many are anxious and poor. Our inventions are offered on Moloch's altar. Our knowledge is irrelevant: there is no master light to all its seeing: it sprawls bereft of integrating purpose. Thus it proposes for final verity that a universe which issued in mind is itself mindless, that a world creative of personality is itself only a dust storm or a black void. There *is* a missing word. In lack of it our little loyalties of home, business, nation, and church are like the stones of an arch without a keystone: the stones break on each other, and the spirit of man finds no door. Dmitri Merejkowsky has lately pronounced this verdict: "If religion were a light in the physical sense, the inhabitants of other worlds would have seen our planet, luminous since the ice age, suddenly extinguished." For our fear and hope he adds: "Never was mankind so near doom as today, but perhaps also it was never so near its salvation."[2]

What *is* the missing word? "We tried to help you," said the man describing his dream, "by calling out the word your lips were shaping; but we also were dumb; and that word was *God.*" And the way to know God? Is He best known "face to face," in the direct venture of prayer? Is there a postern gate into the immediate Presence? Jesus taught that faith and lived it.

I

Perhaps Jesus would tell us that our doubts can be broken only by the direct venture of prayer. The several threads that are plaited to make the binding-cords of our misgivings are not hard to disentangle. One is our new concept of the world: God seems lost in vastness. The old cosmogony—earth a tiny room, hades just below the floor, heaven just above the ceiling—left God near and real; but the new concept seems to exile Him in remotest distance. Another thread is the new science, now becoming old, with its doctrine of natural law. God is shut off, not only by distance, but by an immense steel cage of inexorable uniformity which He cannot invade and in which we are held like prisoners. Still another strand in our denials is the new psychology with its theory of religion as "escape" and "projection." To these issues we shall return. But by far the strongest thread in our skepticisms is our perversity, the twisted fashion of our conduct—our anger, greed, and pride.

As long as our argument is with weapons and blood, so long will life seem a jungle. As long as trade-scramble denies the brotherhood of man, so long shall we doubt the fatherhood of God. As long as in pride we build cities ugly, impersonal, oppressive—away from the elemental forces of earth and sky by which men truly live—so long shall we miss the brooding Tenderness immemorially mediated through the simplicities of nature and friendship. We have tried to usurp the sovereignty of the world: therein is the core of our misgiving. Prayer has therefore seemed a spasm of words lost in a cosmic indifference.

But we begin to doubt our doubts. We are like the wistful ones in Thomas Hardy's poem "God's Funeral." It describes the procession of mankind carrying God's casket. They go to bury Him; and, as they march, they tell His fate:

> . . . . tricked by our own early dream
> And need of solace, we grew self-deceived;
> Our making soon our maker we did deem,
> And what we had imagined we believed.
>
> Till, in Time's stayless stealthy swing,
> Uncompromising rude reality
> Mangled the monarch of our fashioning,
> Who quavered, sank; and now has ceased to be.

But the wistful ones begin to yearn over lost days of faith:

> How sweet it was in years far hied
> To start the wheels of day with trustful prayer,
> To lie down liegely at the eventide
> And feel a blessed assurance He was there!

They insist soon that they are burying, not God, but a counterfeit of straw. They declare, with hopeful finger pointing, that they can see on the world's edge a faint line of dawn. So with us: there is a homesickness, the sense of a missing word, and a wondering if perchance

the night may lift. Perhaps we may soon be willing to
admit that Jesus was both honest and sane.

II

We turn now to him. It seems clear that we can learn
more about prayer from him than by searching in dim
history for prayer's origin. For how, with but scant records to guide us, can we hope to enter sympathetically
into the primitive mind? How can we dogmatize, saying,
for instance, "prayer began in fear"?[3] How can we ignore the fact that in prayer, as in any other agelong
process, newness constantly emerges? This fact of newness makes it impossible fully to understand anything
from its origin, even supposing the origin could be isolated. Great oaks do *not* "from little acorns grow": they
grow from little acorns *plus* sunshine, *plus* soil, *plus*
wind and rain, *plus* the whole mysterious co-ordination
and vitality of the universe. Plato insisted that we can
interpret life only in "wholes." An analysis is useful
only as prelude to a new synthesis.

There is a sharper question about the analysis of
prayer: who can understand music but the musician, or
prayer but the man who long has prayed? The objective
and scientific study of prayer is valid and valuable—but
only as a supplement. In itself it is always partial and
flat, like a photograph compared with life. An objective
description of a man's mother would be true—and foolishly untrue. An attempt to explain her by her prehistor-
ic origin would be worse: she is her own interpreter. If
origins, supposing we could ever trace them, could yield
central meanings, medicine would be the incantation of
a fakir, a *Fifth Symphony* the yap-yap of a primeval
ape, and a cathedral only a hole in the ground. Some
irreverent mind claims to have discovered a rare duck
which flies backward because it cares nothing about
where it is going but must know whence it came. Actually the breed is not rare: the rivers are full of them.
This cult of origins, the strange assumption that priority
in time gives clearer meanings and truer evaluations,
leads almost inevitably to oversimplification—as, for in-

stance, to the notion that prayer began in fear or that religion is merely a tribal custom. For a truer understanding of prayer it would seem wise to turn to some master of prayer.

III

So we turn to Jesus. Many would agree that he is earth's sovereign soul. We might disagree about his titles. For some of us that disagreement would not shake our faith. We would still seek vaster titles for him than earth gives to our fellow men. Truth seems to demand for him some ultimate honor—so deep are his self-revealings, so unaccountable otherwise his grip on history, so inescapable his aliveness for all who have dared deeply to ponder him. But, apart from all titles, he is earth's sovereign soul. His thirty years of life bring forth harvests of light generation on generation. Nay, such a statement, though it would be tremendous tribute to any other, seems of him an understatement—like the attempt to measure the sunrise with the span of one's fingers. Great music is consecrate to him, as in Handel's *Messiah;* great architecture, as in Rheims Cathedral; and great art, as in Raphael's "Madonna" or Munkácsy's "Christ before Pilate." Why should that latter picture, displayed in an American department store each Lent, bring shopping crowds to silence—as though they were in church, as though Someone were over them like a sky and around them "like a breaking sea"? Jesus lived so deeply and so mightily that he has become man's unquiet conscience, secret strength, and sheltering home.

What *is* his secret? Wise men ask, for wise men must learn to live, and he is master of life. The nobles of Florence knocked at St. Francis' lowly door, saying in effect, "You have a secret." With deeper constraint the world knocks at the door of Jesus. Wherein is he different? The question may bring us to some unfathomable place; but, even so, it may yield some final answer. The factor of difference is not in the outward fashion of his days. He lived our life. His friends knew him as the "carpenter's son," and later as "the teacher," just as they knew many other men. Nor is the distinction to be found in the letter of his teaching or even in the substance of his ethic. "Thou shalt love thy neighbor as thyself" was an old commandment. "The meek shall inherit the earth" was an ancient truth. Only 18 verses of the 111 verses which comprise the Sermon on the Mount are without rabbinical precedent.[4] Others had said, at least in scattered fragments, just what he said; and they left the world not much better for the teaching. This fact a recent biography of Jesus again makes clear:

> Jesus did not proclaim a new morality, since to the rich men who asked what he should do to inherit eternal life he replied by quoting the commandments of the Old Testament. The principle of the ethic of Jesus does not differ from that of Jewish morality, that is, obedience towards God.[5]

But the writer acknowledges nevertheless the factor of difference, and endeavors to trace it:

> There have been some who have tried to argue that the teaching of Jesus on moral questions lacks originality, and it is not difficult to show that he owes much to the tradition of his people. But a mere similarity does not constitute a conclusive argument. What makes the originality of the moral thought of Jesus is not the amount of new material, whether great or small; . . . . it is the way in which he has linked this moral teaching with *a new religious conception and a new religious experience.*[6]

The uniqueness of the teaching of Jesus is in its wholeness, its proportion—that is, in what is made central or circumferential—and, particularly, in some subtlety of spirit—a "new religious experience." In short, we must go behind the teaching to find the secret. We must go behind the deeds, even behind the miracles. For there is some evidence that other men were credited with power to work miracles. Jesus asked the Pharisees concerning the exorcising of devils, "By whom do your sons cast them out?"[7] and the Talmud teaches that some rabbis were believed to have power to raise the dead. More-over, Jesus had a certain distrust of what our world calls miracles—"A wicked and adulterous generation seeketh after a sign."[8] This stress is here noted, not to encour-age any hasty conclusion on the hard problem of mira-cle, but only to show that both the comrades of Jesus and Jesus himself would bid us look elsewhere for the secret of his power. Where shall we look? Not even to the outward fashion of his death, for many had died by crucifixion—there were two others on the first Good Friday—and their death laid on mankind no signal blessing. His death has power because it is *his* death. What was *his* secret? Other men's words are like wire: the very same words on his lips are like charged wire. Other men's days are like winter trees: his days with the same deeds are like a tree breaking in blossom or heavy with fruit. Other men's death is death: his death is life. The difference is not wholly traceable to earth. But this can be seen, even by earth-bound eyes: his spirit was completely dedicated to God *in prayer* and *therefore* made vital. So attuned was he to God by secret com-munion that his words are as God's words. He did what other men had done—trudged the road, taught his truth, healed the sick, and flinched not from martyr-dom—but, oh, the difference! The disciples tracked down the secret to its hiding place—"Lord, teach us to pray. . . . ."[9] His secret is indeed a "new religious ex-perience."

IV

A rich man once invited St. Francis to his home so that he might spy upon the saint's praying. All night long he heard him say, "My God and my All," "My God and my All," and was so moved that forthwith he became a disciple.[10] Veit Dietrich tells of overhearing Luther pray in the fortress of Coburg with as much pas-sion of entreaty as if God were before his eyes. Crom-well's valet reports his master's deathbed prayer, a plea not for himself, but for his country, yet ending human-wise as any man's prayer might end: "And pardon the

folly of this short prayer: even for Jesus' sake. And give
us a good night if it be thy pleasure. Amen."[11] But we
have almost no account of the lonely prayers of Jesus.
Of the fact of them there is ample testimony, but of the
method and substance only a scanty record. On the
Mount of Transfiguration he spoke not only with God
but, according to the description given us, to Moses and
Elijah. In the Garden of Gethsemane he prayed, "O my
Father, if it be possible, let this cup pass from me."[12]
That prayer Jesus himself perhaps reported, for his
three companions are described as being asleep. Or did
some other overhear? Those fragments tell us virtually
all we know of the secret prayers of Jesus. Earlier in his
ministry he sent away the five thousand who had
thronged about him, bade his twelve disciples also set sail
across the lake, and then walked back into the hills:
"He went up into a mountain apart to pray: and when
the evening was come, he was there alone."[13] We see
him there, a kneeling Figure. The red gleam fades. He
is silhouetted now against the wheels of stars. The silver
wheel slowly turns, but still he kneels. His hands are
raised in entreaty. His upturned face catches the dim
light. Is he speaking now as if God were on the other
side of that ledge of rock? Does the sky ever seem
brassy to him, his only answer an echo? What is he saying? We may not know: the place is holy ground. We
hear the words, "Thy will . . . . thy will." Once as he
prayed his face was so transfigured that his very gar-
ments were luminous.

This is clear: we cannot separate his praying from his
life to treat it as a mere addendum. It is the bread and
wine of all his days. Luncheon clubs hail his "Golden
Rule." But do they pray? The Golden Rule can mean
almost anything, bribe for bribe, trade for trade, when
divorced from his spirit. We cannot keep the Golden
Rule and discard the prayer. The prophets of social justice proclaim him champion of the poor, and they are
right. But do they pray? We cannot keep his compassion and discard his prayers. Poets see in him a poet.
There is a fine biography entitled *The Poet of Gali-
lee,*[14] written by a poet; and another poet has sung,

> A poet lived in Galilee
>   Whose mother dearly knew him—
> And his beauty like a cooling tree
>   Drew many people to him.[15]

But do the poets pray? We cannot keep his love of
lovely things, his poignant sense of clash between the
soul's vision and the world's stark contradiction, and
discard his prayers. He himself would have told us that
God is also Beauty, and that the love of loveliness is
nourished only in God. Strong men repudiate the effem-
inate portraits we have drawn—

> Give us a virile Christ for these rough days!
> You painters, sculptors, show the warrior bold[16]

Strong he was in truth. He refused the opiate on the
cross, choosing to die as he had chosen to live—with
open eyes. But do our strong men pray? We cannot
keep his manliness and discard his prayers. He would
have told us that true and enduring strength is in God.
Even the best biographies fail to do full justice to his
practice of the Presence. It has become a fashion to acknowledge his sovereign character, his white and gleaming ethic, his courage to expose and resist the hoary lies
of trade and statescraft, his love unto death—and
meanwhile ignore his praying. That fashion is here challenged. It does not deal with facts in true proportion. If
his ethic is true, it is a fair assumption that his faith in
prayer cannot be false. His life and death had their secret springs, like a river, back in the hills where he was
wont to pray.

V

His teaching about prayer is reiterated, yet rich and
varied, like some peal of bells. If we remember that not
more than one hundred of his days, and possibly as few
as forty, receive any mention in the fragmentary record
of the four Gospels, the oft-repeated reference to prayer
is a portent. When the scattered counsels are gathered,
we have clear-cut and almost detailed guidance. Always

there is a girding of our faith: he calls us to a glad expectancy: "Ask, and it shall be given you; seek, and ye
shall find; knock, and it shall be opened unto you"; "If
we have faith as a grain of mustard seed, ye shall say
unto this mountain, Remove hence to yonder place, and
it shall remove; and nothing shall be impossible unto
you"; "What things soever ye desire, when ye pray, believe that ye receive them, and ye shall have them."[17]
We shall later try to trace the features of this essential
faith.[18] It is enough now to remark that it *is* an essential of prayer and of all high endeavor. The scholar believes that truth hitherto unknown will answer the call
of the sincerely questing mind; and the man of medical
research is sure, without either possibility or need of
proof, that even the most stubborn disease can finally
be cured. So the praying man must make his venture,
scorning all insinuating doubts. He must believe that
man is free, that God is near and good and mighty, and
that the world will yield to their coworking. He must
cleave to the faith that any good thing is too good to be
*un*true, and that God will bring it to pass. These were
the assumptions Jesus made: we shall see hereinafter if
they can withstand the challenge. Meanwhile we notice
his ringing *sursum corda,* "Have faith in God."[19]

Always there is the demand for reality, lest faith
should become a poor make-believe. Prayers that are
ostentatious, like the blowing of trumpets on a street
corner, are self-condemned. Prayers that are a parroting
of words, "vain repetitions" or a lengthy "pretense," are
always unanswered except in their own chaos. Prayer
must be honest: let the true man go into his inner
chamber, or to some lonely mountain, where he cannot
strut or pose; and let him there speak out his heart in
simple, direct sincerity. Let a man there remember that
prayer is but one gift and power. It is intended to com-
plement and sanctify other powers, not to cancel them.
It is not a lazy substitute for work and thought: fields
are not plowed by praying over them. But let a man
remember also that fields become a drudgery, or a
botched labor, or even a greed and a bitterness, unless
the plowing is done in prayer. Men should work and

pray. Men should think and pray: God guides them, not
in lazy refusal to think, but through their thinking and
mercifully in the tired or joyous respite from thought.
Men should watch and pray. Men should forgive and
pray, since it is worse than unreality to ask for pardon
while hugging the grudges of enmity. Men should suffer
and pray. We read the record with filmed eyes if we
miss this reiterated demand for reality.

Faith, reality—and always the plea for humility.
Prayer must be "in my name"; that is to say, in the
nature of Jesus, for whatever is outside his radiance of
soul is rashness and rebellion. We are creatures, and
know not anything. We cannot create: we can but fashion clumsily from materials which God gives to hand
and mind. We cannot stretch the tent of sky or set life
within the seed. We dare not lift our childish plans before Eternal Eyes, except we also pray, "Thy will be
done." Moreover, we are people of broken conscience.
The self-righteous finds the gate of prayer forever
closed; but the penitent, even though he has no prayer
but to beat upon his breast and cry for mercy, returns to
his tasks in peace. That truth Jesus scored deep in a
vivid parable, the story of the Pharisee and the publi-
can.[20] Prayer must live in lowliness.

But persistence should be linked with lowliness. Men
should pray with the dogged resolve of an unbefriended
widow pleading her case before a heartless judge, and
with the not-to-be-denied importunity of a man knocking and knocking on his neighbor's door at midnight.[21]
These two parables of prayer are in some respects difficult to construe. We can be sure that Jesus does not
mean us to regard God as either a callous judge or a
grudging neighbor, for such a translation would flatly
contradict all else taught by the Gospels. Some items in
the story are only for verisimilitude. But the require-
ment of persistence in prayer is unmistakable. Why this
demand? Is it because we honor nothing cheap and easily gained? Gold is not often given in nugget, but in ore
which must be mined, smelted, refined, and wrought
into loveliness. Is it because prayer is a great art? Music
is an arduous training, its gifts reserved only for discip-

lined seekers, and we may not hope to enter the treasures of prayer in the casual asking of a casual mind. Is
it because by persistence our clamorings are purified?
If desires are steadily refused, we may wisely question
their worth. Is it because prayer is a friendship? We do
not make friends by nodding our head to a man across
the street once a month. A friend begins by appearing
aloof. Then through speech and silence, through laughter
shared and danger braved, through the give and take of
unsuspected self-revealings, heart opens to heart and
mutual loyalty is gladly pledged. So with a Friendship
above time: it grows of oft-repeated meetings, contacts,
self-givings, and mutual trust. For whatever high reasons,
men of prayer must knock and knock—sometimes with
bleeding knuckles in the dark.

This light-filled teaching about prayer is focused in
the Lord's Prayer. *"Our* Father": we are children of
one home, and cannot pray well until we try to trace the
Father's likeness in every face. "Our *Father"*: there is
austerity in God, because of His wise fatherhood; and
there is mystery, for we are only children; but the sa-
lience of His nature is personal love of which the love of
a wise and strong earthly father is but the broken shadow.
"Who art in heaven" does not mean that God is not on
earth: it is the adoration and kneeling awe in which all
true prayer begins. Perhaps it could be freely but not
falsely translated, "Whose dwelling is in Light." The
phrase "as in heaven, so on earth" applies to each of the
petitions which precede it: "May thy nature of fatherhood be revered—not abused or used presump-
tuously—on earth as in heaven. May thy realm come—
through me and through the comradeship—on earth as
in heaven. May thy will be done—on earth as in
heaven." The next petition raises the whole problem of
petitionary prayer, which question we shall not
evade.[22] For the moment we may understand it to be
an acknowledgment of our dependence and of God's
faithful providence: "Give us day by day our bread for
the morrow." The prayer for forgiveness[23] does not
point to a *quid pro quo,* as though God were the keeper
of celestial ledgers carefully allowing just so much for-

giveness to men as they are willing to grant to their enemies. It points rather to a living law whereby a cherished grudge in a man's heart perforce and of itself
closes the door against an ever-pleading God, and
whereby man's grant of pardon of itself opens the door
to God who ever waits and loves. "Lead us not into
temptation" is obscure in meaning in the original, and,
in our customary translation, a source of bafflement
and misgiving. Does God seduce men? It is clear that
the word in the Greek manuscript, as also the word
"temptation" at the time of the Authorized Version,
meant testing rather than evil enticement. Dr. C. C.
Torrey claims that the Greek phrase is a somewhat
stilted rendering of the original Aramaic idiom, and
suggests as our equivalent today, "Grant that we fail not
in the time of testing."[24] That phrase then would be a
confession of besetting weakness; and a plea to be
saved, not from the battle, but in it and through it. Thus
our translation might read somewhat as follows:

Our Father, whose dwelling is in Light,
  May thy Nature be revered,
  May thy kingdom come,   } on earth as in heaven.
  May thy will be done,
Give us our bread day by day.
  Forgive us our debts, we forgiving our debtors.
Grant that we fail not in the time of testing,
  but deliver us from the Evil One.

The Church added, with a true insight which we are
wise to copy, "Thine is the kingdom, the power, and the
glory, forever." Jesus taught the prayer, not necessarily
as a fixed pattern, but as a type. Yet we are right to use
it in liturgy, as abundant blessings have proved. Jesus
told us that such prayer has healing power: ". . . .
this kind goeth not out but by prayer."[25] It has reconcil-
ing power: "Pray for them which despitefully use you,
and persecute you."[26] It has interceding grace: the man
who knocked on the door was knocking, it is worth remembering, that he might satisfy the needs of a journeying friend. The range and content of Jesus' teaching
about prayer leave us the more amazed that his biogra-

phers should have given it only marginal honor. Beyond
doubt prayer to Jesus was vital and regnant in the whole
venture of life.

VI

His example in prayer has persuasive power even
when his precepts leave us unmoved. Or, rather, in this
issue as always his deed and word are an indivisible
flame. Often and by habit he prayed in solitude. Often
and by habit he prayed in comradeship. That latter
fact should be stressed in a generation which easily neg-
lects and discredits public worship. For a man to argue,
"I do not go to church: I pray alone," is no wiser than
if he should say, "I have no use for symphonies: I believe only in solo music." Prayer is like life, for it is a
life: it swings between the poles of aloneness and comradeship. He prayed in the routine day. He prayed under provocation of crisis. Luke's Gospel, which tells us
more than the other Gospels about the prayer life of
Jesus, seems intent to underscore these crisis prayers.
He prayed at his baptism, in a great initial act of consecration. He prayed—so the context would encourage us
to believe—when the crowd clamored around him to
hail him as a wonder-worker: there in solitude he asked
to be saved from the two impostors, success and failure,
and to inquire into the deeper will of God. He prayed
all night before he chose his disciples: judgment is blind
except in the light of prayer. He prayed on the Mount
of Transfiguration: that prayer, as scrutiny quickly
shows, was a renewal of his initial consecration, an acceptance of the dark baptism of the cross. He prayed
after the feeding of the five thousand, which, by any
interpretation was a miracle of the sovereignty of his
spirit: he was on guard lest he abuse his power and try
to reach heaven's ends by earthy means. He prayed in
the Garden of Gethsemane: "Father, if thou be willing,
remove this cup from me."[27] This, so far as we know,
was the only prayer in which he asked respite from the
terms of righteous living; and it was absorbed at once
into a deeper prayer, "Nevertheless not my will, but

thine, be done." The prayer began in agony, but ended
in a calm strength which not even Calvary could break.
He prayed on the cross. Of the seven "Words of the
Cross" three and perhaps four are prayers. The prayer
of pardon, "Father, forgive them, for they know not
what they do," leaves us "defenseless utterly." This vigil
of prayer, never closely described in the Gospels, but
repeatedly mentioned and reflected is an ungainsayable
testimony. He prayed and prayed—in the "great congregation" of the Temple, in the local friendship of the
synagogue, in the circle of his friends, on the housetop
under Syrian stars, in the fields outside Jerusalem, on
the lonely mountainside, in the "inner chamber"—until
prayer became the climate of his days. The saints said
that "to work is to pray," and they believed profoundly
that "to pray is to work." Jesus said in the language of
deeds that "to live is to pray," and that "to pray is to
live."

We must not dogmatize about the limits of prayer,
though we must recognize certain limits and try to trace
them. For instance, we cannot too quickly conclude
from Jesus that petitionary prayer has no place. Yet the
fact remains that Jesus asked nothing for himself except
daily bread, strength in the testing, and grace to reveal
God to the world. In the Ibsen play *Peer Gynt*, the
hero, committed to the faith that he would "be myself,"
visited the lunatic asylum where, he assumes, people are
"outside themselves." Begriffenfeldt, the director, cor-
rects him:

> Outside themselves? Oh no, you're wrong.
> It's here that men are most themselves—
> Themselves and nothing but themselves—
> Sailing with outspread sails of self.
> Each shuts himself in a cask of self,
> The cask stopped with a bung of self
> And seasoned in a well of self.
> None has a tear for others' woes
> Or cares what any other thinks.
> We are ourselves in thought and voice—
> Ourselves up to the very limit;

> And, consequently, if we want
> An Emperor, it's very clear
> That you're the man.[26]

Jesus asked nothing for himself, neither comfort nor refuge nor name. He worshiped the Will. Selfishness is always lunatic: he alone is sane in a mad world. He did not ask even for continued earthly life. He knew through prayer that God will keep a man until his word is spoken and his work is done, and that no brave man will ask God to stretch his breathing space beyond that day. The word and the work for God are the only issue. So Jesus had a "heart at leisure from itself." His longings were all lost in the longing for God, "in whose will is our peace."

VII

What did he "get out of it?" That is a favorite, but a shabby question. Worthy men do not ask of great music, "How can I turn this to my gain?" That advertisement that used to stand at the outskirts of a little city on a certain lake, "See our million dollar sunsets," was a mild sacrilege. Fortunately the dollar sign can never be written on a sunset, nor can we develop the stars in suburban "subdivisions." When a man says in effect, "See my million dollar prayers," with instances given of how prayer has granted him almost anything he craves, we shall be wise to avoid him by a wide detour. To "use" a friendship is to abuse it—and lose it. What did Jesus "get out of" prayer? The answer might be, "Calvary!"

But the question is allowable if we rephrase it: "What was prayer's natural issue in his life? What radiances were kindled by the ultimate Friendship?" The answer is easy to find, but vast beyond words to tell. We must here try to strike off infinity in paragraphs. Prayer made Jesus "Prophet, Priest, and King."

He is the Prophet of mankind through prayer. He lived in light above the world. Imagine a man walking a forest path at midnight. He cannot walk: he stumbles. The shadows are ominous; a creaking bough is a haunted thing; a twisted root may send him headlong. Imagine the same man walking the same path in sunlight. He goes with glad strength, sees the woodland "flecked with leafy light and shade," and hears in every bower a canticle of praise. Everything is the same as at midnight, yet everything is transformed by the miracle of light. Jesus walked in light that same path along which others stumbled in darkness. Often in the vigil of prayer, lifted to an eagle-ridge, he would see all the paths of the world—the luring path whose end is dead end, the "primrose path of dalliance" issuing on bitter wastes, the pride-filled path that runs to "the perilous edge of battle," and that one road, mountainous indeed and lonely, yet brave and free, whose pilgrims catch glimpses of the distant City. It is no accident that the prophets have repeatedly foretold national destiny with clearer vision than the statesmen. The prophets' view is not local: they live before the face of God. It is not strange that the words of Jesus are still our guiding torch: he prayed.

Jesus is the Priest of mankind through prayer. He stood between God and man, revealing God to men, and by his own manhood justifying man to God. We assume that social service is an earthborn altruism. Actually its roots are in faith beyond the earth. Why lift a sot from his gutter to care for him in a hospital? The reason, beyond all our little reasons, is that the man has some touch of the eternal and must be saved; and that some ultimate tide of compassion moves us to save him. This faith is nourished in prayer. Otherwise it flags, so that social service without religion loses momentum, just as religion without social compassion becomes arid in selfishness. People are lovable only when we love them, and we can love them unswervingly only in faith—that is to say, in the practice of the presence of God. In a fine passage Ruskin[29] explains the destiny of the elements of a muddy road. The clay, left long enough, hardens into a sapphire; the sand becomes by refraction of light an opal; the soot is a diamond in the rough; and the water when it freezes, is a snow-white star. There is a finer destiny for muddy humanity, but earth cannot reveal it. "For love is of God; and every one that loveth, is born of God."[30] Only in God do we understand, in a wisdom deeper than knowledge, the red law whereby bad people are made good people by righteous sacrifice. Only in God are we willing, in love's "touch of madness," to pay the price. Jesus became our Priest by prayer, who alone was pure enough to offer a perfect sacrifice.

Jesus is the King of mankind through prayer. "King" is "Konig"—the man who can, the man who is able. Kings were once a democratic choice. They earned the crown by consent of the crowd through demonstrated power. We have strange notions of power. A transcontinental plane has a wingspread of one hundred feet, a length of sixty feet, a weight of twelve tons, and its engines can hurl it through the air at two hundred miles per hour. It is to us a token of power. But if the plane carries a man who has just learned of his mother's death, the plane has no power to mend his broken heart. Earth's power is very helpless power. But Jesus had real power—"power over all flesh, that he should give eternal life."[31] Other men spoke and their words died with their echo: Jesus spoke the same words, and they shook the world. Other men died martyr deaths and were not long remembered; he died in the same outward fashion, willing to be forgotten, and his cross now stands against every skyline. He is the true King, the "Man who can." He has power—like dawn's banners, like the unseen constraint of tides, like a fragrance, like great music, like buried seed, like that Spirit in history which litters time with the debris of proud empires and wills that the "meek shall inherit the earth." He is "Konig"—the only man who can lift our transitory flesh into an eternal light. He is Prophet, Priest, and King, because his days were hid in prayer.

VIII

"An awful thought of Ruskin's," comments Burne-Jones, "that artists paint God for the world. There's a lump of greasy pigment at the end of Michelangelo's

hogbristle brush; and by the time it has been laid on
stucco, there is something there that all men with eyes
recognize as divine." Our age has marvelous pigments,
brushes, walls—such magic instruments as Aladdin in
his magic city would hardly have dared to dream. But
our airplanes carry us no inch nearer peace, our skyscrapers no inch nearer heaven, and all our money cannot shrive our souls. We have everything—except God.
Therefore we have nothing. Said that man of his dream:
"I thought that I saw you standing on a hilltop, and
we . . . . were crowded around waiting eagerly for
what you might say. We could see your lips framing the
word, but no sound came. . . . . We tried to help
you . . . . but we also were dumb; and that word
was—God."[1] The direct finding of God is in prayer. In
that way Jesus found God in every closer friendship.
Jesus is the only fully rational soul, for he only is fully
delivered from the insanity of selfishness. He is mighty,
for he has his main contact: dynamic light and power
stream through him. He is creative, for he has indwell-
ing life: his desert blossoms like the rose. He is eternal,
for by endless intercession he is lifted above the fret of
years. With the pigments of time and on the stucco
walls of earth he has painted God for all men to see.
The open secret is: His days were steeped in prayer.
The missing word is God, and only by prayer can we
find it.

PART TWO

PRAYER AND THE WORLD

Chapter III

SOME DEFECTIVE THEORIES OF PRAYER

IT IS NOT strange that prayer should draw the sharpest attacks of doubt, and that in every generation misgiving or scorn should allege that prayer is less than communion with the Divine. The spiritual fact, the world beyond our eyes, is always "our dearest faith; our ghastliest doubt";[1] and prayer, which goes behind argument to cry openly on God, is always the most daring assertion of that Unseen Realm. Thus prayer has defended the pass for all religion—since religion is conquered when prayer dies—and has gathered all the spears of skepticism into its own heart. How sharp the spears: "Perhaps prayer is a mere soliloquy, a self-deception, a cowardice that dare not face the unheeding world!"

I

What *is* prayer? "Babes" have shared Jesus' simple faith that prayer is friendship with God, but many among the "wise and prudent" have been skeptics. Their theories are many, often sincere, never radiant. One theory has contended that prayer is animistic fear—stark fear in early times, and nowadays only refined fear. Thus Alfred Maury: "Fear is the father of religion and love its late-born daughter";[2] and Dr. Lewis Browne in his widely read *This Believing World*[3] glibly asserts, without much hint or mention of any alternative surmise, that religion sprang from primitive terror. Three rejoinders, among others, may wisely be made to this particular account. First, no man can

47

safely dogmatize about the origin of an instinct so deep
and universal as prayer. In the nature of the case the
records are scanty, vague, and far removed. Even of the
present-day Polynesian Maoris, they are psychologically
far removed. The early pages of ethnological religion
give poor foundation for a dogmatism. Moreover, this
inchoate material shows traces of other prayer motives
than fear. There are marks of affection and glad ecstasy; and G. K. Chesterton is not alone in his contention that the early savage was not dominantly savage or
terror-striken, but peaceable.[4] Dr. Mario Puglisi quotes
from Dr. Friedrich Heiler an evening prayer of the
Kekchi Indians:

Now I shall sleep under Thy feet, under Thy hands, O
Lord of the mountains and the valleys. Tomorrow the day
will return . . . . and I know not where I shall be. Who is
my mother? Who is my father? Thou alone, O God, Thou
who seest me, Thou who defendest me, along my journey
in the darkness which is above me, and in every hindrance
which Thou canst remove from me, O my God, O my
Lord, O Lord of the mountains and of the valleys! I say
what I think, but do Thou pardon, O Lord, do Thou forget
my mistakes.[5]

Another such prayer comes from ancient Egypt, from a
time when magic was threatening the evolution of true
religion:

O Great God, Lord of all truth, to Thee I came to contemplate thy blessedness. I have known thee. I have always
spoken the truth, take away my faults.[6]

These prayers, and many others, are assuredly not un-
differentiated fear.

A second rejoinder might be as follows: the essential
nature of prayer, whatever its origin, is not shown in its
beginnings. The nature of a hyacinth is seen not in the
bulb but in the bloom. At every stage of process, especially a human process, veritable newness emerges. The
music of Beethoven is not explained by a recourse to
tom-toms in an African forest, nor the maternal instinct

by probing a rudimentary impulse, nor High Mass by an analysis of totemism. Dr. George A. Coe has rightly argued:

The claim of Dewey that a thing is fully explained as soon as its genesis is described is true on condition that "genesis" is made sufficiently broad to cover the whole evolution of function. But if "genesis" refers merely to the earliest functions, and if genetic explanation consists in classifying the later-developed functions under earlier ones, then we have the kind of oversimplification that reveals similarities but conceals differences.[7]

Since that warning was penned the name "emergent evolution" has been exalted. It is a hybrid, almost a contradiction in terms, for an unpredictable upthrust is hardly consonant with a presaged unfolding. A form of creationism would seem a more consistent theory. But, in any event, prayer, like any other agelong impelling, is constantly recreated. It has "emergents" throughout its history. Its "ground" is in upheaval; and the question, "What is prayer?" is better answered by contemplation of the present bloom than by dissection of the ancient root. The study of primitive man is here no safe guide.

Third, it might be urged that even if religion did begin in fear—even assuming what cannot rightly be assumed—fear is hardly a single motive unadmixed. Imagine the "savage" standing at the mouth of his cave; imagine that raging elements and wilder beasts terrorize him. He lifts entreating hands to some god-in-the-sky. He placates the capricious deity with blood: "God, save!" But what does such fear imply? Mere fear of extinction? The fear is really an avowed faith in man: "There is worth in me and other men which ought to be kept!" and an avowed faith in God: "Thou, the Mighty, the Mysterious, art bound up with my life! Forsake not the works of Thine own hands!" Thus Dr. William E. Hocking has written:

If we should venture to name this deep-set desire which we call religious it might be represented as an ultimate demand for conscious self-preservation: it is man's leap, as individual and as species, for eternal life in some form, in presence of an awakened fear of fate. Religion is a reaction to "our finite situation." . . . . This reaction seems to be, at its heart, as instinctive as a start or a shudder.[8]

In short, if we must imprison ourselves in any one theory, this ultimate reaction of man to his universe, this "start" or "shudder," seems to be more wisely described as a *mysterium tremendum, a basic awe*, as Rudolf Otto[9] has described it, than as a primeval fear.

II

Another theory maintains, with sincerity and significance, that man prays, not to God, but to a personalization of the race, or of ideal humanity, or of the needful cohesive mores of the group. We may conveniently examine this theory in the form advanced by Émile Durkheim, the French sociologist, who argues impressively, with parallels brilliantly drawn, that God is really the sanctions of community life. After careful study of primitive tribal festivities and totemism, he asserts: "The God of the clan . . . . can be nothing else than the clan itself."[10] Honesty, wisdom, and gratitude alike require us to admit the measure of truth within this theory. Though we may doubt that God is *identical* with the group, we cannot deny that He is often *mediated through* the group. One gain in recent thinking has been its re-emphasis of the social term of our human (individual-social) paradox. The emergence of individual self-consciousness, we now believe, was possible only in "friction" with other selves: the challenge of the "them" occasioned the sense of the "me." No man can be fully blind to the essential blessings bestowed only through the cummunity. A hermit life, if it were possible, would be truncated to the point of nonexistence. Actually such a life is neither possible nor for long conceivable. A hermit's hut implies a skill in building slowly learned by men through generations. His garden, his clothes, and his very thoughts echo the common life. Presumably he could not recognize sunrise and sunset except he had heard others say, "I also see." He is not a hermit: he is only an exile. Robinson Crusoe is never alone: there are always memories of comrades, and always footprints on the beach. Doubtless this gregariousness involves every individual in compromise and limitation. If we live in a city we cannot with impunity play a calliope in the main street at three o'clock in the morning. But the gain outweighs the loss. From society the individual receives the shelter and stimulus, both in labor and thought, by which to make his own excursions. Community is the camp from which he adventures and to which he returns—the "Little America" of his manhood in which he finds both the spur to effort and the welcome home. From community deeper blessings also have come—a shared awareness of the Eternal. Not without cause have men supposed that prayer is only the reverence of the individual for the social bond, only the homage given by the cell to the blood and beat of the organism.

Even so, the theory raises doubts which cannot be laid. Why should the leaders of the clan make appeal to a nonexistent god beyond the clan? It is hardly scientific to assume in them a Machiavellian cunning. Why this apparently instinctive homage to a Beyond? And why the apparently instant, unquestioning obedience of the tribe, as though every man in his own right had already vaguely sensed an Ultimate to which he and the clan must bow? It would seem more rational to accept the Beyond as our instinctive interpretation of the world rather than call it a devising of priests, far ahead of the sophistication of their age, of which devising all men became at once the witting tools or the unwitting victims. Of course there is always a tendency to deify the state, as witness present Germany.[11] Society is ingrainedly conservative: those who receive its prizes and powers are intent to keep them, and therefore plead that social forms and laws have divine sanction and finality. The eager rallying of the predatory to "the Constitution" and their anger against subversive doctrines— anything being "subversive" which threatens the injustices of *laissez faire*—are sufficient evidence. It has been shrewdly suggested that even the Ten Commandments may have been unduly influenced by the "haves," with the "have nots" still outside the door— "Thou shalt not covet they neighbor's house. . . . ."[12] But the suggestion is token of a Spirit at work in the world which challenges all laws: "Time makes ancient good uncouth."[13] There's the rub! Why on Durkheim's theory should the customs of the tribe ever have been challenged? The prophets arose to champion the poor, and One came to earth to declare his word with quiet thunder: "Ye have heard that it was said by them of old time. . . . . But I say unto you."[14] Laws are graven in stone or written on parchment only as they are first inscribed on the "fleshly tablets of the heart." How any ideal emerges, how man ever imagines anything better than he sees, is still a mystery. Slums do not of themselves create the vision of a Plato's "Republic." It seems more consonant with history and present experience to affirm a Beyond, mediated *through* the clan but forever judging it, appealed to by priests—perchance unworthily—but instinctively honored by all men.

Notice more carefully this stone of stumbling on which the "Collective Soul" theory of prayer seems irreparably to break. The individual is never merely an adjunct of society. In body and selfhood, in craftsmanship and danger, in love-longing and death, he is his own man, walking in solitude. How can prayer ever be only a social control? The individual resists the communal pressure—at risk of martyrdom. By what compelling? Evidently by a higher "must" than the tribal law. Similes, however apt, cannot be driven to extreme; and to describe the individual as a cell in an organism may easily make us victim of a simile. In this instance the cell has a veritable and distinctive selfhood. It says to the organism, "Here stand I!" Its rebellion becomes for the organism a new trail to worthiness. Thus Antigone, in the Sophocles drama, when forbidden by the state to give burial to her traitor brother whom the state had not unjustly slain, made her protest though she courted death by stoning as her punishment:

Creon: Did'st thou then dare to disobey these laws?

Antigone: Yes, for it was not Zeus who gave them forth,
Nor Justice, dwelling with the Gods below,
Who traced these laws for all the sons of men;
Nor did I deem thy edicts strong enough,
Coming from mortal man, to set at nought
The unwritten laws of God that know not change.
They are not of today nor yesterday,
But live forever, nor can man assign
When first they sprang to being.[15]

We cannot think of the individual as other than individual, whatever his dependence on society. He judges the social process, presumably by a higher light. Knowing his own shortcomings, he yet says to all humanity, as the thief to his comrade in merited crucifixion, "Thou art in the same condemnation."[16] The "needs must" within the soul is stronger than any tribal demand.[17] Is there a "Beyond that is within," both for society and men, working through both, judging and redeeming both, honored therefore in corporate worship and individual prayer? To such a faith the slowly clarifying facts both of community and self would seem to point.

III

Then is prayer mere autosuggestion? A man need not be a theorist to feel this doubt. Who among praying folk has not sometimes said, "Perhaps I am only talking to myself"? Latterly the misgiving has gained standing as a full-grown skepticism. Prayer, we are told, is a soliloquy: its only objective answer is the echo of its sound. Not all the skeptics would therefore disavow prayer. Some would say that it is still valuable as a self-discipline. It is an inverted form of self-reliance; and beyond cavil the man who says, "I shall fail," is already unnerved; while he who whispers to himself, "I can," is already half triumphant. So prayer, these critics would allow, is a "healthy lie of life" which pours new confidence into the reservoirs of the subconscious.

But again the theory breaks upon the rock of fact. In strict sense there is no autosuggestion, for whatever we propose to ourselves takes rise in some measure beyond ourselves. If in a dream we see our house attacked by green unicorns each with a tail like a meteor and eight legs shod with lightning, the dream would still draw for its material upon a world beyond ourselves. The combination may be ours, but not the ingredients: we have seen, in picture or in actuality, green, lightning, meteors, and unicorns. It is not in man's power, even in his thoughts, to make something out of nothing. Autosuggestion is not an inner spring: it is the hidden channel of a river with far objective sources. As has been well said, it would be more accurate to affirm, not that prayer is autosuggestion, but that autosuggestion is a form of prayer. If a man suggests God to himself, presumably that august idea also had its fount beyond the pool of man's own life.

Furthermore, if prayer were only a "healthy lie"—supposing lies could ever be healthy—it would be detected, and noble spirits would renounce it. But prayer has been the central faith of many a noble spirit; and souls as realistic as Jesus, "brave Son of fact," have found in prayer their vital breath. "Murder will out." A lie, even "a healthy lie," cannot long pose as truth. The movement of the universe seems to be an unfolding: it cannot keep a secret: "there is nothing . . . . hid, that shall not be known."[18] A modern proverb insists that "it is fun to be fooled," but it is fun only when we know we are being fooled, and then only as test of our defenses. Facts have their coercion, and human nature its fundamental honesty. If prayer were a pretense it might have endured a generation: it could hardly have been an agelong rapture. Many who have prayed would have repudiated instantly any self-deception. Indeed they have prayed to be delivered from self-deception: "Search me, O God, and know my heart; try me, and know my thoughts; and see if there be any wicked way in me, and lead me in the way everlasting."[19] Thus prayer at its best is itself a fundamental honesty. It has had inward grace of redemption from lies. Age after age it is purified: the tribal deity of the early Old Testament becomes "the God and Father of our Lord Jesus Christ." To propose that the universal travail of prayer, with its throes of spirit and its issues in martyrdom, is only a man talking to himself is not a convincing theory. Jesus, with ethic gleaming white and courage unto a cross, prayed there, "Father, forgive them." Let the critic insist that he was talking only to a white-bearded imagining called God, or indulging a poor self-mumbling: the critic, not Jesus, is then under judgment. Shallowness could hardly be more shallow.

There is a further rejoinder. Mere autosuggestion, with no foundation in fact, would be a force for chaos; for it would be against the grain of reality. Unworthy forms of prayer—pleas merely cowardly or a private selfishness—*have* been chaotic, but worthy prayer has been an integration. Can there be any real doubt that nights spent on a mountainside in prayer sharpened the judgment of Jesus, granted him vision, and confirmed him in that courage and consecration which are the world-abiding miracle? Nor has this wholeness given by prayer been transitory, pending the detection of a self-deception: it is the testimony in word and life of all the saints. The ages have drunk of their loyalty and light. If this is prayer's issue how can prayer be dubbed a chimera? Would that we might all live beneath the mirage! A striking acknowledgment is given in Dr. J. A. Hadfield's "The Psychology of Power":

Speaking as a student of psychotherapy, who, as such, has no concern with theology, I am convinced that the Christian religion is one of the most valuable and potent influences that we possess for producing that harmony and peace of mind . . . . needed to bring health and power to a large proportion of nervous patients. In some cases I have attempted to cure nervous patients with suggestions of quietness and confidence, but without success until I have linked these suggestions on to that faith in the power of God which is the substance of the Christian's confidence and hope. Then the patient has become strong.[20]

This is a fascinating paragraph: it bristles with interrogations. We would like to ask the author: "Then can you any longer have 'no concern with theology'? You would not suggest 'faith in the power of God' without believing in it? Can psychotherapy hope to be genuinely constructive without some basic faith?" But these questions do not impair the verdict. It is supported, as to physical and mental health, by increasing evidence.[21] The integration wrought by prayer goes far beyond health of body and "mind"—as it must to be convincing, for all men must die: prayer grants wholeness of vision and motive. If there is any world-purpose, if Christ in any measure reveals it, and if prayer gathers life's unruly waters into the crystal precipitate of that purpose, how can prayer be merely man's self-proposal? If prayer were only autosuggestion it would be thistledown carried away by the wind, or wrecked like a boat defying the stars; whereas, at its best, it is deeply consonant with man's truest life. Why should we not believe that it is therefore the moving of a Cosmic Spirit?

IV

One other defective theory, very characteristic of an age just dying, almost vocally demands examination. "Projection," "wishful thinking," "rationalization" are a new vocabulary, but they represent a potent and widespread doubt. This psychological onslaught on the citadel of faith did not arise of itself: it was enlisted to explain what skepticism termed the agelong aberration of religion. That is to say, a group of sincere critics, of whom, in America, Joseph Wood Krutch, Eustace Hayden, and Walter Lippmann may be regarded as types and leaders, determined on grounds other than psychological that faith in God is folly. Then, confronted by the immemorial phenomenon of faith, they turned to psychology to account for this "blunder" of the generations. With the skepticism itself we are not now concerned. We have tried elsewhere to trace the natural history of modern doubt.[22] It arose from an overweening and unwarranted reliance on the "scientific" view. It arose from the ancient doubt concerning an apparently unheeding universe, a doubt older than Omar Khayyám but never stated more persuasively than in the *Rubáiyát*. It arose, perhaps mainly, from the pagan life of the modern world, since life shapes our creeds even as our creeds shape life. Our inquiry will lead us again to explore this ground of modern skepticism,[23] but we are presently concerned only with a certain psychological account of prayer. Some account had to be given: if there is no God why have the journeying generations believed in Him? Why have men prayed? The critics enlisted psychological reinforcements, and marched forth to hurl charges of "projection," "wishful thinking," and "rationalization." The contention in brief is this: God, if He exists, is as inert as the moon. But most of the race, too timid to face the fact of a world "blind and deaf to our beseeching," invented a man-in-the-moon—who is really a dried-up ocean bed—to whom age after age prayers have been offered for man's timid comfort.

It might be enough to answer that this view, laid alongside the agelong travail of prayer, has all the marks of a hasty glance and a clever guess. But the view has gained such wide currency that answer must be more specific. Let us admit that there *is* "rationalization" in religion and in every realm. Men have always been tempted to "make the worse appear the better reason"—because of some basic optimism, or for fear's sake, or for quick advantage. There *is* "projection": men have imprinted on the sky for worship many a god made only in man's image. There *is* "wishful thinking": "the wish is father to the thought." That these subtle self-deceptions infect the whole range of man's life—his psychologies and skepticisms, for instance, as well as his religion—no honest man can doubt. In every prayer a man must be on guard, and is perhaps never quite unscathed. But the question is this: can prayer, in its whole sweep and at its best, be stigmatized as a whistling in the dark? For instance, can the prayer of Jesus for his murderers, "Father, forgive them, for they know not what they do,"[24] be dismissed as a timid plea to the man in the moon? When the question is thus sharply stated, the answer is not long in doubt. The projection theory has no grace of profundity. The original skepticisms were weighty and honorable, but the psychological ally is bedraggled and thin.

Man has always wondered if his world is real. The misgiving arises, from the days of the Greek sophists to our day, even of tangible and visible things. It is the more acute of "things unseen." Trees are in doubt: they may exist only behind the optic and tactile nerves. Love is in double doubt. Not strangely solipsism is a recurrent theory, but not strangely its force is soon spent. How do we know that sunrise or great music has its own reality? First, it is faithfully recurrent. If it were a private vagary it would hardly keep its own characteristics. It is doubtful, for example, if the sunrise would always occur in the east. Second, it is attested by the group; and though great music has a different meaning for each different hearer—being one thing to a radio engineer, another to an acoustician, another to a composer, and still another to a music printer—it is yet its "own" in sufficient measure to make a common cause for all hearers. Third, it takes us by surprise. It has its own initiatives. We are sure by some instant tang of consciousness it comes from "out there" as well as from "in here." The same argument holds of man's ideals: they also are faithfully recurrent, socially attested, and have their own instigations and demands. Dr. David S. Cairns has recently written: "In the last resort the great issue as to whether the universe . . . . is fundamentally sub-moral, sub-human, and sub-rational, because impersonal and unconscious, seems to me to turn, above all, on the question of whether I ought to do the highest that I know."[25] "I ought to do the highest that I know" is faithfully recurrent, socially attested, and has its own benign coercions. We no more made "the best that I know" than we made ourselves. How, then, can it be mere "projection"—however locally distorted—mere "rationalization," or mere "wishful thinking"?

There is ultimately no argument for prayer except praying, but there is an argument to rebut the arguments leveled against prayer. Furthermore, there is a basic matter-of-factness, a substratum of sanity, which approves of itself when left to itself the record concerning Jesus: "And it came to pass in those days, that he went into a mountain to pray, and continued all night in prayer *to God*."[26] Prayer in its essence is neither fear, nor social control, nor autosuggestion, nor rationalization. The certitude abides that it is comradeship with God. We turn, then, to the vast assumptions which Jesus made in prayer—God, man, and the world: the "personality" of God, the real freedom of man, and the faithfulness yet flexibility of the world. We shall now ask by what positive right we may hold a similar faith.

Chapter IV

JESUS' ASSUMPTIONS IN PRAYER

To MEN WITH misgivings Jesus seems to beg the questions and assume the answers. Is man free? We wonder, fearful that mankind may be only a casual midge-breed in the cosmic marsh. But Jesus calmly takes our freedom for granted. "Repent ye, and believe the gospel" .... "Go ye" .... "Pray" .... "If any man will to do his will."[1] Apparently Jesus had no doubts of human freedom: man has his Magna Charta, his royal grant of liberty. Is God objectively real? We worry or deny. God, we fear, may be only an image in the mind; or He may be only our own reflection in an automobile windshield in driving rain on a mountainous road on a dark night. There may be no God: only the grinding of aeonian wheels. But Jesus appears never to have asked the question, and therefore never answered it: "When ye pray, say, Our Father"[2]—as though God were much closer than our hand. Is the world tractable to our hopes? We argue with deep concern. The world may be an iron scheme without nerves or eyes, without conscience or heart, without anything to answer our yearning. But again Jesus assumes all that we alarmedly debate: "My Father worketh hitherto, and I work" .... "Whatsoever ye shall ask the Father in my name, he will give it you."[3] This simple faith seems all too simple. It does not make him stranger, as it might, for he still haunts us. But sometimes it leaves us wondering, or impatient, or forlorn. Can it never be written of him that

He faced the spectres of the mind
And laid them; thus he came at length

To find a stronger faith his own;
And Power was with him in the night

Which makes the darkness and the light,
And dwells not in the light alone?[4]

Otherwise how can he have any word for us, children of
tumbled darkness and light? Could it be that every man
by inmost nature must make the assumptions Jesus
made? Perhaps Jesus silently kept under heel the wri-
thing of the doubt. Perhaps our best courage—yea, our
very life, as when a man knows he must not confuse
darkness with light—is in the refusal of any alien assumptions. Perhaps the spirit's axioms are these: man is
free, God lives, and the world is a place for their comradeship.

I

If man is not free, prayer is folly. For then uplifted
hands are but antics of a marionette, and sacred words
only the turning of a phonograph. Our generation
brings converging battalions against faith in personal
worth. Science deliberately ignores individual differences in quest for general laws—a method valid in the
scientific realm, but deadly in the interplay of human
life. Astronomy speaks of light years, medicine of cor-
puscles, biology of chromosomes, and psychology of
complexes: the man John Smith is easily forgotten.
Sometimes he is lost. The mass formations of our dubious civilization are a graver threat. Cities herd men in
mean streets and jostle them in crowds until identity
seems to vanish. Industry regiments men, and makes
each personal equation the servant of the machine with
its million "goods" in dreary replica. In the Middle
Ages local apprenticeship and the craft guilds enthroned
the individual or at least educed selfhood; but our mass
production glorifies the cog-in-the-wheel. Meanwhile
war robs a man of even his name: he is a number on a

metal disc. Wholesale murder in daily announcement—
"it is estimated that ten thousand were killed"—spreads
a cynical doubt:

> Raving politics, never at rest—as this poor earth's pale
> history runs—
> What is it all but a trouble of ants in the gleam of a
> million million of suns?[5]

It is nowadays easy to think of man, but hard indeed to
think in terms of this man and that man.

Even so there is small fear that the machine will ever
become a Frankenstein robot. Individuality persists, the
apparent sign-royal of freedom. The very depersonali-
zations of modern life came, paradoxically, with the
genius of singularly "nonconformist" minds: natural
science from Francis Bacon, modern astronomy from
Nikolaus Copernicus, psychoanalysis from Sigmund
Freud, and modern industry from James Watt and his
epoch-making engine. Even the regimentation of current wars is traceable to personalities as sharply distinctive as Adolf Hitler and Benito Mussolini. Life itself
seems to insure that mass pressure shall splinter again
into its units. Real conversations are not stereotyped.
Artistry is an individual gift. Thoughts are intimate.
Memory is essentially personal. Love knows its own.
Prayer is selfhood aflame—the more itself because it is
lost in God: at Pentecost every man was heard speaking
"in his own language."[6] In this wide realm where sepa-
rateness reigns, people are valued not only because they
are like, but more because they are unlike: friends are
dear for their idiosyncrasies of gesture and thought. To
a stay-at-home in America the Chinese are just Chinese,
but to an American who has lived for twenty years in
Shanghai the Chinese are individual faces and names. It
is a rule that ignorance and indifference see men in the
mass, while knowledge and love resolve the mass into
remembered friends. The Good Shepherd "calleth his
own sheep by name."[7] If God is Wisdom and Love, He
knows his own, as a Father knows his children. Is that
why conscience is so acutely individual? Is that why

compassion whispers each man in the ear? Is that why every man has his own fingerprint and original spirit? Despite the onslaughts of a machine age individuality persists.

Moreover, individuality *assumes* its freedom. The assumption may not be as untrammeled as in Jesus' mind, but it is always made. Perhaps Omar Khayyám was a pessimist, and perhaps a poet—a poet being one who lives on the bridge between the world's contradiction and the soul's imperishable dream, and sets both to music. But *if* he was a pessimist, *if* he firmly believed that

> We are no other than a moving row
> Of Magic Shadow-shapes that come and go
> Round with the Sun-illumin'd Lantern held
> In Midnight by the Master of the Show,[8]

it never occurred to him that his skepticism also was a mere "shadow-shape" or that his denial itself was a puppet-antic. A thoroughgoing behaviorist might argue that our words and thoughts are only an inevitable response to some external stimulus, but he would not believe that his own pet theory of behaviorism is also an instinctive reflex—a moving of pistons because someone stepped on the starter. A skeptic might say with Omar, "We are 'but helpless Pieces of the Game He plays,'" but he would not allow, except by some tinkering with immediate consciousness, that his bitter revolt is also a pawn moved by the hidden Tyrant. The cynic denies our freedom, but assumes that his denial is free. Thus every time he drives freedom from the front door he invites it back through the kitchen. Only sophistication, dialectic, and despair dispute our liberty; and instantly life reassumes it.

It is easy to frame an apparently punctureproof argument to show that we are bondslaves of heredity and circumstance. Is not any thought provoked, directly or indirectly, by some event beyond our control? And is not that event in unbreakable sequence with other events? Do we not therefore become menials, to reverse a Shakespearian phrase, of

Yesterday and *yesterday* and *yesterday* . . . .
To the *first* syllable of recorded time?⁹

Is not every man thus moved by the dead hand of all
the past? The argument is almost unanswerable in
"logic," but it is constantly answered in life. For, however convinced we may be by the dialectic, we promptly
proceed to live in the assumption of liberty. Every announcement assumes our freedom: "Keep off the grass"
takes it for granted that we may either obey or trespass.
Every condemnation assumes our freedom, and every
approval: why indict a slaughter of innocents if the
murderers are but straws on a stream, and why approve
heroism if the hero is only a marionet? Every memory
held in remorse assumes our freedom: why regret a
treachery if it is not treachery but only an automatism?
Every crusade against tyranny assumes our freedom:
why suffer if we and the tyrant are only going through
the motions? A famous attorney¹⁰ defended a young
criminal on the plea that the boy could not help himself.
The brief broadly suggested that no man can help himself, and then eloquently entreated the jury to render a
verdict favoring the defendant—forgetting that by the
very argument the jury could not help themselves, but
could do only as they were foreordained. Enough: there
is no need to argue an axiom. The burden of proof is on
those who deny, and they promptly reassume freedom
in the denial. Jesus was deeply wise. He quietly kept
faith with the axiom. It is against nature to rend our
nature.

Obviously the freedom is within limits. No man can
change the calendar of the tides, or divert Neptune on
his orbit, or cancel the law of gravitation, or grow lolli-
pops on cabbages. Paul did not say, "I can do all things
through Christ which strengtheneth me."¹¹ The accurate translation reads, "I am able unto all things
through Christ who makes me strong." Man is still the
creature of time and space; but, however mysteriously,
he is a free creature. In succeeding chapters we shall
plead that his prayers also have free though limited
power. In the building of the old cathedrals the masons,

stonecutters, and woodcarvers were allowed an individual liberty within the total plan. The design was not thus impaired but made rich, as witness original masonry lines, grinning gargoyles, and wood screens that are the spirit's rapture. So we are free within the plan. To deny the freedom is, at long last, akin to the perversity that declares light to be darkness.

II

Is God personal? Jesus quietly assumed it. To a skeptical age it is almost incredible that Jesus, at least in the records left to us, never argued the existence of God. He took for granted that "Spirit with spirit can meet." Other leaders have offered proofs of Deity. Such arguments are the theologian's routine. But Jesus did not offer them. The Sadducees, who were infidel concerning immortality, tried to impale him on a stock question: "Therefore in the ressurrection whose wife shall she be . . . .?" They hoped thus to involve him in a denial of heaven, and, by implication, in a denial of God. But once again he startlingly begged the question: "Ye know not . . . . the power of God."[12] Must we admit that his wise sympathy, elsewhere so clear and ample, in this issue suddenly failed him? Or was he more deeply wise?

There is little doubt that sincere prayer has always assumed that God—or the god—is in some sense personal. Sincere prayer would hardly have been possible in any other faith. A man cannot pray to Dr. Alfred North Whitehead's "Principle of Concretion"[13] or to Dr. Henry Nelson Wieman's "Integrating Factor in Experience."[14] The fact does not impugn the value of these philosophies. They give light and leading, and serve particularly well our present age. But the fact remains that we can hold no comradeship with an abstract noun. We cannot talk to "The Life Essence" or "The Power Not Ourselves That Makes for Righteousness," or even to "The Good, the Beautiful, and the True." Some may claim that they pray in vaguest understand-

ing to "The All" or to the "World-Ground," and the
claim is sincere. But, since it is not in human nature to
discuss life with a wall, or to plead earnestly with a fog,
these agnostic souls must assume, however dimly, a
"Spirit" in "The All"—a "Spirit" which, however unlike their own, has some kinship with them.[15] The savage worshiped not the idol but the god in the idol. The
modern man worships not an abstract Truth, but a
Truth already known in vital impact. "Abstract" means
"torn away from": an abstract noun is torn away from
life. If it is left stranded, it languishes and dies. The
field of second-rate religion is strewn with the corpses
of abstract nouns.

Proofs of God have value, not for what they purport
to be, but because they score more deep a faith already
held. An argument does not establish an axiom: the axiom validates the argument. Logic does not clinch truth:
truth integrates logic. Proofs do not certify God: God
certifies proofs. If God is, we cannot deduce God from
anything, except we have first deduced all things from
God: "In him we live, and move, and have our
being."[16]

> Your music's power your music must disclose,
> For what light is 'tis only light that shows.[17]

It is not surprising that the time-honored proofs, the
cosmological, ontological, teleological, and others,
should each reveal on examination a *petitio principii* or
some other flaw in logic.[18] The arguments for a First
Cause, a Purpose, a Designer, or a Fountainhead of our
highest ideas, can each be shown to assume "the thing
to be proved"—because the "proof" itself marches by
the power and light of "the thing to be proved." There
is in all the world no proof of God, for He proves all
the world. The best we can hope to find—it is enough
"for human nature's daily food"—is not a proof or an
ironclad argument, but rather the opening of clay-
shuttered eyes, a pointing finger of sudden insight, and
a voice exclaiming, "There! Do you see Him?"

> The angels keep their ancient places;—
> Turn but a stone, and start a wing!
> 'Tis ye, 'tis your estrangèd faces,
> That miss the many-splendoured thing.[19]

We "catch" our freedom only in that immediacy in which we *assume* freedom. Freedom cannot be analyzed or proved: we use it to prove it. How can we "catch" the sense of God? Only in the instant consciousness in which we assume God. He is the inevitable postulate. This Jesus knew. This he made the ground-verity of his teaching.

Every man wittingly or unwittingly makes this same assumption of a "personal" God. Dr. George Albert Coe quotes Stanton Coit regarding the survivors of the "Titanic" at the moment of their calamity. They were not stunned, they reported, but "lifted into an atmosphere of vision where self-centered suffering merges into some mystic meaning. . . . . We were all one, not only with one another, but with the cosmic being that for a time had seemed so cruel."[20] The same author quotes also William James' analysis of his own feelings and those of other people who were at Stanford University during the California earthquake. The description runs:

As soon as I could think, I discerned retrospectively certain peculiar ways in which my consciousness had taken in the phenomenon. . . . . First, I personified the earthquake as a permanent individual entity. . . . . Animus and intent were never more present in any human action, nor did any human activity ever more definitely point back to a living agent as its source and origin. All whom I consulted on the point agreed as to this feature in their experience. "It expressed intention." "It was vicious." . . . . To me it simply wanted to manifest the full meaning of its name. But what was this "It"? To some, apparently, a vague, demoniac power; to me an individualized thing.[21]

It appears that when life is broken by tragedy God shines through the breach. Tragedy perchance is fully tragic only to the onlooker. To the victim it may be

apocalypse through tragedy. Even when life is not rent
by crisis it is not opaque. The ordinary day reveals,
however dimly, the "Shadowy Third." Why, in some
foolish, momentarily uncontrollable anger, do we rail
against a world that brings sorrow? Why, when we are
becalmed on the lake and a breeze suddenly comes to
fill the sails, do we exclaim, "That's fine"? Why do we
feel grateful on a perfect summer day? Gratitude is a
person-to-person reaction. Is there not a story of Har-
riet Martineau, who was not too positive in faith, that she
exclaimed on a bright spring morning, "I'm so grateful"; and that her more believing friend, replied,
"Grateful to whom, my dear?" Why do we feel accused
and convicted after our treacheries, or glad and "whole"
when we keep faith in temptation? Accusation and
judgment, approval and vindication—these again are
person-to-person relationships. The Ancient Mariner
was not in the hands of the crew only, or only in the
avenging claws of the albatross. There was no need that
his fellow sailors should hang the dead bird around his
neck. He had gashed the kindly grace of the scheme of
things. That "scheme" was more than "things," for "it"
accused him. Why do we feel of any new item of knowledge that Someone knew it from the foundation of the
world? When insulin was discovered we all said, at the
back of our minds, "It was waiting there, and *known,*
all the time." Why do we feel of mountains blue in distance, or of any loveliness, that Someone saw it long
before any human eye? The Genesis story is true to life:
"And God saw that it was good."[22] Why do we constantly suspect of our experience that Someone planned
it? Its million chances and changes, its momentous turns
hinging on trivial happenings, its myriad meshings with
other lives, are quite beyond our wit. Then whose wit?

> There's a divinity that shapes our ends,
> Rough-hew them how we will.[23]

It was a fine insight which prompted Paul to say: "Now
I know in part; but then shall I know even as also I
have all along been known."[24] There is a touch of the

Eternal on every common hour. Each workaday thought or mood has its fringe of glory. Why do we try to deduce God from "causality" or "purpose"? We could not try unless God were already at our elbow. Why do we try to infer God from "The Good, the Beautiful, and the True"? These are but abstractions, the torn remnants of His seamless robe. There is small fear that we shall lose Him. So long as life endures He will take us unawares. Atheism is an impossible venture, for atheism also is an unconscious testimony: it could not occur to men to deny what never was, or is, or ever can be. To deny light is to confess that already we have found it.

We can partly understand why God should reveal Himself by gleam and hint rather than in dazzling light, by shadow and footfall rather than by indubitable presence. An obtrusive God, His "I" written in a mammoth letter in every sky, His thunderous tones drowning all human speech, would not be Godlike. Besides, we would be "blinded by excess of light," for our sight is yet dim. If He is intent on our perfecting He cannot coerce us. He cannot terrorize men into goodness. We cannot drive them with bit and bridle and whip. "I will guide thee with mine eyes."[25] It is a token of grace that God comes in the breach of tragedy. It is Godlike that He should come like the celestial visitor of Greek myth who was never seen, but whose presence was known because now a fountain gushed where yesterday there had been barren sand. It is the sign-royal of divinity that God should come, not in browbeating cataclysm, but as an unseen Traveler whose kindness is understood only in the memory of the journey, or as a Carpenter at a village bench, or as a Man dying on a cross.

Dimly we can understand also why God should seem inflexible, harshly indifferent to our fond desires. Dr. Hocking rightly maintains: "It is just in this character of ultimate opposition to me and my wishes, of high superiority to any doings or thinkings of mine, that Nature begins to assume for me the unmistakable aspect of Other Mind."[26] Even on the human level the other person is always a paradox of like and unlike, and by both terms of the paradox we are drawn to him. In some

ways he is like us: we share, for instance, an interest in
athletics and music, and a yearning for the outlawry of
war. In some ways he is unlike: we cannot understand
his taste in books, or denominational choice in worship,
or almost moody preoccupation. If we were completely
alike there could be no comradeship, only the mergent
death of identity. Friendship lives by both its tensions
and its affinities. Even so with the friendship called
prayer. On a spring morning, or in any of life's million
amenities, God is "like"; but in tragedy, or the seeming
heartlessness of the skies, or the stern imperatives of
conscience, or the bafflement of unanswered prayer, He
is unlike. He comes, says Dr. Herbert H. Farmer, in
the seemingly opposite but not contradictory aspects of
"succor and demand."[27] There is always a "dark line
in God's Face," and always lines of great mercy: "For
my thoughts are not your thoughts, neither are your
ways my ways, saith the Lord. For as the heavens are
higher than the earth, so are my ways higher than your
ways, and my thoughts than your thoughts."[28] It is a
foolish fear that the adamant of God will drive us from
Him. This friendship also lives by its tensions as well as
by its kinships. If there were no "Other" in God, no
darkness, no repellent crossing of our creature desires,
we could neither love nor worship Him.

"Personality," applied to God, is admittedly a poor
word. What word can be anything but poor? All our
words of speech and architecture and music, all our
words of courage and heartbreak in daily life, all words
joined in one word, would still be poor. Earth has no
net of language in which to snare the skies. "Personality" as a word attributed to God is easily confused with
the body—as though God were trammeled in flesh like
a man, though that confusion may not all be loss, since
personality ought to imply some instrument for the Spirit's expression. More unfortunately "personality,"
linked with the noun "Deity," is easily confused with
the fussiness of *our* personality—with our angularities,
foolish tangents, fragmentary will, and clouded vision.
"Personality" has misled would-be praying people to
think of God with grotesque and irreverent familiarity.

Yet, despite all dangers and all the abuse which the word has suffered and to which it is always exposed, it is still the best word. It is a finer word than "Spirit," which is both too misty and too much under threat from a false occultism. It is finer than "Soul," which is both too vague and too remote from earth's actual hungers. It is a finer word than "Law," or "Purpose," for these words are almost meaningless when torn away from personal mind. It is finer than "Absolute" or any other philosophical vacuum or abstraction, for we are ultimately betrayed and forsaken by anything "abstracted." Moreover, all these alternate titles fail to do justice to the basic assumption of our human days. However we may perversely deny God in speech, we always assume Him as the dominant chord of earth's music. Jesus was deeply wise. Why argue the Truth which alone makes possible and validates the argument? Therein is the reason why Jesus offered no proofs of God. He eschewed all high-sounding abstractions. He said instead, "God is like a Sower, like a Gardener, like the Father of the prodigal." He was simple, and his simplicity was profound. He "knew what is in man." His injunction was, "When ye pray, say, Our Father." He bides his time while men debate: "Heaven and earth shall pass away, but my words shall not pass away."[29]

III

The third assumption made by Jesus in prayer holds peculiar difficulties for the modern mind. Can we take for granted that the universe is both flexible and faithful to man and God? In Jesus' age every event was a miracle; that is, it was attributed to the direct agency of spiritual powers residing just above a flat earth. But in our age every event is law: it is attributed to the unalterable energies of the universe. That these so-called laws are in their essential nature a foggier mystery than miracle has not often occurred to us. For we also are prisoners of our date: we live under the dominance—or blight—of the scientific view.

That the universe is *faithful* both for man and God

we would quickly agree. Invariably the sun rises in the east; invariably spring follows winter; invariably Newton's famous apple falls instead of taking wing. This inflexibility is at once the postulate and native air of the scientific quest. The botanist assumes that an oak tree will not over night change its identity to become a potato. The astronomer assumes that Saturn will not break out with an attack of the zigzags, but will keep its orbit. The chemist assumes that two parts of hydrogen and one part of oxygen will not suddenly become the formula for sulphuric acid, but will continue to be the constituent parts of water. Knowledge would be impossible in an eccentric world. Nay, self-consciousness itself requires a certain constancy in nature and in human nature. If John Smith were one moment Jim Jones and the next moment Bob Clark, life would be much more fantastic than a hall of mirrors. We have sometimes failed to see that our freedom and our very prayers can breathe only in a faithful scheme. If the sun chose not to rise next Tuesday, if bread suddenly became poisonous, if half the race returned in three days to infancy, if noses grew six feet long, if treachery became a virtue, if spring reverted to winter and gravitation took to drink, the world would be a phantasmagoria and God a surrealist figure seen in nightmare. In such a world sanity would become mad, and life would explode in death. We trace a cosmic faithfulness. It is necessary to life both in man and God. It is everywhere evident. It implies certain limits to the power of prayer, which limits we shall try to define. But without it prayer would not be possible, for man could not be free.

We would grant also that the world is in some measure pliable under man's hands. We build boats and catch fish. We seed fields and reap harvests. We design houses, and in them make water run uphill. We reforest to enrich the soil. We build dams to control irrigation. We remove a diseased appendix. We refine serum taken from horses, and use it to make counterattack on pneumonia. We turn the onset of death. The story of civilization is the record of the world challenging man, and man wrestling with the world to bend it to his will. The challenge comes in the beckoning of seas uncrossed, healings not yet discovered, and truth not yet revealed. Man, accepting the challenge, has built liners and airplanes, devised medicine and surgery, and voraciously pursued knowledge. There can be no doubt that man shapes a pliable world. The faithfulness of the universe abides, the materials are given; but, within limits, man works changes.

The real issue then is this: Is the universe, so faithful to God and men, and so pliable under man's hand, *open also to the controlling act of God?* The question seems to answer itself, but it is a focus of misgiving. God presumably can do as much as He challenges and enables men to do, but still we doubt. The doubt obviously involves us in contradictions. If nature, created by God, now resists or nullifies His will, if nature is a belt of inertia impervious to all the divine initiatives, He is no longer God: He is partial impotence. Or if He does not care, if He has fashioned a realm from which He is self-exiled, He is no longer God: His creatures are more capable and Godlike. Again, if nature is closed to God's invasions, man also is forsaken; for by many bonds of the body man is one with nature, however he may be also above nature. Yet we do not feel ourselves forsaken. We constantly, through perchance unwittingly, assume His presence. Thus whenever we imagine God barred from the natural order, contradictions throng. Yet the doubt persists. It is in some regards the crucial mistrust of our generation.

Where is the answer? Deeper than the doubt of human freedom, we assume freedom. Deeper than the doubt of a "personal" God, we know Him in His subtly "personal" impacts; and whenever our agnosticisms are off guard He is there—the "Grand Perhaps," far stronger than all our denials. Now: deeper than the doubt that God can change the world, we *assume* His active presence. Nor can we forebear: the assumption is constitutional. Is His initiative affected by our prayers? If so, how and to what measure? Can His activity be reconciled with "natural law"? These questions we shall later try to answer.[30] We are now concerned only with

our basic assumption that God is constantly busy in his
world. The instances of the assumption, and the occasions of it, are legion. For there is an impromptu character in nature as well as a faithfulness. "Constantly
busy" is the accurate description—there *is* constancy
with unpredictable newness and change. The world
wears a paradoxical appearance of law and liberty. The
surprise is as marked a feature as the pattern. This fact
even science now acknowledges, despite a predisposi-
tion for the regular, and calls it "contingency." Why
does sunlight suddenly fall on *that* hill? Why should lu-
pines stain *that* dell with a blue glory? Why should the
angel of death visit *that* home at *that* hour? Why should
that man stumble on *that* stone to his gain or loss? Why
should Columbus, rather than some other man in some
other age, see driftwood on the shore instead of wheat
in a field? And why should he see it at just the psychological moment, and so change the history of the race?
Why should Esther "come to the kingdom for such a
time as this,"[31] or Garibaldi at the pivotal hour of Italy's need? Why should Jesus visit our narrow valley in
"the fullness of the time"?[32] A man maintains his nature, but his words and actions are nevertheless extempore. The "living universe" likewise has the dual aspect
of fixity and change. The cosmos is as full of surprises
as it is law-abiding. We must do justice to this dual fact.
Such justice would be epochal: it would spell a revolution in thinking, and not least in our philosophy of
prayer. We cannot reasonably assign the regularity of
the world to God, and the extemporaneousness to
chance or some alien will, for the two aspects are a
manifest unity. If science fails in full acknowledgment
of his spontaneity in nature, we shall be wise to suspect
the scientific view, at least as an interpretation of life;
for the spontaneity is so marked a feature that without it
life, becoming always predictable, would turn to
routine-death.

The fact that nature is an "improvising" within a
faithfulness accounts, together with our basic assumption of God's presence, for man's persistent belief that

the whole world is a "sign-language." Always our race, troubled and saved by the sense of "Someone passing by," has asked, "What if Earth be but the shadow of Heaven?"[33] and has surmised that "nature speaks in symbols and in signs." Men of old read the stars—"By night an atheist half believes a God"[34]—or strove to interpret the flight of birds. Macbeth saw in the night storm the token of heaven's condemnation, and Francis Thompson found in the setting sun another picture of Jesus on the rood. These are but instances of a universal practice. The world is speaking to us, sometimes straightly, sometimes in code for which we long to find the key; and we must listen and obey. Hence the persistent belief in miracle. For miracle, in its essence, is not something grotesque, not a rending which leaves the natural world in tatters, but an event so shaped by God that it pierces life with his personal meaning.[35] The only true faithfulness is miraculous faithfulness. The fluid surprise of nature is not merely in general or beyond our eyes: it is addressed specifically to each man. Nature creatively shapes not merely the race in mass, but every individual will. As William James's comrades said of the earthquake, so each man says of each pondered and uncontrolled event of his days: "It expressed intention." However quickly we rebel against the death of a friend, it is probable that our sense of a Presence is ever quicker: we are instantly aware that Eternity now has dealings with us. Certainly it is true that within the moated walls and secret hold of personality each man finds his own meaning in events. The unpredictable changes and onsets of the world have their special and continuous word for him, their special and continuous shaping of his spirit. So the conviction remains, dim or clear, that God is "constantly busy," not only in the world, but with each man. There is small fear that the conviction will vanish. It is unanalyzable and primal. Without it we could not live. If science contradicts it, to that measure science is unreal. The sequence of events for every man is, "Someone passing by," yea, Someone stopping at his door.

IV

We have tried to show that the assumptions which
Jesus confidently made in prayer we also make in our
more timid faith: man is free, God is "personal," and
the world is both faithful and plastic to their comradeship. How can our timidity become confidence? By
prayer itself—and by faith. As for faith, some comment
is here in proper place. Because the issue is vital, a
fuller inquiry will follow.[36] Faith is basic confidence. It
informs all our life. Faith is the certitude that the universe is intelligible, learning being grounded in faith; or
that disease can be conquered, medicine being grounded
in faith; or that God can be known, religion being
grounded in faith. Faith becomes active and potent
when we affirm this basic confidence, and "highly resolve" to live in it.

"Projection" may not be unworthy. Rightly conceived, it is essential. If "projection" implies "I make
believe," it is dangerous because unreal. But if "projection" means "I believe the basic though apparently eva-
nescent assumptions of my nature," "projection" is the
highway to life. Granted a prior "out-thereness" on the
part of God, granted the onsets of a "Shadowy Third,"
our brave and creative answer is an ejaculation of the
spirit. The word "ejaculation" is derived from *jacula,* a
spear. "I believe" is a spear-thrust of the spirit of man
in answer to a Beckoning. It is worthy "projection."
Life waits upon this venture of faith, as Jesus constantly
declared. Our modern demand, "Prove it to me," easily
becomes cowardice. That kind of mind sits at home to
receive all arguments about God. The gravedigger, the
mystic, the novelist, and the chemist call in turn. The
prove-it-to-me mind is scientifically polite to all, and
serves afternoon tea. When the guests have gone it pon-
ders the arguments, and concludes: "I find no convincing proof: I am an agnostic." A recent instance of the
prove-it-to-me mind was that of the popular novelist
who on a public platform dared God to strike him dead;
and who, when nothing happened, denied the existence

of God. It would have been just as reasonable to infer that God exists, since only God could have been so patient with such folly. The defect of the proof-demanding mind is that it can never reach any conclusion. It can never reach anything, because it does not move. It just sits, and waits for certainties. It is hardly a mind. It is a pumpkin into which the world shoots its arrows black or white, a cash register for ringing up pros and cons, an almost mechanical lie detector; but hardly a mind. In fine weather it tends to believe; in storm it doubts. Its universe is always in tantalizing equipoise—snakes and butterflies, summer and winter, laughter and tears. It cannot strongly believe or disbelieve, for it is noncommittal, and may therefore end by being trivial. The apparent equipoise of life is tipped to the side of *certitude*—not necessarily *certainty*—only by the courage of faith. The mind also must take its risks. "He that cometh to God must believe that he is, and that he is a rewarder of them that diligently seek him."[37] So Dr. Hocking writes with penetration:

For the proof of . . . . my God-idea is this: that in meeting my world divinely it shows itself divine. It supports my postulate. And without such an act of will, no discovery of divinity could take place. . . . . Impute then to the world a living beneficence: the world will not reject this imputation. . . . . He who waits his assent till God is proved to him, will never find Him. But he who seeks finds—has already found.[38]

The faith of Jesus that man is free, God "personal," and the world a sphere for their creative comradeship was not naïve. His apparent "begging the question," and his refusal to argue, imply no lack of understanding and sympathy. The world has dealings with us, and there is always enough evidence for Jesus' basic postulates. *Enough* evidence, but never too much. Too much would not be proof: it would be coercion. Proofs that battered the mind to pulp, leaving it helpless, would spell the death of courage and the end of growth. Jesus had no time for dialectic, for to dialectic the world is always in balance. Jesus lived in faith. He kept under heel every insinuating doubt. He met his world divinely, and "it showed itself divine." He met his world through prayer.

Chapter V

THE PROBLEM
OF PETITIONARY PRAYER

BY PETITIONARY PRAYER is meant, in loose definition, prayer which asks God to change things. Its immediate object, though perhaps not its ultimate concern, is to affect the interplay of natural forces and human will. Few people doubt that prayer cleanses and ennobles the spirit of the man who prays:

> Lord, what a change *within us* one short hour
> Spent in Thy presence will avail to make![1]

But can it "avail to make" a change *outside* us? And, supposing it can, is such prayer really justified? That is our question.

It is not the final question about prayer, but for many it is the first; and we cannot end until we begin. It may not be the deepest question, but it is for many the most debated. It is the focus of prayer's doubt. "Focus" in the Latin means "fireplace," and here in truth is a burning issue. "Focus" in pathology means "the point of injury or lesion," and here in truth the life of prayer has suffered a deep wound, as witness the present sharp division among honest minds. Mario Puglisi in his book *Prayer*[2] broadly hints that all petition is eudaemonistic (savoring of magic, and selfish), and that we need not be surprised therefore if arguments offered to support it break logic and deepen confusion. In a similar vein Dr. A. L. Lilley quotes Cicero as an example of pagan prayer: "We do not pray to Jupiter to make us good, but to give us material benefits"; and insists that "those for the Christian are just the things for which . . . . no one would think of praying to God."[3] Likewise Dr. Alva W. Taylor, writing in an interesting symposium entitled *We Believe in Prayer,* clearly affirms, "If prayer means the direct interposition of Providence to favor us in material things, I can no longer believe in it."[4] But Ulrich Zwingli said that prayer is "a begging for the necessaries of life." Friedrich Heiler declares that "the kernel of prophetic prayer is . . . . the simple request for deliverance from an evil, or the granting of gifts and favor," and that "the Lord's Prayer is . . . . exclusively petition."[5] The widely read writings of Dr. Glenn Clark are in large measure a testimony to the power of petitionary prayer.[6] In more searching mind Dr. Herbert H. Farmer holds that the word "prayer" in most languages indicates that "petition is the heart of prayer,"[7] a point of view which he himself defends and advocates. Thus we are in No Man's Land. It is a good locale from which to view the battle, but somewhat exposed; and it is only small comfort to know that if we are killed, we shall be buried in good company, whoever conducts the interment.

Far more compelling than all these voices pro and con is the dictum of Christ: "When ye pray, say, ... Give us this day our daily bread." The Church Fathers interpreted "bread" to mean spiritual food. But, without full warrant, they allegorized all Scripture, as, for instance, the parables of Jesus; and it is now generally agreed among scholars that "bread" in the Lord's Prayer means just what it appears to mean. Nor is its testimony blunted if we say with a recent commentator: "The right prayer for a thing should put us in the way of the proper process for producing or delivering that thing. Can a farmer get the answer to his prayer for a crop without farming?"[8] The question is not whether Jesus proposes prayer as a lazy substitute for work: we all know that he would be the last to deny that worthy men must work and share. Yet the world shortly before harvest is only a few weeks from starvation; and, however faithful a man may be in toil and planning, a million changes intricately interwoven rule and threaten his daily bread. In the final issue a man does not feed himself: the "world" feeds him. He is guest of the Spirit who informs nature and orders the whole adventure of human life. In any event, petition seems to be enshrined in the Lord's Prayer, and it is supported by the command "Ask!" which Jesus was apparently wont to use. Shall we say, then, that Jesus encourages petition? Can we rightly "pray for things"?

I

Plainly we may not *dogmatically* rule petition out of court. To dismiss it as "childish" is not convincing. There are gifts which earthly parents cannot wisely grant until their children ask for them. Indeed, a child's askings are a self-disclosure. They must often be denied or "turned"; but sometimes they must be gratified, even though they are not fully wise, because to acquiesce is at that moment the best honoring of a child's personality and the best road of guidance. Are we not children in God's sight? To dismiss petition as "absurd and presumptuous" is also not convincing. A yearning agelong and deep rooted cannot be slain by a couple of adjectives. Emmanuel Kant made the attempt: "It is," he said, "at once an absurd and presumptuous delusion to try by the insistent importunity of prayer, whether God might not be deflected from the plan of his wisdom to provide some momentary advantage for us."[9] The comment is full of assumptions: the pedantic philosopher, taking his meticulously punctual daily promenades, was often but not always vast in mind. Petitionary prayer is more than "insistent importunity": often it is a cry *in extremis*. Moreover, "the plan of his widsom" may conceivably be to work *through* our prayers, as we work through a child's askings. Moreover, petition may involve not merely "momentary advantage" but issues of life and death. Moreover, by Kant's reasoning in this instance, it might be "absurd and presumptuous" to plow a field, for plowing deflects God from His plan to let the field run to seed. It might be "absurd and presumptuous" for us to think and purpose; for God in His wisdom can fulfill His plans better if He is spared the meddling of our poor brain cells—or even Emmanuel Kant's brain cells. "Oh! but," someone might vigorously and rightly object, "we have learned concerning our thought and labor that God has provided a realm of the uncreated, in which man, for man's growth, is co-worker with God." Granted: but by the same token God may have provided a realm of the uncreated in which the human-divine *friendship* may be fulfilled.

Other hasty dogmatisms should be equally suspect. For instance, to dismiss petitionary prayer as "selfish" is not convincing. "Selfish" is a wide word. In a certain sense Edith Cavell was selfish when she risked and lost her life in Belgium: she did as she deeply wished to do, like any saint. The word "selfish" derives its meaning from a cleft in our nature. "For whosoever will save his life [his lower life] shall lose it [his higher life]."[10] The higher selfishness, which we rightly call unselfishness, is a constant cleaving to the higher self. But this self, not less than the lower, is entangled with the world of things. If a young man's best service to mankind is plainly through an early-evidenced genius as engineer, would he be "selfish" to petition God to grant him opportunity in books and training? To dismiss petitionary prayer as "unnecessary, because a good God will give me what is good, nor wait for my asking" is unconvincing. If an earthly father dealt with a child thus he would spoil him in very truth and in every sense of the word. A gift requires a receiver ready and able to accept and use as much as it requires a giver able and willing to give. The "Preludes" of Chopin are rich treasure, but they can be fully given only to someone of attuned spirit disciplined in music. How otherwise with God's gifts? Prayer is the attuning of the spirit, and is besides its own high discipline.

One other hasty dogmatism, highly favored in our particular era, requires special mention: to dismiss petitionary prayer as "unscientific" is not convincing. It is quite *un*convincing, for it is an outright and unwarranted stealing of a main issue. A recent writer thus affirms: "It would be unreasonable to expect God . . . .

to make direct intervention anywhere in a cosmos made possible only by certain laws which he himself has established. In our world, God can work only by the laws that he has made."[11] An irreverent mind might answer, "How do *you* know?" But that would be hardly fair to a book, which, while it appears strangely insensitive to our creaturely needs and compellings, almost rash in its overturning of time-honored convictions, and certainly not too profound in the sweeping changes which it proposes for the life of prayer, has nevertheless a provocative gift and a most honest realism. Yet the questions throng. How does anyone know that the cosmos is "made possible only by certain laws," or that "God can work only by the laws he has made?" Nature's changing face and our own experience combine to teach us that God works in a paradox of unpredictable newness and trustworthy faithfulness. The spontaneity is as marked an aspect of His ways as the fixity.

In any event, what are we to understand by the "laws" of God? The word is no longer a solving word, for it is foggy and ambiguous. It does not answer our questions, but rather confuses them. The average man thinks of "natural law" as an inexorable steel framework of the world, but that conception even the scientist himself now hastens to disown. He tells us that "natural laws" have a strange affinity with the categories of our own mind; and that every event, far from being a foretellable link in an iron chain of cause and effect, has always an element of creative surprise. He now speaks of "contingents," "emergents," and "charges in the field of force." The universe is not steel girders: it has a fluid and extempore character, almost like drama or music. Sometimes the average man thinks of "natural laws" as roughly resembling the laws of a city or state. He derives their meaning from the social edicts which gave science the word. Our laws in brief are customs to which we consent: they are ordained by personal minds, and persist only by the agreement of personal minds. Are the "laws" of God the customs and consistencies of *His* mind? If so, the problem at once assumes another cast. We might then be constrained to say, as G. K. Chesterton is reported to

have said, "The sun does not rise by natural law. It rises
because God says, 'Get up, and do it again.' " We must
inquire further on this issue: it is the focus of misgiving in
our generaion concerning prayer. Meanwhile we pause
only to notice that the dogmatism, "Petitionary prayer
is unscientific," or, "In our world God can work only
by the laws that he has made," does not answer our
questions: it only erects a signboard to hide what may
be a mystery. We ourselves must guard against dogmatism. Our present plea is solely this: we should not dismiss petitionary prayer offhand as "childish," "presumptuous," "selfish," "unnecessary," or "unscientific."
The whole issue is vast, complex, throbbing: we cannot
resolve it by quick adjectives.

II

Everyone has cried aloud in petition. We ought to be
able, by probing this experience, to uncover its essen-
tials. What shall we say? Petition seems to be instinctive, part and parcel of our nature, almost beyond our
power to repress. Petition springs from crisis. Perhaps it
should not be so, and certainly it should not always be
so; for every worthy man recognizes that prayer should
be more than a "fire escape." Yet the fact remains that
prayer is most urgent in extremity or pent-up emotion.
The crisis need not be one of danger. Any crisis throws
us back on God. Thus a mother exclaims in the crisis of
the joy of childbirth, "Oh, God!" The prayer is both
thanksgiving for God's delivering care, and a plea for
His favor toward her child. Thus a poet exclaims in the
psychological crisis brought by sudden beauty:

> Lord, I do fear
> Thou'st made the world too beautiful this year;
> My soul is all but out of me—let fall
> No burning leaf; prithee, let no bird call.[12]

In crisis of love, or moment of plighted troth, no man is
completely an atheist. His native language then is
prayer: skepticisms come when the mind is aloof from

life. Any crisis carries us beyond ourselves. A man suddenly and undeservedly bankrupt will cry, even though he may be quite alone at the moment, "It isn't fair!" Nor is he addressing the world at large: he has found, however dimly, that Other whose ways are strange and whose Will is not always our will. Yet, though in any straits, glad or sad, "deep calleth unto Deep," it remains true that petition springs most naturally from need and anger. It is the cry of creaturehood: it is man's pitiable finitude, in weakness or guilt, knocking in entreaty at the door of Infinite Resource. Petition is more than a plea for inward grace: it concerns our world as well as ourselves. "O God, save me!" means "Save me from this wave!" or, "Save me from this fire!" Perhaps we should strive to outgrow such prayers. Perhaps, if we could foresee the danger, we would pray, not for safety, but for strength. But one of the traits of a crisis is that it cannot be foreseen; and it is likely that man will not outgrow petition until he outgrows his earthbound creaturehood. The essence of petition is this:

> All my trust on Thee is stayed,
> All my help from Thee I bring;
> Cover my defenseless head
> With the shadow of Thy wing.[13]

Perhaps prayer *did* begin in fear, as critics suggest. The theory will not dismay us if we realize that fear is an implied faith.[14] Perhaps primitive man, standing at the mouth of his cave amid some howling of wolves or clash of storm heard a cry wrung from him, "Lord, save!" The fear was more than fear: it was sudden faith in the Beyond—"There is a Power greater than wolves and storms." It was faith in his own worth—"There is treasure in my spirit, known to Thee; and I have claim on Thee for deliverance." At any rate petitionary prayer seems to be as instinctive as a shock, a shudder, or a leap in peril. Dr. Charles E. Jefferson has written: "I have noticed that wherever I am in a situation in which no human help is sufficient . . . . I pray spontaneously."[15] It is everyman's experience. The Japanese

fisherman, picked up far out at sea after clinging for
three days to his wrecked boat, explained, "Oh, sir, we
could do nothing but pray." In ordinary days we turn to
what we choose to call "higher forms of prayer"; but
when we are at "our wit's end," whether for ourselves
or for others, we cry out, "Lord, save us: we perish!"[16] Petition is our native response when life is rent,
when in some terror or glory we realize that the world is
infinite. Our boat is little, the sea is vast, the Spirit is
Everlasting—from these ingredients, age after age, petitionary prayer is compounded. It is worth remarking
that human defenselessness has not passed. The airplane baptized, by our characteristically foolish human
pride, "The Skymaster" is not quite master of the sky;
nor do our skyscrapers quite scrape the sky; nor is the
"Queen Mary" quite monarch of the seas. Our science
is so poor a bulwark against life's terror that in any war
science sharpens terror and invites ambushed death. We
still stand at the mouth of the cave amid clash of storm.
Life is still torn open by remorse and sorrow, danger
and gladness, to provoke us to pray. A saving realism
will admit that petition seizes us despite all our safeguards and sophistications. It is as elementally human
as a cry.

III

This question must again be asked: How, in any kind
of prayer, can we hope to divorce ourselves from our
world? We have quoted,

> Lord, what a change within us one brief hour
> Spent in Thy presence will avail to make;

and we have asked if prayer can "avail to make" a
"change" outside us as well as within us. But can we be
sure that there is a gulf between the "outside" and the
"within"? Again, we must not dogmatize but it would
seem that even what the mystics call "internal prayer"
carries in it at least the seeds of petition. For how can we
ask God to change us without asking Him to change our

world? We are not disembodied spirits. Hold whatever
theory we may of the relationship between brain and
thought—that they are "parallel" or "co-ordinated," that
the mind uses the brain as Kreisler uses a violin, or that
thought is only the play of phosphorescence on the be-
havioristic energies of the brain—no one would propose
that brain and thought are forever alien. In this mundane
existence they are assuredly linked. Then is it not true
that the man who prays God to change his evil thoughts
is also asking God, even though by unguessed inference,
to refashion his brain? Thus every prayer may involve
petitionary prayer. People sometimes commend a sermon
or book because it is "so spiritual." If they mean that
the book or sermon carries life back to its ultimates in
God, the commendation is high praise. But it is to be
feared that often they mean "so vacuous," so stratospheric, so unapplied to daily life. Sermons that apply
ultimate Verity to our ordinary day—as, for instance, to
a man's pocket-book—have never been in popular favor. Christianity is not merely a "spiritual" religion:
"The Word was made flesh"![17] Christianity is a religion of spirit and flesh: its truth shines through our
earthy day.

No discussion of prayer can be honestly blind to this
yoking of personality and things. Without doubt God
has His own direct access to man's spirit, as, for example, in the instant stab of conscience; though that stab
also, because man is not a disembodied spirit, is somehow subtly communicated through flesh. But often God
chooses to come mediately through the instrumentality
of matter. How does God reach us? By a Bible? But the
Book is ink and paper. By the sunset flight of homing
birds? But the sunset is light rays and dust, and the
birds are feathers and bone. By the agelong word of history? But history is planet changes, plowed fields, clash
of swords, and all human yearning. By an infinite un-
dertone to the music of human love? But human love is
mediated through lips, eyes, and hands. We know God
as we know man, not only directly—if any revelation
can be direct while we are embodied spirits—but as an
elusive Verity glinting through matter. We know Sibel-

ius through his massive frame and lowly speech,
through his log house in the pine forests north of Hel-
sinki, through his "Finlandia" or "Swan of Tuonela."
Pine forests, notes on a piano—these are not Sibelius.
But without them we would not know Sibelius and
without them he, perchance, would not fully know himself. In some such fashion we know God: we translate
Him from—or He finds us through—the majesty and
meekness, the faithfulness and surprise, of all nature
and humanity. He is greater than nature and humanity,
as Sibelius is greater than his music; but He is known
through nature and humanity, and without them we
might not know God in this world. "The Word was
made *flesh.*" The Word was made the hands and voice
of Jesus; the Word was made the woods and nails of the
cross. For prayer to imagine that it can shake off the
trammels of earth and flesh is vanity and delusion.

William James makes rightful protest against any
conception of God as a Celestial Rarefaction, and un-
mediated Thought or Absolute:

We owe it (we are told) to God that we have a world of
fact at all. *A world* of fact!—that exactly is the trouble. An
entire world is the smallest unit with which such a God can
work, whereas to our finite minds work for the better ought
to be done within this world, setting in at single points. Our
difficulties and our ideals are all piecemeal affairs; but if
God can do no piecework for us, all the interests which our
poor souls compass raise their heads too late.[18]

The essence of petitionary prayer—and, perhaps, indirectly of all prayer—is a plea to God to work "within
this world, setting in at single points." Not even the
most abstract thinking can for long escape particu-
larity—nor the most abstract praying. When people advise, "Pray for your own spirit, but not for things," we
may reply, "How can you separate them? Who gave
you skill to live the disembodied life?" When people
counsel, "Pray for inner grace, not for outward
change," we may answer, "Who has wit to draw the
line?" Trace any prayer to see if it can be inwardly im-

prisoned. "Lord, save me from the curse of drink." That prayer is worthy. But salvation from drink for any man depends not only on his spirit, but on how many men offer him a drink, how his nose reacts when he passes a saloon, how his taste affects him as he drinks the sacramental wine. "Lord, grant me peace of mind." That prayer also is worthy. But the mind is not a vacuum: it is co-ordinated with the brain, and therefore with the whole outer world. Peace of mind depends, at least in its occasions and issues, on the body, on the weather, on the grace of friends. We cannot leap out of our skin to live in some philosophical stratosphere: we are creatures, and petitionary prayer is the acknowledgment of our creaturehood. The creation is not ours to control; and therefore every prayer, though it may not be *of* the world, is still *in* the world. Our journey has thus brought us, so far, to this truth: petitionary prayer is as inevitable as a cry in the night, and it seems to be perforce an ingredient in every prayer.

IV

Our journey has been by life, not by theory. We now travel on, our eyes still set on the stuff of experience, not on mere notions or argument. What happens to us in petitionary prayer? Most of our petitions are not granted. The rather misleading plea that every prayer is answered with a "yes" or a "no"—a favorite plea with a certain kind of preaching—is of course true if the word "answered" is made sufficiently wide. What we here mean by "answered" is what people usually mean: answered according to the hopes and terms of the asking. In that sense, most petitions are not answered, at least for most people. Why deny fact? There are those who pretend that every clamoring of their prayers is straightway fulfilled. We may be pardoned if we suspect that they will say anything except their prayers. For the saints such a claim of answered prayer may—or may not—be true, but not for the ordinary man. Recall Huckleberry Finn's account:

Miss Watson she took me in the closet and prayed, but nothing come of it. She told me to pray every day, and whatever I asked for I would get it. But it warn't so. I tried it. Once I got a fishline, but no hooks. It warn't any good to me without hooks. I tried for the hooks three or four times, but somehow I couldn't make it work. By and by, one day, I asked Miss Watson to try for me, but she said I was a fool. She never told me why, and I couldn't make it out no way. I set down one time back in the woods, and had a long think about it. I says to myself, if a body can get anything they pray for, why don't Deacon Winn get back the money he lost on pork? Why can't the widow get back her silver snuffbox that was stole? Why can't Miss Watson fat up? No, says I to myself, there ain't nothing in it.[19]

People have prayed for fine weather, and it has rained in torrents. People have prayed for health, and their sickness has become chronic. People have prayed for deliverance, and danger has turned only to imprisonment and wounds. People have prayed to live, and they have died. People have prayed that loved ones might be spared, and loved ones have perished even while the prayer was being offered:

> O father, whereso'er thou be,
>   Who pledgest now thy gallant son,
>   A shot, ere half thy draught be done,
> Has stilled the life that beat from thee.

> O mother, praying God will save
>   Thy sailor—while thy head is bow'd,
>   His heavy-shotted hammock-shroud
> Drops in his vast and wandering grave.[20]

Why deny these facts? It is doubtful if people would ever fall sick and die if all prayers were answered. In how many instances has faith been lastingly injured because preachers have assured people that every prayer is granted according to ardent and sincere desire! The answer is not forthcoming, and faith flags. Jesus never made any such unqualified promise. His assurances were wide as time and eternity, but they carried always a condition: "If ye shall ask anything *in my name,* I will do it"; *"If ye abide in me, and my words abide in you,* ye shall ask what ye will, and it shall be done unto you."[21] This condition is usually explicitly stated, and where it is not stated it is implied.[22] Any man writing honestly on this topic to honest folk must beseech them to be realistic, if only for the sake of integrity in mind and life, and to face the fact that many petitions are not answered after the fashion of the asking.

But there is another side, and a saving grace, to our experience. There are people lowly and genuine, with neither desire nor bent for self-deception, who are sure that their crisis prayer, "Lord, save!" has been answered in marvelous deliverance. Let us grant that in this issue it is easy to fool ourselves. A woman, distraught because her son in another city was rooming with people whom she considered undesirable, asked her friend to pray for the son's rescue. Then she vilified the people in letters sent to them, and slandered them in letters sent to their friends, until in justifiable anger they bade her son begone. Then she thanked the friend and praised God that prayers—which, incidentally, had not been offered in the form suggested—had been so signally answered. It is easy to "rationalize," and perhaps doubly easy in respect of prayer. But people claim answers to their petition who are as free as most folk from the hidden canker of "rationalizing." Their testimony, "Only prayer brought it to pass," is too humble, too heartfelt, too freighted with conviction, and too agelong a testimony glibly to be gainsaid. There have been answered prayers for deliverance in ill health: Dr. E. Stanley Jones is sure that God restored his physical weakness through the power of prayer, and he is but one of a multitude who believe themselves similarly blessed. There have been answered prayers for deliverance in danger: the sudden shift of wind for a man trapped in ice floes or forest fire—Dr. Grenfell's experience is here typical—or, even more striking instance, the quick weaving of a spider's web across the mouth of the cave in which Scotch Covenanters were hiding, so that when the persecuting horsemen saw the web they concluded that no one had recently entered the cave, and went their way. There have been answered prayers in regard to human action: George Muller was convinced that he built his orphanage by prayer. Let it be granted that, once it becomes known that a man like George Muller trusts only to prayer, that knowledge is itself the best advertising, the story of George Muller nevertheless has a core of testimony not easily dismissed.[23] So sober a student as Canon B. H. Streeter has written:

As a matter of fact, whether it is because when we pray for others we are less blind to their real and highest needs . . . . or whether it is because such prayers, being more disinterested, are more truly prayers "in His Name," it is the experience of many with whom I have spoken on this subject that such prayers are answered too often and in too striking a way to make the hypothesis of coincidence at all a possible explanation.[24]

Luther writes in language characteristic of those who are sure that God has made specific response to their prayers:

No one believes how strong and mighty prayer is and how much it can do except he whom experience has taught, and who has tried it. It has raised up in our time three persons who lay in danger of death, myself, my wife Katha, and Philip Melanchthon in 1540 at Weimar.[25]

And Kierkegaard thus:

The archimedean point outside the world is the little chamber where a true suppliant prays in all sincerity— where he lifts the world off its hinges.[26]

The word of Dr. Douglas Mackenzie has been endorsed by multitudes of praying folk:

It is a fact that prayer is answered abundantly and in infinitely varied ways. No people who have practiced

prayer faithfully and rightly have any doubt of this. They
know that God has come to them in prayer. They know
that He has come in outward answer to prayer, thousands
and myriads of times in the history especially of Christian
prayers. The mathematical probabilities are all against the
theory that these answers are mere chance coincidences.
Therefore, as one who has prayed for many long years and
has known alike the personal influence of prayer and the
strange, often startling, phenomena of "answers to prayer,"
I must go on to the end in its practice.[27]

We can dismiss this concerted testimony as mere "wishful thinking," if we so choose. But there is no reason to
assume that these witnesses are less honest than their
critics. Granted that the witnesses are men of prayer,
and therefore perhaps "prejudiced," it remains true that
many of the critics are *not* men of prayer and are therefore like tone-deaf men judging music. It is hardly "scientific" to dismiss so staunch and so far-flung a testimony. The witness is agelong: "This poor man cried,
and the Lord heard him, and saved him out of all his
troubles."[28] It is well-nigh universal: almost every man
who has prayed has known strange turns in life in
which, with surging gladness, he has traced God's hand
in answer to his prayer. He has been sure, in some stab
of truth, that there is more at work in our world than
"natural law." "Prayer ardent opens heaven."[29]

V

We are therefore brought to a clear verdict. Some petitions, perhaps most, are not answered. But some petitions are answered, at least in the throbbing conviction
of honest folk. The conviction is an instant thing. It
does not come by deduction. It is primal—like an immediate recognition, like the scientist's flash of truth,
like a sob of joy, like an instinctive reverence. We cannot well deny it: it would be as easy to deny light or
love. This double issue of petition, a reply sometimes
forbidding in its refusal and sometimes winning in its
benediction, is precisely as we might expect. A human
friend, we have said, has two sides. He is unlike us, an-

other spirit, and therefore in some measure alien. He is like us, and therefore kindred. Like and unlike—such is the paradox of friendship with God. He is like us, and comes in blessing: "In all their affliction he was afflicted, and the angel of his presence saved them."[30] He is unlike us, and meets our pleadings with seeming indifference or refusal: "How unsearchable are his judgments, and his ways past finding out!"[31] Some prayers He can answer, and some gifts and guidance He can grant, perchance only through our asking. But some prayers He cannot answer except in denial. If there were no "clouds and darkness round about him," if there were no mystery in the Godhead, He would not be God. If we understood His every "yes" and "no," we would not be man. Dr. Herbert H. Farmer recalls an anecdote concerning Tolstoy. A skeptic asked Tolstoy, "How can I believe in God in face of a cholera microbe?" To which Tolstoy replied, "Don't be flippant!"[32] A God without concealings or rigor, who always kept pace with our pedestrian minds, would not be God. His worship would be trivial, and the worshiper merely flippant. We see God as a sailor might see a promontory—now in sunshine, now in storm, the tiny visible only a sign of a vast Unknown. Some petitions are not answered, and if they were we could not worship Him, for His ways are higher than our ways. But some petitions are answered: He is surprise of Mercy, outgoing Gladness, Rescue, Healing, and Life.

Chapter VI

PETITIONARY PRAYER AND
NATURAL LAW

AN OBVIOUS QUESTION now confronts us: How can we reconcile with natural law this agelong conviction of answered prayer? Perhaps we cannot reconcile them, for in finite knowledge there are always wide gaps of ignorance. How can we "reconcile" a textbook in algebra with a spring landscape? But prayer and science are such lively issues that some attempt must be made to relate them. Though ignorance remains, changing but not disappearing with each new disclosure of truth, we must always seek some fairly consistent picture of our world. To the modern man petitionary prayer and natural law are contradictory and incongruous: he cleaves to his modern dogmatism of natural law. That is why in our time an almost fatal blight has fallen on the life of prayer. We repeat: the honor given to scientific method and natural law has blighted prayer, and almost threatens the wholesome life of man. This obeisance is a root of skepticism, whose final fruits are the pride and violence which now disfigure the world.

I

Glib and merely plausible reconciliations will not avail us. It is not enough to assert, "If man can manipulate nature's laws to change their effect, as in air-conditioned trains, how much more can God skillfully contrive His whole creation!" This is a favorite escape from the dilemma, especially among liberal theologians. Actually it is not an escape. It is not even a wriggle. For it leaves God at the mercy of His world: whatever His skill as a Mechanic He must forever tinker with wires in order to reach men. Nay, it degrades God into a celestial Tinkerer. The proposed solution is worse than the original problem. Why not confront the issue? We must surrender either prayer's certitude or our current concept of natural law. But how can we surrender petitionary prayer? It is as elemental as a cry in danger, and age by age it has found its frequent or infrequent answer. Then let us not shrink from a necessary counter-revolution in thought: let us deliberately disavow dogmatic interpretations of science's natural law. The cosmos is not a realm of necessity; it is a realm of free spirit. It is patterned only on its surface: its prime trait is spontaneity. Its foretellables are only poor meteorological readings: its mystery is still an unpredictable though faithful sky. We have accepted Browning's "All's law," and forgotten that what he really said was, "All's love, yet all's law."[1]

II

This proposed disavowal is not a bigotry; it is an emancipation. It does not detract from the grateful esteem which modern science has assuredly earned. Science in its applications has wrested whole kingdoms from distance, darkness, and disease. Science in its spirit has been so rigorously truth-loving as to be in itself almost a religion, and so sacrificial that it now has written its own roster of heroes and martyrs. Indeed, in purity of motive and devotedness of service, science has often put religionists to shame. Our quarrel is not with science, but with the philosophy and theology which have turned its fractional truths into wholesale dogmatism. The scientific view is actually so limited as to be almost false, but it has been made totalitarian. Perhaps this is the ground totalitarianism in which all others have their root! Blindly and totally accepted, it is the end of human freedom and of any worth in life.

The scientific view is inadequate because it is too *external*. Take the son of a scientist as instance. Hide the boy's identity: call him Exhibit *X*. Now describe the boy as a physical process; describe him in chemical constituents; describe him biologically, eugenically, psychologically; describe him by weight, by displacement in water, and by blood count. Then chart and graph the description. The scientist, given no other account, would never recognize *X* as his own child. In short, if the scientist overcomes the man, manhood becomes an automatism. Science defines a tear as "a drop of saline liquid secreted by the lacrymal gland, ordinarily conveyed away by the lacrymal canal to the lacrymal sac, whence it passes into the meatus of the nose and mingles with the mucous secretion." But, in spite of science, that is not a tear. The description is so external as to be almost false, as any weeping man could tell us.

> For a Tear is an Intellectual Thing,
> And a Sigh is the Sword of an Angel King,
> And the bitter groan of a Martyr's woe
> Is an arrow from the Almightie's bow.[2]

The scientific world-view is inadequate because it is also too *fractional*. Its portrayal of man's life and destiny is not much more convincing than a lifelong prisoner's description of a continent. The mere psychological description of prayer, for instance, is comparable with a description of the universe from within a closed room. That knocking on the door is a vibration of a wood plaque and of air waves, that voice an effect on the auditory nerve, and that window an amorphous substance consisting of silica and potash and lead oxide. True; but how untrue to dawns and sunsets, the music and march of men, and all the starry vastness of the world. The scientific view wears horse blinkers: it can see only an arbitrary segment of a world.

Beyond doubt science is too *analytical* to provide a world-view. The dissection of a flower is not the flower. Except as material for a new and richer synthesis, the dissection of a flower is the death of the flower. No scientific axiom could be less true, save in a very lim-

ited sense, than the Euclidean, "The whole is equal to
the sum of its parts." The whole is more and other than
the sum of its parts. The whole has its own peculiar
properties, like self-consciousness in a man. The besetting sin of analysis is that it ignores the subtle grace and
genius of the whole. So Goethe has written in some dis-
dain:

> To understand the living whole
> They start by driving out the soul;
> They count the parts, and when all's done,
> Alas! the spirit-bond is gone.[3]

All this we have known, but we have not faced its
implications. We have lowered our guard against its un-
due encroachments. We have fallen prey to a sterile totalitarianism against which the finest scientists would
warn us. As long as we approach the world and man,
and the relation of man to his world, through the external, limited, and analytical eyes of science, so long shall
any deep truth elude us. As long as we deny the primary fact of personality under the mysterious prompting of a universe which is personal enough to find us at
the very point of personality, so long shall the scientific
world necessarily seem inert and fixed, a process of
inexorable law. But introduce personality, even though
it be but human personality, and this calculated and
patterned world of science becomes impromptu, like
breeze music or a dancing fire. On a summer day I saw
my garden-loving wife move a small locust tree, and
then I spent a week pondering the mystery of the act.
"This," said I, "is a miracle." She, now painfully used
to my ruminations, suggested that I had been slow to
understand, like any husband, that any wife must be a
miracle worker, especially when living with an amateur
theologian. Ignoring this pertness with Olympian un-
concern, I spoke again: "This is a miracle. By natural
law that tree could never have moved of itself. In moving it you have presumably moved the center of the
earth, and shifted the balance of all worlds. You have

> . . . . troubled the gold gateways of the stars,
>   Smiting . . . . on their clangèd bars;
>   Fretted to dulcet jars
>   And silvern chatter the pale ports o' the moon.'

This is a miracle. You have changed the world, doing what natural law of itself could never do. Yet your prompting was by natural law, the tree was moved by natural law, and now that it is moved no natural law has been broken. This is a miracle!" Then I reassured her that she did not intend this cosmic revolution, but was just grubbing in a garden, and that it would not be held against her. Thus the dim awareness came that if human personality, using natural law like a garment, like a very body, could make life as impromptu as a dancing fire, the personality of God—using natural law as a body, shall we say?—could make life like swift mercury, like light, like the inescapable constraint of a Cross. It may be that the scientist's account of life is only a tintype photograph—valuable, even precious, but fixed in two dimensions. By comparison, a dramatist's or musician's account of life may be a portrait in oils— almost in three dimensions, and enriched by an interpretation. Perchance the praying man's account of life is *from within the living spontaneity itself*, where the will of man blends with the creative will of God! Our plea is this: we must cease parroting, "All's law." It would be much more true, though still not adequately true, to say, "All's spontaneity." If we must speak of law, when the simile is certainly worn and possibly outmoded, let us regard the law as only the keyboard of the piano. The universe then becomes in our thinking just what it appears to be in our experience, a mysterious and tremendous improvising on this temporary and earthbound console of law. Granted there could be no present music for us without the console, it is more deeply true that the console would be meaningless without the composition and the Composer.

III

Then how can we reconcile answered prayer with natural law, spiritual certitude with scientific generalization? It would be problem enough to try to reconcile man's free act with natural law! Perhaps there is no full reconciliation in theory: perhaps the reconciliation must come in some welding arc light of life. In the instance of our praying Covenanters, we cannot dismiss the spider's web at the mouth of the cave as "coincidence."[5] The word does no justice to the Covenanters' instant conviction that God delivered them, for the conviction is as primal and elemental as the scientist's recognition of truth. It is obviously true to reply that the spider's web might have been spun if there had been robbers in the cave, or might not have been spun at all; but that answer is merely academic, an argument after the event. Hindsight is an easy wisdom. We have admitted the many apparent denials of petitionary prayer, the times when the spider's web is not woven. But what of the times when it *is* woven. The word "coincidence" does not cover the heartfelt joy of men who are sure they have seen a miracle. In fact, the word does no justice even to the scientist's own inadequate faith. The universe is either an order or a "happenstance." The scientist says it is an order. If so, it is an order in its coincidences. The word seems to be an escape from thinking, yet competent and honest minds continually use it. A splendid psychologist, whose work enriches Christian faith, explains answers to petitionary prayer as being due to "lapse of memory, unintentional exaggeration, ... and coincidence."[6] That blessed and saving word "coincidence"! A conversation with an advocate of natural law might well proceed as follows:

The preacher: Why did the walls of Jericho fall just when Joshua's trumpets blew?

The scientist: They didn't fall.

The preacher: Yes, they fell. They have been found, the bricks in courses such as are made only by an outward falling. Nor is there good reason to doubt the identity in time of the blown trumpets and the falling walls. Such identities occur. Why did the wall fall when the trumpets blew?

The scientist: Probably an earthquake.

The preacher: Possibly, and perhaps probably. That portion of the planet's surface is known to be an earth fault. But why did the two events happen together?

The scientist: Mere coincidence.

The preacher: Coincidences are never "mere." What does the word mean?

The scientist: It means they happened together.

The preacher: We began with that fact. Why did they happen together?

The scientist: It was coincidence.

Blessed word! But it is still an evasion—or an honest confession of limited knowledge. Thornton Wilder's novel *The Bridge of San Luis Rey*[7] grapples with the problem. The bridge fell, and its fall could be explained by natural law. But such and such people were on the bridge when it fell. Why were just these people, and not others, on the bridge? The novelist's answer is naturally fiction, but it is a better answer than the word "coincidence."

Then how shall we reconcile natural law with answered prayer? We must acknowledge facts even though we cannot make them dovetail, even though we must live with a hiatus in the mind. Real reconciliations are made only in life. A man who is all man, can be also a scientist, but a man all scientist is no longer a man. That is to say, free spirit can use scientific method without betraying it, but scientific deduction can never include free spirit without killing it. As Fernand Ménégoz has written:

Liberty can easily subordinate necessity to itself without falsifying it. On the other hand, necessity cannot subordinate liberty to itself without destroying it. Religious knowledge possesses enough amplitude and flexibility to incorporate the findings of scientific knowledge, but rigid scientific knowledge would not know how to assimilate the affirmations of religious knowledge without turning them into the vapor of illusion.[8]

This quotation shows how urgent is the call for a counter-revolution in our present thinking. Science inevitably begins with life—the vital life of the scientist himself under stimulus from the vital life of the Cosmos. Then let him return to life; there is no home for us in the famine-land of scientific generalization discovered by the abstract mind.

If theories are demanded by which to reconcile prayer with law, even though such theories, being merely theoretical, must disappoint us, several have been advanced. They are affairs of abstract thought rather than of full-orbed personality. They are only arrows shot at a mystery, as are all our theories. Even so, they are more kindling to mind and heart than the word "coincidence."

One such theory[9] would persuade us that if we could be certain of all the antecedents of any natural event, and if we were wise enough to comprehend them, we could exactly predict the consequents. But, says the theory, we can never be sure of the antecedents, since natural law is indwelt by human freedom and by God's will. Prayer enters into the antecedents as one of the unknown factors, thus influencing the result. The short-comings of this theory are obvious. It still conceives history under the concept of cause and effect, and still binds God and man within the concept. Science itself now disowns any rigid theory of causality. Any new event *is* new, an emergent evolution, an uprush from primal wellsprings. It is not merely a recombination and issue of old elements. Nature is by nature unpredictable, even in the primordial energy of the quanta. Man under God is a vital agent, above nature even while he is within nature. This theory fails to incorporate these radical facts. It tries to explain a Copernican sky in terms of a pre-Copernican astrology.

Another theory, brilliant and thought-provoking, closely associated with the name of Henri Bergson, would argue that science always deals in past time, and can therefore regard all its laws as fixed; but that present and actual life is never fixed. In short, the only fixity in the cosmos is an apparent fixity given to the eyes of retrospect. Past time is like a waterfall: it is frozen in distance. Thus science can weave whatever happens, once it has happened, into generalized patterns. When an event occurs to disturb accepted patterns, such as the discovery that uranium changes ino lead, the patterns are made more widely schematic, more thin, more aloof from life. But the laws of nature are in reality only observed regularities in the fixed field of past event; and the regularities must, even then, be attributed to the categories of our mind as well as to the fixed field. Thus science can never *predict* by natural law any event, especially one that is involved with man's vital spirit. It can only observe in retrospect. It cannot predict, for instance, that a spider will weave a web just after pursued Covenanters have entered a cave, or that Edna St. Vincent Millay will be caught by the loveliness of an autumn tree, and exclaim:

> My soul is all but out of me—let fall
> No burning leaf; prithee, let no bird call.[10]

Imagine life to be like a woven rug. Science sees the patterned threads from the earthbound side of the frame, not in their weaving but only when they have been woven, and traces their regularities. Great art in music and drama stands likewise, and glories in the color and imagination of the design. But prayer stands with the Weaver as He works. The Weaver says in graciousness: "You shall help me in prayer and thought and labor, though for your own good I still must guide. Some of your wishes shall be granted, for through the granting you shall more surely learn: and I will still guide. Some of your wishes cannot be granted. When the design is complete, and you can see it from the other side of time, you will understand. And your best prayer is still the prayer of Christ, 'Not my will, but. . . .' " This theory is not offered as ultimate. In our finitude nothing is ultimate. But it is a more coherent theory, covering more wisely the facts both of science and of the daily experience of honorable folk, than the theory of "coincidence" or "natural law."

But it is not ultimate. It builds on a cleft—the cleft between the apprehended nature of time past and time present. Is there really a cleft, time being one mystery? Are there not high moments when even prosaic minds are set free from the treadmill of moments when they apprehend all Time, past, present, and future, as the medium of the Timeless when they also can write:

> Life, like a dome of many-coloured glass,
> Stains the white radiance of Eternity?[11]

It is better to build a theory on a living mystery than on bricks and mortar, but it is best to choose the central Mystery. The prime facts are not those of our sense of a cleft in time, but those earlier cited[12]—the real though limited freedom of man, the personal providence of God, and the faithful flexibility of the world. A satisfying theory will presumably begin with these facts, not with a philosophic doctrine of time. In short, Christian *faith* must carry philosophy to its goal, affirming that the world at its core is Holy and Loving Will. The fixities of nature then become the fidelities of God's Spirit; the unpredictabilities of nature then become the play of His word and act. Our own life is still the best poor adumbration of God's life. Science and theology alike are inescapably anthropomorphic: it is wisdom to accept the bond. Human personality shows this paradox of fixity and fluidity. We are sure of a good man that he will act in such and such a way—he will not suddenly become self-centered, and grab, and lie—but we cannot know what specific word or act new circumstances may provoke. We accept this parable: it is a ladder by which to climb from man to God: "How much more shall your Father which is in heaven. . . . . "[13] There are fixities of faithfulness in God's nature: science calls them "law." But there are surprises in God's nature by which "he sets in at single points": religion calls them His very word and deed. He is adamant Truth and intimate Love—never-changing and ever-changing Life.[14] Gregor Holtum[15] has suggested that we are confronted by an alternative: we must interpret the universe either as miracle or inertia, either as God's constant grace or as an iron structure of natural law. By miracle he does not mean any incongruous rending of the scheme of things, but God "setting in at single points" in such a way that man knows that he has been found by the Eternal. Some of us are sure that, granted this more vital definition of the word miracle, life is a constant miracle—flashes in faithfulness—of divine good will. Thus Fernand Ménégoz again:

From the scientific and natural point of view: no miracle. But from the religious and spiritual point of view: miracle everywhere and in everything. It is a free and self-consistent God who sets up the world sovereignly with its immanent order and who utilizes this order sovereignly, without violating it, being himself the transcendent and omnipresent cause of all. It is a free and self-consistent God who sets up sovereignly the primordial relation between himself and his spiritual, free, and responsible creature, and who utilizes the universal order without violating it, taking his creature as a partner with whose co-operation he can realize those designs which are at one and the same time those of sons won to his cause, and his own. . . . If to the eyes of faith miracle is permanent and an ever-renewed granting, it is not because Liberty is forever breaking the iron circle of Necessity, but, on the contrary, because absolute and sovereign Liberty, enfolding everything with gentleness, knows how to use and bring into co-operation for his own ends the whole appearance of necessity, the totality of physical and psychical laws, without in any way altering their deep and mysterious economy.[16]

Our only exception to this avowal is that in its language, though not in its purport, it seems to make the natural order an instrument of God, and therefore in some sense alien and inert. Why not affirm that "law" *is* a living Faithfulness? The return of the seasons is sure, not because of some earthy necessity, but because the goodness of God is sure. The picture which Jesus gave,

"Our Father," is not only the most glowing but has most verity: it answers best to the impacts and beckonings of our daily life. Let us repeat: the reconciliation of scientific law and religious certitude is not in any theory, but in a welding arc light of life. That arc light is prayer: one electrode is the transcendent Personality, the other is man found-of-God. The light welds all life, and makes us, though timebound, citizens and friends of the Eternal.

IV

What then? Some petitions, wrung from us by our defenseless creaturehood, are answered. Such is the reiterated conviction of honorable men. The conviction is too instant, too vivid, too honestly recurrent to be doubted.

> God answers sharp and sudden on some prayers,
> And thrusts the thing we have prayed for in our face,
> A gauntlet with a gift in't.[17]

It seems probable that if petitions had not been answered, such prayers would long since have vanished in man's despair and pain. On the other hand, many petitions are not answered. Paul prayed that the "thorn in the flesh" might be removed, and it was not removed. Jesus prayed that the "cup" might pass, but it did not pass; though, be it said, strength was increased both to the Master and his disciple, and was made equal to the burden. Many petitions in their direct aspect are not answered: Covenanters have been trapped in a cave with no spider's web to save them. If we knew why some prayers are granted and some are denied we would have the wisdom of God. Actually our deepest wish is *not* to know: God is God, and men are men. If there were no "dark line in God's Face," no inscrutable mystery in His providence we could not worship. To ask God to keep our pedestrian pace would be, as Tolstoy said, merely "flippant." Furthermore, there are obvious kindly and constant limits to the power of petition—

limits fixed *not* by any falsely conceived isolation of natural law, but by God's faithfulness. Not all our praying will change the position of the planet Neptune, or make winter follow spring, or cause a new arm to sprout at the place of amputation. Just where these limits run we broadly observe, but cannot finely trace. Our prayers are bound also by our own dark motives; and, as our motives grow purer, we shall hesitate more and more to lift before Eternal Eyes our wishes born of ignorance.

Thus the plea that nearly all our petitions are answered—and Dr. Glenn Clark's books,[18] for instance, appear to savor somewhat of such a plea—not only is unconvincing, but leaves us morally and spiritually uneasy. For who can be sure of human wisdom, and who could worship so indulgent a God? God is still the Almighty "Other," and "clouds and darkness are round about him." But the plea that no petitions are answered, and that prayer is only aspiration—perhaps toward some "external power" or perhaps toward "some part of our own nature . . . . ordinarily submerged," as Dr. Kirsopp Lake has suggested—is also unconvincing. "This poor man cried . . . . and the Lord heard him": his name is legion, and his testimony has the ring of truth. We must still "cry out," when the weaving of the tapestry of life's terror and triumph seems to cut across our fondest hopes, for we are still creatures and defenseless. Then God sometimes denies: all men must die at last. But God sometimes grants the prayer because we offer it, guiding us through the answered prayer. Thus God enlists our prayers, together with our thought and labor. But as in closer and closer friendship we watch His weaving our very petitions are redeemed, and we exclaim: "All Thy ways are mercy. In Thy will is our peace. Not my will, but Thine be done."

Chapter VII

THE PROBLEM OF INTERCESSORY PRAYER

IF YOU WERE to ask the man in the street, do you believe in intercessory prayer?" he might echo blankly, "Intercessory?" If you were then to explain that theology is fond of long words and that you meant prayer on behalf of other people, he might answer in a silent skepticism. Even among church folk the sea of faith is at the ebb. Behold the intercessor. He kneels in some church to pray for our chaotic world. He pleads divine protection for his son who, let us suppose, is a newspaper correspondent in England or China. There he kneels—alone so far as eyes can see. What can *he* do? Can he stay this natural calamity or that national aggression? If a shell should fall on London, can he shield his son? To our skeptical sight the intercessor may be a lovable and even a saintly figure, but he is pathetic and futile. Airplanes might help us—though we would be nonplussed to prove it. Preparedness might help us—though generations of preparedness (and war) are poor evidence. A new law might help us—though, again, experience gives scant encouragement. But the intercessor: how can his mumblings redeem a violent world?

The doubt is more acute because Christian minds disagree. Thus a recent writer[1] in the church says bluntly, "Intercession is not real prayer." Confronted by the fact that the New Testament calls Jesus our Intercessor and High Priest, he explains that the title is only a figure of speech coined by an age of priestcraft. Faced with apparent answers to intercession, he suggests that they are due to "chance" or "clairvoyance." Intercession makes *us* ready to speak and act, he says: that is its only virtue. Granted that the book in question is too hasty and sweeping in its judgments, it is honest, and it represents a widespread view within the church. Friedrich Heiler, on the other hand, argues with abundant illustration[2] that intercession is integral in genuinely Christian prayer. There is a cleavage in Chistian belief. What shall *we* think?

I

Two facts provide a setting for our inquiry. One is that our life is a paradox of individual and social. Wise men do not try to split a paradox, but the attempt to split this paradox is rife and unrelinquished. The hackneyed truth that we are "members one of another" is accepted in theory, but stubbornly resisted in practice. It is strange indeed that we should try to isolate our lives. Our individual being is drawn from the total human process, and that process is girded and fed by the total process of the natural world. Each of us is the child of the whole creation. We arose, as Tennyson said,

> Out of the deep,
> Where all that was to be, in all that was,
> Whirl'd for a million aeons thro' the vast
> Waste dawn of multitudinous-eddying light.[3]

Dr. Francis G. Peabody tells us that the freshmen of a certain university, at its three hundredth anniversary, carried a banner with the inscription, "This university has waited three hundred years for us." They were not totally wrong. There is a sense in which the universe has waited millennia for us. In such a world any resolve on sharp "individualism" is doomed to fail. Indeed, psychology now assures us that our consciousness was not first individual and then by deduction social. It seems likelier that we were first social—that we became aware of ourselves only by the contrast and comfort of the world of nature, only by the friction and co-operation of other wills. Assuredly we were born in the paradox of

social-individual, and we always live in it. Nothing we
say or do can be cabined in ourself. Take any word—
nay, that very phrase will serve: "Take any word."
Take: we cannot, except from God or man. *Any:* any
street implies all streets, and streets are where our
neighbors walk. *Word:* we are introduced to the whole
realm of common speech, and thereby to all history. "A
man's home is his castle." It is? Not when his child
catches the measles without knowing who bestowed the
favor! Even a wall is the sign of people living on both
sides:

> Something there is that doesn't love a wall,
> That sends the frozen ground-swell under it,
> And spills the upper boulders in the sun;
> And makes gaps even two can pass abreast.[4]

In a day when distant revolution shakes domestic mar-
kets, world news is dispensed by radio in any home, and
any man's son may be killed by the rebound of a pistol
shot in Tientsin or Bengasi, we need not belabor the
fact of the social bond. The bond is daily drawn closer
by the machinery of mass production, and by the science that conquers distance. The ends of the earth are
in every room. It is hard for us to realize these facts.
We have but lately emerged from the pioneer age. That
is why present transitions in political and economic
thought seem so startling. But we *have* emerged—on
the day when somebody spoke about "the preservation
of natural resources." "What wages I pay," says someone, "what quality of goods I make, what volume of
production I choose, what price I charge is my concern." But it is not that kind of world, and the world
does not stop rolling for any hitchhiker. Our life is a
paradox of individual-social. That is one prime fact in
the setting of our problem.

The other is that our life has striking mutualities.
Within the comprehensive net of our common life is an
endless number of strands which we might label "thee-
me." Conversation is a mutuality, even when it is one-
sided. Reading a book is a mutuality, for it is a conver-

sation between the mind of the author and the mind of
the reader. Listening to music, or playing it, is a mutuality. So is marriage—both in body and spirit. Who
could measure the wealth which God has given us
through the instigation and devotion of mutual minds?
A man was walking in academic procession with a well-
known bishop. Aware of the bishop's fondness for
mathematics, he pointed to the back of the man ahead
of him and said, "That is the professor of mathematics."
The remark cost him his processional partner: the
bishop was now walking with the professor. The two
were busy over a mass of figures on a grubby paper.
"What would you do with this?" one was asking. Only
the shepherding of kindly Providence brought them to
their proper places on the platform. It was an instance
of problem solution. Problems are solved, deeper than
mathematics, only by the give and take of friendship.
We might never believe our raptures, we might doubt
our eyes regarding ocean or sunset, except for friendship's corroboration, "I also see." Thus social life validates the higher meanings of our world, and our mutual
life makes them dear. When Elizabeth Barrett wrote to
Robert Browning,

> I love thee to the level of everyday's
> Most quiet need, by sun and candle-light.
> I love thee freely, as men strive for Right;
> I love thee purely, as they turn from Praise,[5]

she confessed that their mutuality opened a path
through earth to heaven.

Why do we here stress the fact that our life is not
merely individual, but social and mutual? For this reason: to make clear that it would be strange indeed if
such a profound and universal fact as prayer lived only
in the separate self. Life in its very nature predisposes
us to believe that prayer also has its social and mutual
bonds. Intercession accords well with the pattern of
man's life. It is a fair assumption that prayer cannot be
merely individual: others share its yearnings and are
held in its petitions. We must be content for a moment

with this tentative claim: we must not jump to conclusions.

II

Then what befalls our intercessor? There is little doubt that he himself becomes a nobler man. His night becomes day: he steps with the assurance of those who forget themselves in the remembrance of their neighbors and God. His winter becomes summer: a new climate conquers the snows, and brings buried seeds to glory. His weakness becomes power: he is strong, not in the pseudo power which slays an enemy, but in the real power which slays the *enmity* and turns the enemy into a friend.

There is gain also in the direct line of his intercession. Grudges are canceled, for bitterness and intercession have no common dwelling. Human need is more clearly understood, for intercession gives insight and a purer sympathy. His practical help now has added wisdom. His very prayer provokes him to help, for he could hardly pray for a destitute family in the next street without being prompted to visit and aid them.

These facts few people would question. They are a benison. They are, quite literally, a godsend. If there were no other good in intercession, these gains would make it a fountain on our pilgrimage. But, to be blunt, they are not the main issue. That father, kneeling alone in church, asks *God* to help his son. His prayer is not only, "Help *me* to speak and write." It is rather, "I beseech *Thee* to bless him." Suppose he does not know where his son is, except that he is in danger. Is he then to stifle his prayers as futile vaporings? Or suppose he is burdened with woe for suffering folk whom he cannot reach. Is he to remain despairingly prayerless? Are these folk to be cast out utterly from his pleadnigs? *That* is the real issue. If intercession is only a self-discipline, however valuable, its light will fail. If the man for whom we pray is to be blessed only in *our* feeble power, the prayer will have no urgency. When Monica prayed for her son she was asking more help than *she* could give—even more help than could ever flow *through* her life. She was laying hold, as she believed, on the robe of God to turn *His* eyes and hands to Augustine. So all the saints have prayed. Has intercession any grace beyond the intercessor's reach? That is the central issue.

III

Ever since gentleness entered our world worthy folk have practiced intercession. These are man's most ardent prayers. A blasphemer will cry out for himself in physical or moral disaster, "Oh, God!" That cry is not mere blasphemy: he must call on something beyond the human, and the word "God" best answers his need. But when his child is under threat his prayer is doubly intense. There are not many people, whatever their faith or lack of faith, who have not sometime been driven to their knees to plead with God for someone dear to them. To intercede is an ancient impulse with vital roots. The dying Alcestis in the Euripedes drama prayed to Hestia, goddess of the hearth, for her son and daughter:

> Queen, for I pass beneath the earth, I fall
> Before thee now, and nevermore, and pray:
> Be mother to my orphans: mate with him
> A loving wife, with her a noble husband.
> Nor, as their mother dieth, so may they
> My children, die untimely, but with weal
> In the homeland fill up a life of bliss.[6]

Alcestis could not reach her children after death. Was her prayer therefore only a blunder or wishful self-deceit? A prayer of Athenaeus has come down to us from the third century. It is a plea for his city:

O Pallus Athene, sea-born Queen, keep this city and its citizens from discord and from all calamities and also from untimely death, thou and thy father.[7]

In Grecian mythology Athene was the child of Zeus. Thus Athenaeus carries the entreaty to the ultimate god: "thou and thy father." In the seventeenth century Oliver Cromwell interceded on his deathbed for his country:

> Lord, though I am a miserable and wretched creature, I am in covenant with Thee through grace. And I may, and I will, come to Thee for Thy people. . . . . Lord, however Thou do dispose of me, continue and go on to do good to them.[8]

That prayer echoes the great intercession of Moses for *his* people: "Yet now, if thou wilt forgive their sin—; and if not, blot me, I pray thee, out of thy book."[9] There is a striking prayer of Giuseppe Mazzini in the nineteenth century on behalf of the slaveholders:

> God of pity, God of peace and love, forgive, oh forgive the slaveholders! Great is their guilt, but infinite is Thy pity. Open up in the desert of their souls the living fountain of charity. May the angel of penitence descend . . . . and between them and his sentence may the prayer arise of those who suffer, as I suffer, for Thy holy cause, Thy sacred truth, for the emancipation of nations and the human soul![10]

Enough of instances. They are legion. Each century is crowded with them, almost as the sky with stars. But, lest it should seem that compassion is now cold and faith everywhere dim, here is an instance from our own time: Dr. Edward A. Steiner, of Jewish origin, was lecturing at the Roman Catholic college, St. Catherine's, at St. Paul, Minnesota, and told the principal, Sister Antonia, of the critical sickness of Dr. Ozora S. Davis, a Protestant, in Chicago.[11] She called two other nuns, who with her had once visited Dr. Davis, and asked Dr. Steiner to join them in prayer for Dr. Davis' recovery. Thus a Christian Jew and three Catholic nuns prayed for the health of a Protestant minister. Intercession canceled their differences, as the sun overleaps the fences between our fields.

Not only is intercession apparently universal but—and this is a vital consideration—it lives in our worthiest motive. There are today many earnest folk who are burdened by the war-madness of the nations, but who cannot speak any conspicuous word, or lay any potent hand on the levers of state action. From very pity they are driven to their knees. Human motives are always mixed, but their motive in that pang of prayer is nearly selfless. In a yearning akin with the motive of Christ, they would gladly die if the world thereby might live. Are we to conclude that our world is a mockery so grotesque that it defeats us at the place where life is purest? Parent is parted from child, husband from wife, friend from friend. Each for the good of the other would gladly count all gain but loss. They pray, and are delivered as they pray from the canker of selfishness. Is our planet so distorted that mere distance is stronger than the soul's compassion offered as a sacrifice to God? If that were true, we might have to say, as a French skeptic said of some blind and cruel theology, "*That* God is my devil."

So the universality of intercession seems to argue the reality of its faith, and the purity of intercession's motive seems to reinforce the argument. We might add that the very closeness of the social bond brings further confirmation. We are "members of one another" in truth, not merely in metaphor. We are joined more closely than stones on a beach, for stones only touch; more closely even than the intertwining roots of grasses in a field, for roots are still individual. We could not live without the common life. We are *organs* one of another[12] —that is the Greek word—living cells in one body of mankind. The little finger cannot be hurt, the least tooth cannot throb, without the whole body feeling pain. If one man is guilty of robbery, locks must be placed on every home. If one man collects a false insurance claim, the premiums are raised for all his neighbors. So close is this vital oneness of mankind that Dr. George A. Coe has suggested that "as the same umbrella may shield two persons from rain, so one brain might conceivably be 'mine' to more than one self."[13] Is the mind of mankind

one Mind? Our common life in its very nature cries aloud
for intercession. Facts seem to justify more than our
tentative claim.

III

There is one understandable objection which might
seem to break our chain of evidence. Let us state it
thus: If by secret prayer I can secretly change my
neighbor's life, am I not dishonorably breaking his freedom? To which answer might be made: it is easy to
cloak a fallacy in a right-sounding phrase. The right-
sounding, but mistaken, phrase in this instance is "dishonorably breaking his freedom." In the case of most of
us, we did not build our house: the contract and labor
were without our knowledge. Its walls, we might argue,
"dishonorably break our freedom," for if they were not
there we could stride directly into the open air. Probably we did not make the clothes we wear: we did not
drive the sheep to the hills, nor shear them, nor clean
and card and dye the wool, nor weave the threads into a
garment, nor carry the garment from factory to store.
Probably we do not know the name of any of the toilers
in all this sequence of toil. They worked unbeknown to
us, and they have changed our life. Have they therefore
dishonorably broken our freedom? Every word spoken
without our planning or desire, every law drafted, every
book printed, every song and every martyrdom is, in a
way of speaking, a coercion—an invasion of our liberty.
But that would not be a true or wise way of speaking.
In point of fact, there is no such creation as "individual
freedom"; and, unless all the signs mislead, the future
will not provide it. We have a richer gift—not individual freedom, but *individual freedom within the corporate bond,* the corporate bond likewise being *caught up
into the life of God.* Plainly we are dependent on one
another's unknown *toil:* we do not know what hands
tilled the fields to provide our sustenance. Plainly we
are dependent on one another's unknown *thought:* we
would be in sore case if our parents had not planned for
us during our helpless years. Why should we not be de-

pendent on one another's *prayers?* That commonalty would fit well the pattern of our common days. The planet then would seem complete in comradeship. Instead of speaking about a dishonorable breach in another's freedom, why should we not say that freedom is made perfect in love?

IV

Faith in intercession has another ally: the prime fact that Jesus practiced it. He said to Peter, "I have prayed for thee, that thy faith fail not."[14] Mothers brought their children to him that "he should put his hands on them, and pray."[15] He interceded for "the people which stand by . . . . that they may believe that thou hast sent me."[16] If answer is made that these prayers were within sound of voice and reach of hand, we might reply that it is hard to believe that Jesus did not pray for Peter, for children, and for the crowd when nobody was near. Are we to believe that his midnight prayers were only for himself? Did he not urge us to "pray for them which despitefully use you, and persecute you?"[17] It would be arbitrary to suppose that such prayers are to be offered only when the persecutor watches and listens, or that he recommended them only as self-discipline. Did he not call his disciples to the apostolate of intercession: "Pray ye therefore the Lord of the harvest, that he will send forth laborers into his harvest"?[10] Was that prayer merely an oblique, and therefore somewhat deceitful, plea to a gathering of folk from whom new disciples might be recruited? Or did Jesus mean—it would be a breath-taking and glowing meaning—that by prayer we can quicken noble longings and resolves across the world? There is an even deeper instance of Jesus' intercession. Let us assume, as we probably must, the late origin of John's Gospel; and let us allow that its chapters are like profounder Socratic dialogues, the meditations of a reverent mind on the real words and deeds of Jesus. It is still true that the "High Priestly Prayer" of Jesus recorded in the seventeenth chapter is congruous with all we know of him. There we can al-

most overhear him interceding tenderly and earnestly for
his disciples, and "for them also which shall believe on
me through their word."[19] His disciples saw in him the
Intercessor, and learned of him so well that the prayers
of Paul for all his comrades are the soul of compassion
and trust.[20] Jesus believed in intercession and practiced
it. Whatever our doubts, he is on the side of faith.

V

Are intercessions answered? Apparently many are
unanswered. Often life seems to move directly counter
to our beseechings. True faith requires clear record and
recognition of this fact. Some have prayed for loved
ones critically sick, and have opened their eyes to find
that death has come even while they prayed. With such
facts we must be honest: it is better to bare our breast
to the spears of God than to receive them while clinging
in a corner. But there are entries on the other side of the
ledger. In the unshakable conviction of truth-seeking
men, *some* intercessions *are* answered—in the direct
fashion of their asking. The intercessor sees changes in
both circumstances and human nature. It is as if a
Voice had answered, "It shall be so," and he has
praised God. These answers could not be proved in
logic: life's weavings and interweavings are so intricate
that "answers to prayer" can always be ascribed to
other factors or to that blessed evasion named "coincidence." Some years ago the suggestion was made that
prayers should be offered for half the patients in a hospital ward, so that their progress then could be compared with that of patients for whom nobody interceded. The suggestion was as foolish as it was
uncharitable. Who could tell if the unbefriended in
prayer were really unbefriended? It is a wide world, and
no man is completely bereft of friendship. Who could
tell if the promised prayers were really offered? Not all
people pray who say they pray. And who could tell
whether the experimental prayers were really prayers?
Under the circumstances, they were probably more experimental than prayerful. There are no instances from

which all factors except prayer can be eliminated; and if there were, the doubt of intercession's power would not be dispelled. The answers could still be ascribed to "chance," "thought transference," "coincidence," or even to "the unknown." But this doubt is not essentially different from the doubt which besets any spiritual reality. There is no scholastic proof or scientific demonstration of the fact of God. In the final issue, the only answer is this:

> Whoso hath felt the Spirit of the Highest
> Cannot confound, nor doubt Him, nor deny:
> Yea with one voice, O world, tho' thou deniest,
> Stand thou on that side, for on this am I.[21]

The best proof of answered intercession is precisely this quality of conviction in those who intercede, and in those who consequently have been blessed. A recent commentator offers his testimony with both wisdom and certitude:

I have no evidence to offer beyond the religious interpretation of history, the example and instruction of our Lord, the revelation He gave of the Heavenly Father, and the testimony of those who have been so helped. These are sufficient to give vigor to an assertion that every earnest act of intercession affects the situation towards which it is directed so vitally as to create a new situation. Through it circumstances are often changed, and even if these are unchanged hearts are changed, and when hearts are changed circumstances are transformed, till temptations become altar stairs, and a cross becomes a gate into life. No situation remains the same when prayer is made about it. There are influences of many kinds, good and evil, operating in every cause and in every soul, and each of these has power as an element in the battle between good and evil, but the decisive and essential factor in each case is the loving power of God called forth, or rather made way for, by the intercessions and prayers of Christian folk. For a time things may seem to go on much as before, but the decisive power has entered in, and even mountains must move. *Prayer always creates a new situation.*[22]

This the intercessors have known. They neither make,
nor need to make, any deduction, inference, or argument. They know God and His ways— more deeply
and surely than an artist knows that a blossoming lilac
bush is beautiful, than a musician knows that Mozart
has some secret of rippling sunlight, than a scientist
knows the flash of truth, or even than a child knows his
mother's heart. The instances of this knowledge are agelong and manifold. They cannot be dismissed by a cap-
tious denial. Neither may the believer stubbornly pretend that all intercessions win a reflex answer.
Sometimes they seem to the observer, and perhaps to
the intercessor, to be bluntly refused. But even then,
there is in hidden ways, such is our faith, a "new situation." Meanwhile some intercessions are answered according to the terms of the intercession, and the Spirit's
secret sign is given for surety. Then the man on his
knees exclaims: "This is the Lord's doing; it is marvelous in our eyes."[23]

V

Dr. George S. Stewart of Scotland affirms in the paragraph just quoted that "circumstances are often
changed" by intercession. This power of prayer over the
event we have examined and underscored in an earlier
chapter. He further asserts that, even when circumstances are left unchanged, "hearts are changed." Can
we give any further account of this power of intercession to change the heart? Not very much: these journeyings elude our eyes and thoughts. We can speak only
in surmise and parable. Telepathy has sometimes been
proposed as the instrument of intercession. But we
should be on guard against any too-strong alliance with
thought transference, lest we should later cry, "Defend
me from my friends." Many psychologists still doubt the
existence of telepathy. To the layman the evidence
seems multiplied and vivid, but many experts hold that
the phenomena in question can be interpreted better by
known factors than by an "unknown" factor called telepathy. Thus Dr. Karl Ruf Stolz roundly affirms:

The evidence for telepathic marvels is scientifically untenable. The most competent students of borderland psychology reduce the so-called telepathic occurrences to a hopeless jumble of suggestion, unconscious perception, chance and coincidence, hallucinations and illusions, defective observation, exaggeration, imagination, musclereading, deliberate or unintentional fraud. . . . . Thought is not a vibration of the ether set up by sensitized brain cells, but an immaterial condition, a state of mind.[24]

He then proceeds to give instances of alleged telepathy which on inquiry yield easily to other and more satisfying explanations. Psychology may revise this appraisal. So sweeping a dismissal is not fully convincing: it relies too much on scientific proof, and assumes without full warrant that a troubling of the ether is the only account to be given. But the dismissal is widely characteristic of present psychological thinking, and should therefore give us pause. In any event, even if telepathy were surely proved, we would need to remember that the transfer of human thoughts is not necessarily a blessing. Evil thoughts could be transferred, and our extremity might be worse. Indeed, we might have to spend our time, as Mrs. Eddy spent her declining years, in fear of "animal magnetism."[25] Even *man's* good thoughts could not save us. There is ultimately no salvation in *man*. That is why prayer is prayer to *God:* we are aware that even the best human power is not enough for human need. Wherein, then, would we be blessed by telepathy? We cannot tell how intercessory prayer finds its way into a neighbor's life. Can we *ever* tell how God is mediated? How does He come through nature? Or through the whole process and urgency of human love? How does a sense of the Timeless visit our time-held minds? It does. We yearn over

> . . . . old, unhappy, far-off things,
> And battles long ago.[26]

We feel pity and resolve for people not yet born:

Red helpless little things will come to birth,
And hear the whistles going down the line,
And grow up strong and go about the earth,
And have much happier times than yours and mine:
And some day one of them will get a sign,
And talk to folk, and put an end to sin,
And then God's blessed kingdom will begin.

God dropped a spark down into everyone,
And if we find and fan it to a blaze
It'll spring up and glow, like—like the sun,
And light the wandering out of stony ways.
God warms His hands at man's heart when he prays,
And light of prayer is spreading heart to heart;
It'll light all where now it lights a part."

How comes this sense of the Timeless to men who are
in the category of time? How *is* God mediated? We do
not know. Nor can we tell how intercession finds its
way. We must be content to know that intercession is in
God, and that no one "hath known the mind of the
Lord. . . . . For of him, and through him, and to him,
are all things."[28]

A *parable* of intercession's journeyings is possible,
but not a *parallel*. Let us suppose that a person is sick
with pneumonia, that the infection has been located in
the lower lobe of the left lung, and that a decision has
been reached to use serum. Where is the serum injected?
Not in the lobe of the lung. Perhaps in the crotch of the
right arm. Now suppose there is a boil on the mid-arm.
The doctor does not inject pneumonia serum into a boil.
The right arm provides the locale only if it is healthy.
Now suppose the injection well made. The serum spreads
through the hidden channels of the whole body, and thus
attacks the area of infection. Its benefience shows a decline of fever. That is our parable. But it is a parable, not
a clinical diagnosis. We do not know the hidden channels
of our common life. But perhaps we may fairly say that
when a "clean member" is offered to God He grants some
new injection of His spirit, and that health spreads by the
hidden channels of our common life to attack and con-

quer the areas of disease. That assumption lays rightful stress on purity of motive. Perhaps our intercessions fail because we offer God an arm with a boil. If we pray for the poor but make no gift and show no neighborliness, or for the chaotic realm of toil and attempt no reconstruction, how can we rightly hope for answer? The prayer is not then a prayer: it is only shadowboxing or self-deception. Noble prayer imposes a rigor on our deeds. Bobby Burns wrote to a friend on New Year's Day as follows: "This, Dear Madam, is a morning of wishes: and would to God that I came under the Apostle James' description: 'The effectual, fervent prayer of a *righteous man* availeth much.' In that case, Madam, you would welcome in a year full of blessings."[29] Checkered character and stubborn motive block the channel of our prayer. The beginning of any true intercession is a word of Christ, "For their sakes I sanctify myself."[30] But the parable still has its gleam of truth. It is like one of the realistic visions of St. Gertrude. She saw Jesus showing his arm wounded on Calvary, and heard him say tht his arm was healed whenever she prayed for certain malicious men who had been guilty of vandalism against her monastery. She was aghast: "But, Lord, how canst Thou call such men thine arm?" The Lord answered, "I call them so in truth, because they are members of the Body of which I glory to be the Head."[31] To our sophisticated eyes that vision has a certain medieval bareness, but it is an "image of the true."

VI

Can we give any closer account of intercession's journeyings? Only by surmise, not by sight. Perhaps we may justifiably assert of intercession that, because it lives always in purest and most self-forgetting motive, its best answers are in the same realm—in the area of *motive*. How do noble thoughts arise in an ignoble mind? Whence our sudden tendernesses? Whence "flashes" of new truth, or undreamed of access of courage? Surely these are sometimes the gift of prayers offered for us! Sherwood Eddy has written: "We can prove the reality of

prayer only by praying. No philosophy can prove or dis-
prove it. No philosophy or science has ever shown that
God cannot put a thought in the mind of man. If he
cannot, he is more helpless than a little child."[32] Why
should we not believe that worthy impulses and brooding insights came through the intercessions of devoted
friends? Such thoughts and persuasions, be it noted, are
no breach of our freedom. For our response to these
"openings" is still our choice. They invite us to organize
our freedom around a higher focus: we may accept or
refuse the invitation. Here is Vida Scudder's word:

I think desire is the strongest force in the world; it is
desire that shapes empires, molds characters, alters the
course of events. Human desires degrade and stifle, they
inspirit and they heal. And surely they are never so dynamic as when uplifted into unison . . . . with the Mind
of the Most High. God invites our co-operation in carrying
out His purposes. . . . . Prayer is an energy as real as the
energy that binds the planets to the sun.[33]

"Pray ye therefore the Lord of the harvest, that he will
send forth laborers into his harvest." What could Jesus
honorably mean except that his disciples by prayer
could quicken noble vision and true resolve across the
world? If *that* is the power of intercession, the man on
his knees might do more to stay the aggressions of earth
than twenty treaties or fifty battleships!

VII

Then are our intercessions answered? We ourselves
could not wish them answered when motive and life are
insincere. In that instance they would not be prayers,
but rather excuses and evasions. But are intercessions
answered when men are penitent and sincere? Often not
in the way asked by the intercessor. God cannot perjure
Himself to answer a blind prayer, nor destroy a neighbor's essential freedom. Even when all the circumstances of intercession seem *to us* to be consonant with

the mind of Christ, the prayer may still not be answered
so far as our eyes can trace, though our faith remains
that all sincere love-in-prayer "creates a new situation."
His ways are higher than our ways, and "past finding
out." But some intercessions are answered in direct response. Let other men speak about "rationalization"
and "coincidence." We shall still remember with a smile
Zona Gale's parable of the tadpole: "What!" exclaimed
tadpole to tadpole. "Do you mean that when you put
your nose above water, there is actually something *else*
than water to breathe? Absurd!" Let tadpoles chatter:
there *is* another climate constraining and governing our
little pool of earth. Great art knows the hidden might of
intercession. Thus Robert Browning claims that David's
intercession prevailed for Saul, and gives David that faith
for utterance:

Do I find love so full in my nature, God's ultimate gift,
That I doubt his own love can compete with it? here, the
    parts shift?
Here, the creature surpass the Creator, the end, what Be-
    gan?—
Would I fain in my impotent yearning do all for this man,
And dare doubt He alone shall not help him, who yet alone
    can? . . . .

I believe it! 'tis Thou, God, that givest, 'tis I who receive;
In the first is the last, in thy will is my power to believe.
All's one gift; thou can't grant it moreover, as prompt to
    my prayer,
As I breathe out this breath, as I open these arms to the
    air.[35]
David could not enrich Saul, nor raise him from sorrow.
But he could pray, having done what he could, and he
could be sure that in the prayer his service was made
perfect. There is another poem of intercession, even
more dramatic and breathtaking in its faith, which af-
firms boldly that one man's intercession can save a
world. Written by James Stephens, it is entitled "What
Tomas an Buile Said in a Pub."

I saw God. Do you doubt it?
Do you dare to doubt it?
I saw the Almighty Man. His hand
Was resting on a mountain, and
He looked upon the World and all about it:
I saw Him plainer than you see me now,
You mustn't doubt it.

He was not satisfied;
His look was all dissatisfied.
His beard swung on a wind far out of sight
Behind the world's curve, and there was light
Most fearful on His forehead, and He sighed,
"That star went always wrong, and from the start
I was dissatisfied."

He lifted up His hand—
I say He heaved a dreadful hand
Over the spinning Earth, then I said: "Stay—
You must not strike it, God; I'm in the way;
And I will never move from where I stand."
He said, "Dear child, I feared that you were dead,"
And stayed His hand.[26]

VIII

"But does God rest my neighbor's good on my prayers?" we may ask, shrinking from the burden of so great an obligation. Why should we doubt that God imposes such a burden of love? The responsibility is stern and splendid. God rests our neighbor's good upon our toil and thought. Why not upon our prayers? "But would not God give good gifts in any event?" Apparently there are some gifts which God chooses to give through love's labor and planning—and prayer. God is intent upon the growth of the comradeship. He has so ordered our days that we live in mutual reliance. He yearns to see "The Beloved Community" fulfilled on earth. Therefore He has made us one life. We must not fail those whose weal depends upon our toil and thought—and prayer.

So are we called in sympathy. Sympathy means not only "feeling with" our neighbor's sorrow, but communicating to him our confidence that if we were in the same besetment we could lift a banner above it. How, save by prayer? We must live in purity also, not offering God an infected arm. We must live in work and thought, for prayer is not a laziness. We must live in Christ, for we cannot pray aright for others except as we try to see all men as he saw them from his cross. Then the tiny labors of our hands and the poor gropings of our thought are made perfect in intercession. This mutual pleading is the beginning and end of the Kingdom of God. It is a prime essential in our common destiny. It is, perchance, the first act and the continuing spirit of a new order in the earth. Enter the Apostolate of Intercession!

Chapter VIII

THE BOUNDS AND BOUNDLESSNESS
OF PRAYER

LIN YUTANG, IN his book "The Importance of Living" tells how he was alienated from alleged Christianity by what seemed to him a false theory of prayer. A relative fervently prayed for fine weather for a Chinese funeral, and the questions thronged. If a neighbor's crops need rain or sunshine shall our convenience outweigh his need? Is God so indulgent and foolish that everyone may pray successfully for his own weather? Do we know what is best for mankind? Shall our petty hankerings cloud the Eternal Eyes?[1] We have taken issue with those who claim too little for petitionary prayer, who, under the empty threat of natural law, would rob the individual of his rights and standing as a person. Now we must meet those who make extravagant and unworthy claims. The Maréchal de Villars, taking leave of Louis XIV, exclaimed: "Defend me from my friends; I can defend myself from my enemies."[2] The would-be friends of petitionary prayer sometimes dim its light: their pretensions deter truth-loving minds. Realism, especially Christian realism, requires us to trace, as closely as we may, the limits of petition.

I

Our prayers are limited by God's world: we cannot by prayer pluck stars from the sky or turn springtime into sudden winter. Few people believe that when Jesus said, "If we have faith as a grain of mustard seed, ye shall say unto this mountain, Remove hence to yonder

128

place and it shall remove,"[3] he meant such mountains as the Pyrenees or the Himalayas. A bigot might insist that everything is possible to faith, and that the Himalayas are fixed only because of our lack of prayer-confidence. But some saving grace of common sense would answer: "There have been people with apparently boundless faith, yet the mountains have not moved. Moreover, wise men would not pray to have them moved. We could not live in a capricious universe."

That last fact invites emphasis. The girl who prayed for the torn page of her geography book to be made new, but found it still torn, needed counsel in the full truth concerning prayer. She was not to blame. The fault was in the teacher who had told her that "God can do anything."[4] A *good* God, intent on man's growth in goodness, *cannot* do anything. Suppose a man should say, "I wish I were at the other side of the world," and thereupon should find himself instantly transported from England to Australia. Suppose a man should exclaim in shame, "Oh, that day would never dawn!" and thereby should turn the world dark. Suppose mountains, victimized by myriad prayers, gamboled like lambs. It is clear even to our dim sight that free men can endure only in a faithful world. Indeed, only so can free men pray. The goodness of God is attested in constancy as well as in newness: "Thy righteousness is like the great mountains; thy judgments are a great deep: O Lord, thou preservest man and beast."[5] Men can grow only in a trustworthy realm, for true growth is not growth in cosmic sleight-of-hand but growth in grace. "An evil and adulterous generation seeketh after a sign; and there shall no sign be given to it. . . . ."[6] Religious insight interprets the world's unchangeabilities, on which science and religious faith alike rest, not as an iron fixity "deaf to our beseeching," but as the unswerving fealty of the gracious Creator.

Just where the limits run who can closely trace? The land is fast, and its bounds elude us. If a friend lost his hand in an accident we would not pray for a new hand to grow, but if he were sick with typhoid fever we would pray for his recovery. Where *is* the boundary? We would not pray for the sun to rise in the west, but if we were caught in the track of a forest fire we might pray for the wind to change. We would not pray for a youth to return to babyhood for a new start, but we would pray for good motives to kindle in him in power. Where *do* the limits run? The greater the apparent constancy in nature, the less the power of petitionary prayer: we cannot change the tides by praying. The greater the apparent variability and flexibility, the more instant our prayers: we shall continue to pray about the weather and about physical health. Did not Jesus say, "But pray ye that your flight be not in the winter, neither on the sabbath day"?[7] Lin Yutang writes, "To thank God for a good wind is sheer impudence, and selfishness also, for it implies that God does not love the people sailing south when *HE,* the important individual, is sailing north."[8] But the sentence need not dismay us. It is rife with false assumptions. Men who pray for a favorable wind are *not* necessarily impudent: they may be *in extremis.* They are *not* necessarily selfish: an aviator so praying may be thinking of his wife rather than himself. Several such instances are given, in fact, in the book *Wind, Sand, and Stars.*[9] Lin Yutang might argue that the aviator should think of all wives and of the ageless wisdom of all weather, but he would then make an impossible and almost inhuman demand. Lin Yutang is wrong again when he says that petitionary prayer for good weather assumes an arbitrary God: it assumes, rather, that God deals with us as persons and respects our birthright of selfhood. Helpless human folk will continue to seek God as succor in storm—and continue to find Him. They will know, and accept the knowledge, that in the midst of earth's variabilities there is still a core of the unyielding; for they realize with Lin Yutang that the weather ought not to be in our control, and that death may be more important in its revealings than physical health. But they will not cease to cry from the depths upon a Help out of sight, and God will not fail to answer them—sometimes in denial of the wish but in sure peace in the heart, and sometimes in instant acquiescence. Even a blind and foolish prayer honors Him more than the alleged wisdom that buries Him in His "laws." The variabilities of earth are God's play of impromptu act, which sometimes grants our childish askings and thereby serves our growth. The fixities like-wise are filled with His presence: they are not belts of inertia, but assurances of His unwearied care.

II

The outlines of a reasoned faith about prayer and physical healing have already been hinted, and the question in other aspects will engage us in the chapters on "Prayer and Personality." But widespread interest in the issue and its daily bearing on our life call for some focused word. The discussion of the limits of prayer gives an appropriate place. Flesh and spirit may be a monism: the solidities of an erstwhile science are now resolved into very immaterial "radiations" and "vi-bration frequencies." But for us, in the smart of experi-ence, flesh and spirit are a psychophysical unity *and* tension. We distinguish between "me" and "my body," yet realize that the two are "marvelously compact to-gether."

Physical ills find a rough and ready scale in this area of unity-tension. A skull fracture in an accident comes from the *"body"* side of the tension; while a nervous breakdown due to fear of the court exposure on some crime rises on the *"me"* side of the tension. A stomach disorder may come both from physical susceptibility and from sudden sorrow: it may rise from middle ground. There is no physical affliction without its men-tal bearing—toothache brings depression—and no psy-chosis without its physical issues—sorrow brings insom-nia. The average man, open-minded about prayer, naturally assumes that prayer prevails most on the mind side of the tension. It is a fair assumption. No prayer, however fervent, can restore an amputated limb. We might argue that in a completely spiritual society an arm cut off at the elbow by surgery would grow through prayer, but the argument would be academic. We know that our prayers do not restore the arm. Nay more: we surmise that a dangerous universe is necessary for our growth: we *covet* real risks and stern austerities.

Thus there are limits to the healing power of prayer in physical ills, if "limits" is the proper word. In truer phrase, there is a realm of God's constancy. We grow older and die—"Man goeth forth unto his work and to his labor until the evening."[10] Man cannot labor unremittingly for a year without food or sleep, nor long forestall the onset of death; "And one man in his time plays many parts"[11] from childhood to second childhood. That rule holds. It holds not because it is empty of God but because it is full of God. It is His ordaining, for our good. Where nature seems unyielding to our prayers, nature is not flinty, but faithful. The apparent denial is not denial: it is rather the smiling refusal of a Father to do anything to injure His child, even though the child mistakes injury for good and prays for it.

But when this realism has been honored, another fact, equally realistic, cries for recognition. This fact: the power of prayer in the realm of health has hardly yet been tapped. Even in afflictions which seem beyond cure, deliverance has come—by prayer. The testimony is too poignant, too instant in conviction, too recurrent, and too honest to be ignored or arbitrarily gainsaid. Such instances are proportionately not numerous. They are numerous enough to show that the flesh is not a determinism, and to validate man's freehold as a person under God; but not so many that the Faithfulness becomes unfaithful. There is a vast middle ground of disease where prayer is a strong resource. It can shorten healing time in sicknesses involving long convalescence, such as hip dislocation, for the reason that prayer keeps the whole system toned to health. It can be a determining factor in certain operations: a fear-stricken heart, especially one physically weak, might succumb to an anesthetic, while the same heart calmed by prayer might well bear the strain. In afflictions that arise from the "me" side of the tension—bodily ills due to repressions, complexes, fears, unworthy desire or dark memory— prayer is "very heaven" and medicine only a broken reed. This fact we shall hereafter trace. How many are such ills! In bombed cities people die from fear, the fear that induces uremic poisoning. There we see vivid token of the many fleshly besetments originating in the mind. On that side of the body-spirit tension, prayer has mighty power. There is little doubt that Jesus healed by prayer. There is little doubt that His disciples wrought works of healing in His name. Private and corporate prayers have a wide range of curative power in physical ills. In this ministry to men's bodies the Church has been so remiss and faithless that the therapy has been left to quasi-mystical cults which refuse the realism of fact, make healing almost an end in itself, and, what is worse, rob man of danger and heroism by denying the odds. The cults have their neglected truth, and cannot be answered by attack. The true rejoinder is in a Church which is realistically reconsecrate to the lost ministry of healing.

In physical afflictions which cannot be cured, or which necessarily involve sharp pain or worse tedium, prayer gives deeper healing. One man is embittered by his cancer, while another gains insight; one resents the encroachment of age, while his neighbor greets it as bright destiny. Attitude determines the issue, and prayer is attitude.

> Man was made for joy and woe;
> And when this we rightly know,
> Thro' the world we safely go.
> Joy and woe are woven fine,
> A clothing for the soul divine.[13]

The dark and uphill stretches of the road have their own strange joy—a greater treasure perhaps than the sunlit downslope can give. We blame God for pain and danger, and then proceed to increase the afflictions and the risks. We could stay on land but must travel by sea or air, and we scorn those who bid us live without risk or pain. Thus Mario Puglisi has written concerning "Ethical Prayer":

Instead of negation of the world, visionary aestheticism, literary dilettantism, emotional disturbance (which tends to make the pure stream of religion muddy rather than clear), it chooses the drama of life in which human flesh falls, bit by bit, upon the burning embers of pain; because it is by pain and by pain alone that the garland of victory acquires a matchless glory and life gains a religious quality which it could attain in no other way. Instead of a passive quietism which shrinks timidly from the arena of history in order to escape from the clutches of evil, it adopts a creative activity, both fertile and heroic, which, conscious of the difficult task allotted to human effort, steps forth to meet evil, in order to attain that ideal life which is purified and exalted in pain.[13]

Prayer's greatest healing is therefore not healing, but the courageous and creative acceptance of the terms of mortal life. True prayer does not evade pain, but gains from it insight, patience, courage, and sympathy; and, at long last, makes it an oblation to God. True prayer does not sidestep death, but greets it. This is healing beyond healing. By this prayer we are "more than conquerors": the realism of unanswered prayer becomes the very Presence of God.

III

Prayer has other bounds: *it must keep its proper place within thought and toil.* These powers also serve our growth, and prayer cannot be their lazy substitute. "If wishes were horses, beggars would ride." If prayers were a magic carpet, indolent folk would fly to heaven—and be miserable in a spirit still earth-bound. This is a truism, but it is often evaded by those who thereby claim credit for "faith." The farmer cannot grow a harvest merely by prayer: he must learn farming, and he must work. The would-be musician, though endowed like a second Mozart, cannot compose another *"Nachtmusik"* by petition alone, however ardent: again there must be thought and labor. Some alleged answers to prayer, if proved, would make God a partner in the blasphemy of "get-rich-quick."

Any man who has done an honest day's work, soling shoes or performing a surgical operation, chopping wood or designing a house, knows that he staked out a wider claim to manhood. He is worthier:

> Something attempted, something done,
> Has earned a night's repose.[14]

He has won a certain wholeness, an access of selfhood. Whence this grace through labor? No such virtue comes through waste or warfare, through idleness or easy journeying. Why should the hard task, if worth doing and honestly done, confer integrity of character? Is it because we are thus joined in friendship with our Creator—"My Father worketh hitherto, and I work"?[15] Whatever the hidden cause, "even in the meanest sorts of Labor, the whole soul of man is composed into a kind of real harmony, the instant he sets himself to work."[16] The monastic orders, such as the Rule of St. Benedict, wisely insisted on a discipline of manual and mental toil. Man is set for his growth in an unfinished earth—its fields at first weed-cluttered, its gold held in mountain-ore, its homes mere scattered stones, and its songs and pictures only inchoate in dream and hope. This seems to be by deliberate Intent. We learn by labor, nor can we rightly expect our prayers to spare us that discipline. "O Townsmen," says a modern prayer, "go and see those who write their prayers to the Lord with the great pen of the plow, and see how the Lord bestows His gifts between the lines of that writing."[17]

These facts hold also of the labor of thought which informs all rightful work. A faithful universe does not spare us the pain of thinking through its problems. The stars yield their secrets only to long hours at a telescope, apprenticeship in mathematics, aching thought, and daring postulate. The boll weevil in our fields and the pneumococcus in our body are conquered only by stern research. Problems which are even more difficult, because more entangled with our human foibles—such tasks as a new culture of cities, the banishment of unmerited poverty, and the outlawry of war—demand the

sinew of intelligence. Co-operative thought and labor
are the rule of life. The rule is not remanded by prayer's
pleading. Pure religion does not eschew thought. Cults
which make the mind a blank page "for God's writing"
are no asset. "Thou shalt love the Lord thy God with all
thy . . . . mind."[18]

Such sureties seem to leave prayer in eclipse, as in
the ancient maxim, "God helps them who help themselves." Actually that proverb, like most others, is only
partial truth: God helps those also who cannot help
themselves. Prayer, far from being superfluous, is the
proper air of thought and labor. For man's toil without
prayer is finally meaningless, unrenewed, undedicate—
a treadmill drudgery or a suicidal snare. Man's thought
without prayer is self-enmeshed, blind with pride, forgetful of his ignorance and need. How much of man's
work is hurtful or cheap because he does not pray!
How much of man's thought is robbed by prayerlessness
of the timeless accent which is thought's noblest mark!
The golden issue of thought comes not solely by the
mind's labor, but when the mind is off guard. It arrives
in a flash, by surprise, as a gift. Prayer is the creative
silence in which the subconscious energies of creative
thought are best fulfilled. This we shall try to show in
coming chapters. Here we urge only that the wise rule
of life is neither prayer without intelligent labor, nor intelligent labor without prayer. The wise rule is to work
and pray, think and pray, watch and pray.

IV

There is a darker fetter on our prayers—*the bounds
set by our wrongdoing.* However intense our plea, however clamorous, God cannot forswear Himself to bless
our wrong. The whole question of prayers in wartime is
here pertinent. As these words are written Germany has
conquered most of Europe. Letters pour in upon American Christian agencies to urge special days of united
prayer for peace. These messages agree about the value
of prayer in crisis. They urge with Tennyson's King Arthur:

> More things are wrought by prayer
> Than this world dreams of. Wherefore, let thy voice
> Rise like a fountain for me night and day.[19]

With such conviction Christian faith cannot quarrel. If prayer flows from sincere fountains, even though the fountains have been choked by selfishness and opened only by retributive earthquake, the prayer is not in vain. But when the letters pass beyond that fact they are in strange contradiction. Several suggest prayers for British victory, though a few hint that God this time may be on Germany's side. Some recommend prayer for American intervention with money and men. Some advise repetition prayers: "God bless Belgium," "God bless Norway," and thus through a list of nations—from which Germany has been carefully omitted. These letters are a dramatic instance of the problem which prayer confronts by reason of man's waywardness.

The question is not one of forgiveness after confession. Indeed, very few of the letters propose confession—a fact which is itself a condemnation. We are agreed, let us assume, that a Christlike God forgives freely confessed sin, and for love's sake remits the penalty or makes it a remedial discipline. The question is whether the hasty assumptions in the proposed prayers can ever be upheld. Notice only some of these assumptions. It is assumed, *first,* that certain nations are almost black in character and others almost white, and that we have power to read the inmost character of nations. It is assumed, *second,* that God's purposes are wrought through the mass killings of war; and that His other methods, if any, are subordinate. It is assumed, *third,* that we know how history should move, and that we can wisely plan the immediate and more distant future of the race: God is needed only to endorse our draft of wisdom. It is assumed, *fourth,* that if war is a judgment on us, an open sore proclaiming poison in the blood, the poison can be canceled without any radical change in our central motive or our way of living. The assumptions collapse as soon as they are thus isolated. As to the first, the immediate occasions of war may be

hatefully tyrannical—a recrudescence of Caesarism—
while its causes are involved and world-wide: embittered
poverty inviting demagoguery may be one of several
pregnant causes. As for the second, there is assuredly
no guarantee that God's best blessings are mediated
through military conquest. The history of the Hebrews
seems to show that military defeat turned them to
deeper tasks than victory might have levied. The Christian gospel came from a conquered land. This is written
not to beg a question, but only to show that we cannot
beg it. As to the third assumption, how appalling is our
pretense of wisdom, our thrusting of petty notions before Everlasting Eyes, as if we could turn the axis of
history and sagely shape the destinies of man! As for
the fourth assumption, which is our immediate concern,
we become sure on second thought that we ourselves
would not wish to live in a universe where wrongdoing
goes scot-free or prospers. The words of Lincoln, spoken of prayers during our Civil War, are better guidance than such shallowness:

Both read the same Bible and pray to the same God
. . . . Fondly do we hope, fervently do we pray, that this
mighty scourge of war may speedily pass away. Yet, if God
wills that it continue until all the wealth piled by the bond-
man's two hundred and fifty years of unrequited toil shall
be sunk, and until every drop of blood drawn with the lash
shall be paid by another drawn with the sword . . . . so
still it must be said that "the judgments of the Lord are
true and righteous altogether."[20]

There are doubtful assumptions even in that noble comment: does God "will" that wars continue? But the
words are nearer truth than the flippancy which asks
God to ignore or immunize our still-cherished transgressions. So long as we live for cheap thrills or a false success, so long as we coerce our comrades or neglect their
far-flung poverties, just so long shall we fetter our prayers by our own selfishness. The worst chain on modern
prayer is the false civilization in which we are content to
live. In wartime, as in every time of judgment, the first

prayer must be a confession of sin and a plea for pardon. The second prayer must be a confession of ignorance and a plea for light. The third prayer must be a confession of the comradeship and a plea for a forging of the bonds of love. Then, only then, can we safely offer our specific petitions.

But even in this issue it would be easy to draw the limits of petition too closely, as though they were a straitjacket. In a letter published in a religious journal we can trace this too-harsh drawing of boundaries: "Peace is the result of actions . . . . past. For . . . . religious leaders to call on men and women to pray for world peace today is comparable to a farmer praying for a harvest of a different nature from that of the seed he has sown. It is one way by which the Church is hindering, even killing, the spread of Christian truth."[21] The plea seems plausible. We have no right to ask that criminal blunders be ignored. We cannot worthily pray God to "bail us out" so that we can "flee the country." But the letter nevertheless is the victim of a metaphor. "To pray for world peace" is *not* like a "farmer praying for a harvest of different nature from the seed." A field cannot be forgiven nor change its nature, but men are not thus bound. The letter, desiring to be Christian, is actually sub-Christian: it holds by implication low views of man's possibilities, and lower views of God in His dealing with man. The dying thief had presumably sown weeds through part of his life. Yet he prayed, "Lord, remember me when thou comest into thy kingdom"; and Jesus answered him, "Today shalt thou be with me in paradise."[22] Was Christ also "hindering, even killing, the spread of Christian truth"? Would Christ have been Christ if he had said to him sharply, "You have sown weeds: now reap weeds"? Men are *not* like fields. New light can pierce men's minds. Christ honored that sudden grace in the dying thief: he took the new will for the new deed. It is worth noting that the thief did not ask to be saved from the cross: he prayed to be remembered in the new Kingdom. He might have prayed for physical rescue, and that prayer might or might not have been granted. Instead, and more worthily, he asked that new light should be validated as his new nature; and Christ sealed the prayer with a promise. The cardinal fact is that light pierced the praying man, thus quickening fresh, creative factors in his nature. Such light does come through prayer. Even in our sins prayer may still be, not "limited," but a boundless liberty.

V

We have tried to trace the limits of petitionary prayer. We have found that, though we cannot be sure just where the line runs, the bounds are wide. There is a faithfulness of earth and sky, of life and death, which our pleading cannot touch, and without which we could not be free in life or prayer. Yet that faithfulness is overlaid by a free activity in which men are "workers together with"[23] God. There is an area where man's thought and labor must be fulfilled. Yet in that area thought and labor without prayer are a helplessness and a delusion. As for other limits, prayer cannot cancel God's holiness or our own moral nature; yet only through prayer can our wrongdoing be redeemed and new motives be kindled into regnancy.

In short, the seeming fetters are still a freedom. The promises of Christ concerning prayer are always qualified: "Whatsoever ye shall ask *in my name,* that will I do."[24] When the proviso is not spoken, it is implied. But it is not a shackle. "In my name" means "in my nature." The world is not a resting place for perfect folk, but a pilgrimage towards blessedness. Why should such pilgrims pray for anything outside the nature of Christ? Similarly, the one prayer that is basic to all true prayers, "not my will, but thine, be done,"[25] is not a high enclosing wall; for the will of God for men is not dark shadow, but shining destiny. Jesus called it his food: "My meat is to do the will of him that sent me."[26] Nor does God's will outlaw man's will. If man's wishes are of no account, then manhood is of no account, and the earth is but a camp for robots. God leaves wide room, not only for man's toil of hand and mind, but for man's prayer. The limits are those which we ourselves would covet. In rashness we cry with Omar:

> Ah, Love! could you and I with Him conspire
> To grasp this sorry Scheme of Things entire,
>   Would not we shatter it to bits—and then
> Remold it nearer to the Heart's Desire![27]

But sober afterthought wonders how God can make heroes without danger—or a danger that is not dangerous—and we exclaim: "Who can understand his errors? cleanse thou me from secret faults."[28] The limits of prayer are then desired limits. Being desired, they are no longer limits.

As these lines are penned a written prayer has reached me from a friend[29] whose days are numbered. He has sent a letter, from the borderland of time and eternity, whose ink is courage and faith. His wife independently has sent the prayer which he composed when told that his sickness would be brief—and fatal. Soon he died. His wife has kindly consented to the printing of his prayer:

O Giver of life on earth and in heaven, Thou who hast breathed into me the breath of Thine own spirit, my call to go has come, and I am as one on the edge of a lonely margin. My spirit shrinks, and a great dumbness seizes me. My Father, must it be? How incomplete, how fragmentary, how improverished my life has been! So little attempted, and so little achieved! And Lord, Thou knowest how I have been counting on filling up my emptiness and offering myself body and soul in my remaining years. . . . .

O Gracious and Merciful one, heal me with Thy forgiveness. Restore to me the joy of Thy salvation. Fortify me to meet death as I ought: as Christ would have me. May Thy sustaining grace buoy me up as the waves and billows go over me in the days at hand. Keep me steadfast, patient, radiant, and forgetful of self. O let my dying prove a true witness to thy love and power that others may be encouraged to entrust themselves to Thee in life and in death. Glorify Thyself in me.

O Father, enfold in thy loving, everlasting arms my beloved and gallant wife and my boy and precious little daughters. I know Thou wilt. Thanks be to Thee. Great is Thy faithfulness. Thy love is deeper than the deepest sea, and it has no ebb or flow.

Strength comes to my soul as I pray, Lord. I know that death is only the beginning of a more adventurous life. I had hoped to live out my span of three score years and ten, for life is sweet. But the call comes, and I yield my flickering life to Thee, "That in Thine ocean depths its flow may richer, fuller be."

Receive me as into Thy hands I entrust myself, and to Thy name be glory and praise, through Jesus Christ my Saviour. Amen.

Death is a "natural limit," but this prayer conquers death. The area of man's toil is a limit, but what could toil accomplish more than this prayer has wrought? Our wrongdoing is a limit, but this prayer overwhelms wrongdoing: the praying man is cleansed and clothed in unearthly light. Fetters themselves become freedom. "Most gladly therefore will I rather glory in my infirmities, that the power of Christ may rest upon me."[30]

PART THREE
PRAYER AND PERSONALITY

Chapter IX

PRAYER AND OUR WANDERING ATTENTION

WE HAVE TRIED to trace prayer's power to change the world. What of its power to change the man who prays?

> Lord, what a change *within us* one short hour
> Spent in thy presence will avail to make.[1]

Religion has rightly stressed this "change within us." Prayer *does* change our world, but the change is within limits. For man does not rule either in life or prayer. He is creature, not Creator. The Beyond still governs us in love: "Which of you by taking thought can add one cubit unto his stature?"[2] No prayer evades the physical onset called death. Besides, whatever the outward event, bright or dark, our own attitude largely determines its value and power. The Beyond governs us—through our response. Though "there is one event to the righteous, and to the wicked";[3] yet to the righteous man, Nathanael, the event of Jesus' life was joy, whereas to the wicked man, Herod, it was flaming judgment, "John the Baptist"—whom Herod had murdered—"risen from the dead."[4] Affliction is a drab experience to the merely callous, but to the saints it is "shade of His hand, outstretched caressingly." Thus the "change within us" is an affair of crucial import. A stained-glass window seen from the outside may be drab and meaningless, but seen from the inside it may be an apocalypse in jeweled points of light.

I

The title "Prayer and Personality" avoids the word psychology. The omission is deliberate; but it is neither ungrateful, nor blind, nor self-sufficient. We do not refuse the sharp light which psychology sometimes sheds on dark areas of man's mind: we welcome it. But we wish duly to stress the fact that in the study of prayer psychology is not a thoroughly competent guide. It is a young endeavor, and apt therefore to be dogmatic; and "none is infallible, not even the youngest." Its dogmatisms continue even though, in the present welter of psychological theory, they wage an irrepressible civil war. As a strict science, psychology can probe little deeper than the nerves and muscles, and has been known to mistake mice for men. As a philosophy, it is too subjective and too limited. It has microscope but no telescope. It studies mind "as is," not "as ought to be." It studies only the mind "in its own place," and cannot study the bewildering, wonder-impelling world which age on age plays on the mind and fashions it.

The fractionalism of psychology is not guilt, but virtue. It is the inevitable and commendable rigor of any specialized research.[5] But in the probing of prayer it may easily bring infections. For if prayer has any meaning, the mind is not alone: it is in communion with God. To treat the mind as an entity may yield knowledge not otherwise gained, but the knowledge will not be proportioned or final knowledge. News can be studied in a newspaper office, but such study does not grant a rounded comprehension of the nature of news. Yes, news is in clicking typewriters, busy telephones, the descriptive skill of reporters, the organizing gift of editors, and the roar of printing machines. But news is not merely "in here": it is also "out there"—in the battlefield, the stock market, the "march and fire of men," and basically in the constraint of cosmic powers. So the "authentic tidings" of prayer is not merely "in here," but also "out there"—in the strangely individual pressures and messages of the world. Psychology needs the alliance of philosophy and theology: it must contemplate fields and the eternal sky, as well as mind—on penalty of astigmatism.

In the study of prayer, psychology is under even worse handicap: it is only an observer. It is denied the truth which comes only to the participant. Here the rule runs deep that "spiritual things" are "spiritually discerned."[6] Dr. Hermann Ebbinghaus has proposed that "in order to understand correctly the thoughts and impulses of man, we must treat them just as we treat material bodies, or as we treat the lines and points of mathematics."[7] But that is an impossible approach: man is *not* merely a material body, and his impulses are *not* mathematical lines. Psychology is and must be partly introspective, despite its experimental methods and its resolve on objectivity. To understand prayer, psychology must be more than introspective: it must pray, flinging itself on God. But thus it ceases to be "strict" psychology. Yet a man cannot wisely appraise music by any objective scrutiny. Nor can he thus comprehend love or honor or the worship of God. If he should try to choose a wife scientifically, by medical and psychoanalytical test, forswearing any venture of the heart, he might be eugenically mated but he would never be truly married—unless his heart should finally overcome his scientific head. Impersonality is not completely achieved in any study. Emotion enters, not least in astronomy. Interpretations must be made, not least in medicine. The refusal to be participant, whether in love or prayer, necessarily leads to low or shallow theories of human life, such theories as would make man a material body and his impulses mathematical lines. We must consult the musician if we would understand music, and the saint if we would understand prayer. Nay, we must be musician at least in longing, and we must be saint in the outpouring of confession.

Is there then *no* value in psychology for the study of prayer? There is no *solely determinative* or *final* value. But there is a *contributory* value so genuine and rich that religion is already under heavy debt to this new knowledge. Psychology *has* shed light on prayer—painful, healing, clarifying light—which religion cannot intelligently ignore. Prayer is not stratospheric in the sense that we employ in prayer another self with another kind of consciousness. "Laws" governing everyday attention are not meaningless for religious attention. To withstand the researchers of psychology into prayer is as foolish and ultimately as dangerous as for the physical man to oppose the inquiries of medicine into the body. The anger of some allegedly religious men against Freud and Jung is a sober reminder of the embattled "zeal" which greeted Galileo and Darwin. Such denials of the questing mind turn faith into fear, and the soul's "invincible surmise" into dark superstition. Psychology has codified and organized man's ancient wisdom concerning himself, and has added to its store. This wisdom can *correct* prayer—for prayer motives *may* be a selfishness, concepts of God *may* be poor "projection," and worship *may* be a timid "escape." This wisdom can *illuminate* and guide prayer, as succeeding pages will gratefully acknowledge. As psychology comes of age—dare we prophesy and say, as its Gestalt country is explored?—it may find in prayer the deepest response of man to the deepest constraint of the cosmos, and so become the acolyte of faith. Meanwhile we must be discriminating: in the study of prayer, psychology's present light is partial, broken, and only peripheral. But we must be hospitable and grateful: psychology's light *is* light, sometimes piercing light, and therefore of God.

So in this and succeeding chapters an attempt will be made to relate psychological findings to the life of prayer. The warnings just given, and the guidance just acknowledged, will be heeded. The country is vast, with an ever-changing climate, and a hinterland ever being explored. These chapters cannot cover it. But they may roughly trace its outlines and contours. We turn first to a discussion of prayer and our wandering attention.

II

Our dog has a mission in life against horses. The ragman's horse, which has a bell, is a particular foe. Sandy,

even when profoundly asleep, hears that horse two
blocks away. He leaps to the window ledge, organizes
himself into a reception committee, and begins to yap.
But for the sound of hoofs and bell he would continue
to sleep. An assault upon him from the great outer
world, a sign attracting his attention, provokes his feeling and conduct. Thus with the organism called man:
signs flash and his attention is caught.

Our self is like a pincushion: the world jabs it with
myriad thousands of surprises or reminders. We depend
on these provocations: they spur and prompt us. We
hear a knocking: that is the aspect of consciousness
called *sensation.* We realize that the knocking means
someone at the door: that is *perception.* We feel an-
noyed or glad or curious: that is *emotion.* We consider
what to do: that is *thought.* We reach a decision to get
up or sit still: that is *action.* Psychologists thus speak
about the "flow of consciousness"—sensation, perception, emotion, thought, and will. They are careful to
warn that it is a "flow." Its waters are inseparably
mixed. It cannot be cut into sections. It has aspects
rather than parts, different activities rather than atomic
"faculties." Modern definitions of attention—that it is
an "emotion," or "a change in clearness of ideas"[8]—
show that the whole self is involved. But an apparent
"arc of consciousness" can still be traced. *Sensation:* a
vivid patch of color—*perception:* "It is a peacock"—
emotion: "How beautiful!"—*thought:* "Wouldn't So-
and-so like the feathers for his making trout flies!"—
action: "Please, do you sell the fallen feathers?" Psychologists warn us, further, that to stop a worthy flow,
as, for instance, just short of action, is dangerous: the
dammed up waters may flood and ruin fertile fields. So
William James, for one, urges us not to leave noble feeling untranslated into noble deeds. We are concerned
just now with the primary end of the stream, with attention and its issues.

Ours is a bewildering age. We live amid multitudinous distractions, and it is doubtful if we can say with
Robert Louis Stevenson,

The world is so full of a number of things,
I'm sure we should all be as happy as kings.[9]

He lived in a simpler time. We are beset. Radios blare.
Traffic roars. Neon signs flash and dazzle. Headlines
explode. We are like strangers on Broadway: we surrender sober thoughts, forget our journeyings, and our
attention whirls. Advertising is a vast conspiracy and
competition to make us look and listen. We develop
jumpy nerves and kaleidoscopic minds—if they can be
called minds. Possibly one of the semiarticulate reasons
why people move to the country is in a resolve to be rid
of this besieging battery of sights and sounds and
smells, this myriad assault of man's devising, in order
to surrender again to the gentler stimuli of the world as
God made it. Luther once wrote: "Just as a good,
clever barber must have his eyes and mind upon the
beard and razor, so as to mark distinctly where he is to
shave, so everything, which is to be done well, ought to
occupy the whole man, with all his faculties and members."[10] But Luther would not have found concentration easy in any city in this year of grace. Often the
razor slips. Everyman, not merely the careless driver or
barber, must confess, "My attention was diverted."

III

Of course our attention is basically controlled for us,
not merely by us, by the very nature of the world and by
our own created nature. The world governs us: it has
restful green fields, distance of mountains, blue depth of
sky, and the merciful darkness of night to save us from
too great distraction. Our own created nature governs
us: we can attend to only one stimulus at a time. Thus
the man who does several things at once does all but
one of them automatically. The man who sees several
things at once, such as the letters of a word, or the stars
in a constellation, sees them as a unity.[11] "One thing at
a time" is a law of our constitution. Even then attention
soon flags, especially concentrated attention, and we fall
asleep. If, as we have argued, the world is alive, if the

world is Personal Spontaneity and Faithfulness, is a fair assumption that our attention is and will be controlled for our good, granted always our willingness. In this issue also we are not our own masters.

But we must co-operate, being free. This feeling, thinking, acting organism, our self, can within limits control his clamorous environment. Indeed he does— and must. "But thou, when thou prayest, enter into thy closet, and *when thou hast shut thy door.* . . ."[12] We can close the mind against distractions, and deliberately expose ourselves to helpful signs. This might be called external control. As students we gather about us a library, and may become so accustomed to that "world" as to be unable elsewhere to do thoroughgoing work. As a family, we make a home: it has artistic colors and friendly furnishings, photographs of our friends, a desk for correspondence with other homes, and pictures that make the imagination glow. All in all, we cannot claim to have been very successful in the ordering of a wise environment, as witness the disfigurement of country lanes or the unhealthy congestion of city slums.

More important than external constraints are the internal controls. In the Prohibition era we removed the outward signs. But, because desires were unchanged, old habits returned. Inner defense and inner selection are a stronger bulwark against our clamorous age than the wisest environment. Saints go unscathed through Vanity Fair: sinners find occasion of sin even in a monastery. Attention is by nature selective: it serves our purpose. What is our desired and espoused purpose? That will largely determine what we see and hear. Is it our purpose to read this book, mastering its knowledge? Even our wife may then sit unnoticed on the other side of the room, complaining, "You haven't heard one word I've spoken." Are we clockmakers? Other men may hear the clock ticking without hearing it, but we shall hear only the clock, and almost describe its anatomy from its sound. What is our purpose? Dwight Morrow would enter a Midtown elevator, and say, "Take me to 14 Broad Street"; or he would stand silently absorbed for half an hour and then turn to a stenographer

with, "And make three copies of it." What is our desire
and resolve in life? Fleshliness? We shall see what
piques and inflames our fleshly imagining. Saintliness?
"To the pure all things are pure." Thus our dominant
interest largely decides what shall be focal in our consciousness. Houdini said that professional psychologists
were the easiest group on whom to work sleight of
hand: they were alert, but alert for the wrong things.[13]
Our regnant longing, our habitual thought, selects "its
own" from the multitudinous world. It determines attention, and thereby rules, at least in primary movement, the whole "arc of consciousness."

IV

Then what of attention and prayer. Prayer is itself
dominant purpose, the C major of all this bewildering
music. Such is the Christian faith and witness. Jesus,
praying all night on his lonely mountain, did not claim
to have found the Purpose. He made vaster claim—that
the Sovereign Purpose had found him. Why does the
Universe jab us, ever prodding this living pincushion of
man's life? Where does "It" wish us to go? What does
"It" wish us to see and do? Why have these ever-
changing stimuli playing on protoplasm—ice age and
tropical age, stars and mountains, storms and stillness—
brought forth this intricate organism called man? For
what end was he born? To what destiny bound? He
must make some answer. Nor can he pause for final
proof: he must choose, or be chosen, and journey. By
some faith, meager or mighty, he must live—by body or
mind, by greed or love, by earth seen or heaven surmised. He may erect his own ends, but if they are false
they will fall: how can they prevail against the Purpose
enthroned in the sky and ingrained in his own nature?
even if they are valid, but only limited, they will likewise fall: when a man's chosen end is only automobiles,
how can he confront death since death is an area where,
as in Mackinac Island, automobiles are forbidden? The
dominant Interest that finally governs this distracting

world is not man's but the Will in which both man and his world are made.

Dr. W. P. Montague offers this discriminating faith: "Religion . . . . is the acceptance neither of a primitive absurdity nor of a sophisticated truism, but of a momentous possibility—the possibility namely that what is highest in spirit is deepest in nature."[14] What *is* "highest in spirit"? The Spirit of Christ. Christianity affirms that his spirit is "deepest in nature," the ultimate meaning of man and his world. Therefore the Christian's purpose: "This one thing I do. . . . . I press toward the mark for the prize of the high calling of God in Christ Jesus."[15] This sovereign purpose it not merely man's: it is created "highest in spirit." By faith it is "deepest in nature." It is not false, nor feeble: it fills time and eternity. Through prayer, which is friendship with God, it governs what a man sees and hears. Selectivity and control are the issue of any purpose made central. The absent-minded philosopher is blind and deaf to the small affairs of home and street. To an electrician a lamppost is a demonstration in electrical engineering, to a man searching for a house number at night it is a welcome help, while to an artist it is golden glow in the rain. Interest rules attention, which modern psychology properly describes as "a point of view," "a change in clearness."[16] The Christian's purpose driven deep by habitual prayer, is Christ. His principle of selection is Christ. The sight of slums? They must be changed to "a city that hath foundations." A mountain storm? God's mystery, majesty, and power. A deed of kindness? God "breaking through" our veil of flesh. Affliction? A path of insight and the perfecting of man's spirit. This Purpose is vast enough to cope with all the signs whether of life and death: it can give both saving blindness and saving sight.

V

To shepherd wandering attention, prayer builds external controls, which, in their reflex influence, deepen the life of prayer. Outer guidances are not as strong as inner desires, nor do they suffice of themselves. But they are disowned only at grave risk. In some measure they are indispensable for every man. Prayer needs its reverent setting. To pretend that "we can worship God anywhere" is only a pretense—the pretense, namely, that we are disembodied spirits. Kierkegaard writes thus of the man who claims to commune with God in the countryside: "I do not hear the trees in the wood telling the old legends—no, to me they only whisper the nonsense they have witnessed for such ages, they only pray me in God's name to cut them down, to save them from the nonsense of all the nature worshipers. Would that all those prating heads sat on one neck; I should know, like Caligula, what to do."[17] This simulated anger in one so gentle was not without reason. The nature worshiper hears many a sound, such as the violent mooing of a cow or the backfiring of an automobile, and sees many a sight to distract his attention from God. Music wisely builds its helpful setting—walls to make a silence from the world, instruments, manuscript scores, biographies of the masters—knowing full well that a man cannot anywhere or everywhere attend to music. Education builds its helpful setting—schools, textbooks, laboratories, libraries—well aware that learning demands its proper environment. We are more apt to remember a man's name, as we meet him after years of absence, if he is in the place where we used to know him: the circumstances supply the clue. Experiments have shown that anything learned in one setting is better recalled there than in a strangeness.[18]

So prayer builds its own house. Otherwise prayer would be blind, like the man who claims to worship God anywhere, to the simplest psychology of attention. God is best found in nature by those who have first found Him in prayer. Worship gathers round it external aids. It builds churches in Gothic splendor or Quaker simplicity. It enlists great art and music. It advises that we close our eyes in prayer for greater concentration, since moving and shining objects attract and distract. It suggests that we close our ears, and helps us by erecting walls against the noise of the world. It provides the quiet drama of the chancel and the profound drama of the sacrament, so that when our eyes are open the mind is still held on things divine. It offers successive items of worship, hymns, scripture, anthems, because attention cannot long be riveted, and is kept only by wise change. It proposes that we kneel in prayer and that the hands be clasped, because such physical acts focus attention, just as walking or frowning help the concentration of an author, and because these gestures have been shown both by psychological test and religious experience to be assets in attention and devotion. It recommends that prayer be now audible, now silent; for speech clarifies thought and gives spear thrust to a high resolve, while silence grants that receptivity which is prayer's heart. In all these counsels religious attention is a higher graft on natural attention. It is only obeying the rules which everywhere govern externally the focusing of man's mind.[19]

VI

Prayer likewise establishes internal controls. By prompting of Mystery and by answering faith[20] the praying man affirms that the spirit of Christ is the meaning and purpose of the world. This faith has its own burning emotion—"The love of Christ constraineth us."[21] Emotion brings attention to sharp focus—as any love letter proves. Modern psychology teaches that just as the self is not a composite of separate "faculties"— perception, memory, will, etc.—but is always one self with different aspects and activities, so emotions are not entities: they gather into "constellations" under the regnancy of some dominant desire.[22] The love of the knight Lancelot for Queen Guinevere gathered hope, fear, and even honor into its solar system:

His honour rooted in dishonour stood,
And faith unfaithful kept him falsely true.[23]

Aaron Burr's overleaping ambition for high position in the state carried with it love—which thus became self-

love—courage, anger, and every other mode and mood
of feeling; as his famous letter, challenging Alexander
Hamilton to the duel, clearly shows. A mother wakes
from sound sleep at any whimper from the baby's crib:
her love for her child makes captive even her "instinct of
self-preservation," and becomes both her joy and pain.
Dr. Alexander F. Shand affirms that the "most conspicuous"—and the most powerful?—of these greater systems of emotion is love. The ancient law, validated and
personalized in Jesus, is thus psychologically sound:
"Thou shalt love the Lord thy God with all thy heart,
and with all thy soul, and with all thy mind."[24] This
love governs attention in prayer: it draws all signs into
the focus of its own system. It makes its own anger,
fear, sorrow, and joy. It brings the clamant world into
order and harmony. All love, of home or country, now
obeys the love made known in Christ. Hate now is hate
of wrong. Doubt now is not a canker, but the odds
which love must meet. Fear now is fear of sinning
against Love, and has no other fear. Life now is unified
as a cathedral conspires round its altar. Stone arches
climb, but they also march—toward an altar. Oak
benches are set—toward an altar. Aisles lead forward—
to an altar. The pulpit, the voice of a man speaking
about God, is on one side—a man must not obstruct the
sight of an altar. Even the Book is at one side—it testifies to an altar. The whole scene has meaning, movement, and a vital heart; and much is forever shut out by
walls. When the worshiper leaves the shrine he still carries the Shrine within him, and thereby redeems the
clamorous world. Thus prayer gives selective purpose,
and governs the multitudinous signs of earth and
heaven.

In another way prayer establishes internal control—
by force of habit. Only by habit is life saved from fatal
wear and tear. If we were always conscious of every act
in walking, could we walk? Or of speaking, could we
speak? Is there not a sad story of the centipede who,
when asked how he walked, tried to watch all his legs so
as to give answer—and promptly stumbled? The focusing of attention by prayer is not assured until prayer has

in some sense become second nature. The factors governing piano playing, the habit by which the sight of a musical score becomes the movement of fingers on a keyboard, are reasonably clear. There is first a desire for music, then the guidance of a teacher, then practice sufficiently repeated to give recency and frequency of impress on muscles and memory, and finally a capacity and a fulfillment of nature.[25] These steps of progress obviously apply in the formation of a habit of prayer; and, just as obviously, the habit reacts on life to govern attention. The guidance on the formation of new good habits given by William James,[26] following the writings of Alexander Bain, is sound counsel in the life of prayer. James proposes four rules which we might summarize as follows: *first,* the habit should be started with full self-commitment and with a "burning of bridges"; *second,* the new action or thought should be repeated frequently, and if possible without lapse, especially in the early stages; *third,* the impulse to obey it should be honored without delay, even though the impulse occurs "out of hours"; and, *fourth,* the habit should be practiced beyond routinely regularity and at some "cost." In obedience to these rules, the praying man declares his faith and deliberately chooses a new environment; he prays night and morning, and observes public worship; he prays whenever the impulse comes, silently in street or shop; and he practices an asceticism which does more than a routine prayer life may require. This practice of prayer we shall later discuss. Here we are intent to notice that prayer establishes an inner control of attention, not merely by intrinsic light and power, but by being made habitual.

VII

Does someone say, "But my attention is vagrant even in my prayers"? Whose is not? The saints have not been immune. They, far from claiming power to "worship God anywhere," have despaired of the wandering mind and enlisted every aid to govern their distraction. Even then they have failed: "For the good that I would I do

not: but the evil which I would not, that I do."[27] How
easily we are distracted from our prayers! An unkind
letter curdles the mind, or the thwarting of some small
ambition, or even some unaccountable dark mood—to
say nothing of the insistent radio or newspaper. Perhaps
these perversities come of an undisciplined life: cultivation in prayer will not avail if the rest of life is left to
run to seed. Perhaps they come from some subtle doubt
of prayer itself. Perhaps they are the onset of "the powers of darkness," since there is a malignity in the world
still best described as a warfare between night and day.
Perhaps they are themselves a challenge from God,
since God does sometimes challenge us to change our
prayers, and even to forsake our prayers for the en-
counter.[28] Whatever these moods they are not overcome without prayer, and we need not be distraught if
they seem beyond our control. They *are* beyond our
control. The only sure controls are not ours: they *are*
God's. They are established in His world and rooted in
our nature. Unless our controls are consonant with His,
they are not scepters but only weak reeds.

> O, who can hold a fire in his hand
> By thinking on the frosty Caucasus?[29]

Some harbors cannot be reached at low tide: all man's
skill then is vain. But the tide soon flows, by the sky's
power. Then a man must do what he can: he must set
sail and rudder. That much power of will remains unless the man is sleeping or insane. After that he must
trust a Tidal Power. The Power does not fail. Praying
men have found that their central love, the love of God
made known in Christ, is not alone. It is one with the
tides, gravitation, and the stars. "The evil which I would
not, that I do. . . . . Who shall deliver me? I
thank God through Jesus Christ."[30] Such is the testimony of the saints: their tiny boat is carried on a tide
flowing through the creation and moving in the deepest
mind of man. That is why prayer persists age on age,
and saves mankind from distraction and the threat of
chaos. Let a man set the sail and rudder with such poor

skill as he can command: "If there be any virtue, any praise, think on these things." Then the Tide will flow: "And the peace of God . . . . shall keep your hearts and minds . . . . and the God of peace shall be with you."[31]

Chapter X

PRAYER, SUGGESTION, AND FAITH

BUSINESSMEN SPEAK OF the need for "confidence." Sometimes the platitude is used to hide injustices which break confidence. Sometimes it is a poor substitute for remedial action. But the general truth of the contention can hardly be denied. Without mutual trust, society cannot cohere, but crumbles into alien groups and anti-social individuals. Leaders and governments ask for "a vote of confidence." Nations also recognize an indispensable bond of honor: "We demand guarantees of good faith." That insistence is naïve, for what guarantee of faith is there except what Kant called "the good will"? And how can *that* he produced on demand? But again, the fact that such faith is an essential of a stable world order cannot be gainsaid. "Trust," "confidence," "faith"—it is as subtle as the "something far more deeply interfused" which gives unity to a landscape, or as the spirit-bond which makes one organism among many members. It is as subtle, as requisite, and as vital. William Osler, the notable physician, wrote, too sweepingly but with a proper sense of values, "Nothing . . . . is more wonderful than faith—the one great moving force which we can neither weigh in the balance nor test in the crucible."[1] Jesus would look searchingly at men who had prayed for healing, and would ask, "Believe ye that I am able to do this?"[2]—the faith being an indispensable factor in the cure. He implied plainly that faith is the intrument or channel of salvation: "Thy faith hath made thee whole."[3] He would inquire, with deep pathos, "When the Son of man cometh, shall he find faith on the earth?"[4] thereby inferring that loss of faith invites the "reign of Chaos and old Night."

I

Then what is faith? Not, in initial instance, a theology. Faith frames the theologies. When Paul wrote, "I have kept the faith,"[5] he was discussing deeper issues than intellectual obedience to a creed. He had held inviolate, not a theological belief merely, but his "soul's invincible surmise." Creeds are the successive homes of faith. There faith lives, as man must live—in some home. But there faith, like man, is restless:

> For men are homesick in their homes,
> And strangers under the sun.[6]

So faith is always building vaster creeds, and always using its own primal resources in the task:

> Build thee more stately mansions, O my soul,
> As the swift seasons roll!
> Leave thy low-vaulted past![7]

Then what is faith? Not credulity. Credulity is superstition rather than faith. Credulity is a gaping loafer, faith an eager pilgrim. Nor can faith be identified with any willful blindness, for that comes of fear rather than faith. Said Thomas Moore:

> But Faith, fanatic Faith, once wedded fast
> To some dear falsehood, hugs it to the last.[8]

But he was grossly inaccurate: he should have written *fear* instead of *faith*. There were men in the time of Galileo who refused to look through the famous telescope *for fear* their religious beliefs might be overturned. They were men of fear, not men of faith. The *faith* lived in Galileo as he gazed through his telescope, not in men who refused the sight. Faith is inward truth daring the unknown. Only once does the Bible try to define faith, for the Bible well understands that eagle-verities cannot be enticed into any cage of careful words: "Faith is the substance of [or the giving substance to] things hoped for, the evidence of things not seen."[9] Then the Bible forsakes its unaccustomed role of pedantic teacher, and, resuming the brush and canvas of the artist, paints unforgettable pictures. "By faith Abraham . . . . went out, not knowing whither he went. . . . . For he looked for a city which hath foundations."[10] He dared to believe that men are not meant to dwell in cities of lusts and lies. "By faith Moses" chose "rather to suffer affliction with the people of God, than to enjoy the pleasures of sin."[11] He dared to believe that earth holds no treasure for the man who will not live by an inward honor. Faith is what Wordsworth called it—"a passionate intuition":

> Of one in whom persuasion and belief
> Had ripened into faith, and faith become
> A passionate intuition.[12]

Faith is the axiom of man's spirit, his thrust into the future as memory is his thrust into the past, his courage in the dark, his undying fire. In the days before there were airplanes, J. M. Barrie once wrote: "The reason birds can fly and we can't is simply that they have perfect faith, for to have faith is to have wings."[13] But that avowal is an almost complete instance of the pathetic fallacy. Birds do not fly by faith: they fly by animal instinct. But man, born without wings, by faith has learned to fly.

II

Obviously faith is not our creation, for we ourselves are creatures. It is a fashion of psychology to trace faith to social example, propaganda, and wishful thinking—as if there were no primal hunger called faith. This tracing has truth and value. But the real questions are still unanswered. Whence society's groping faith? Whence our susceptibility? Faith, by whatever evolution, is a bestowal. What is more, it lives by constant prompting. As a species of sight, it would die except for the repeated stimulus of light. As a seed—and that comparison falls short because faith is never separable from any aspect or energy of our nature—it grows by the continuous ministries of wind, rain, and sun. Winter and summer—that is to say, the contradictory and genial forces of the world—both bless it. These provokings of faith from the encompassing universe are called by psychology "suggestion." How are ideas introduced into the mind? Initially by the arrest of attention. A copy of Chaucer catches the eye of John Masefield. He reads it long into the night. Ere morning his faith leaps: "I too am a poet." The "suggestion" was a book of poetry. Like a spark it touched off tinder long gathering in the subconscious. The flame broke: "I too am a poet."

Then how arose our faith in God? It was not man's invention. Even the idea of a cosmos is not man's invention. There was a bestowal, by whatever agelong development. Constitutionally, man has a certain expectancy of spirit: "Oh that I knew where I might find him!"[14] and signs come, spear thrusts from God through nature or through human life, to quicken the soul's surmise.[15] The mountain tempest "suggests" mystery and majesty of power. The sunset "suggests" quiet gates opening on eternity. Fleecy clouds "suggest," at least to a poet's mind, that "angels have gone to worship and left their plumes lying there." The stirrings that come through human life have a sharper and more instant touch. For who can be completely callous to the mystery of birth? That any man should be able to say and feel, "I am," or that through his transmission of life another soul should be born, is token of the ultimate Wonder. Likewise with the sign called death: quicker than the sorrow of death, and quicker than the rebellion, is the sudden awareness, "Eternity now has dealings with me!" These "troublings" from the sky are much more frequent than birth and death: any kindness is a stab of shining doom, and any noble martyrdom is the arrow of God. Thus a Sanctity "breaks through." Then what of the life of Christ among men? And what of the heartbreak and glory of his Cross? This is sign so arresting, a living thrust so sure, that he is become "the author and finisher of our faith."[16]

The constant play of life upon our secret expectancy, like fingers on vital harpstrings, is its own best corrective. Children, being children, are very suggestible: mother kisses away the pain, and presto! the pain is gone. But soon pain becomes a better interpreter than even mother's assurances, and the child exclaims, "But it isn't gone!" For ages men looked casually on the stars: the stars suggested twinkling lanterns strung above a little park called earth. But the stars kept on shining and moving, until they themselves quickened a vaster faith. In the lobby of some New York City apartment houses you may find an imitation fire: electric lights are set within red celluloid to resemble glowing coals. Sometimes a man will warm his hands at them. For a time he may even feel warmer. But not for long: the fire is fictitious, and his body rebels. Thus even emotional people, who are the most easily suggestible, are finally not permitted to deceive themselves—unless by their deliberate blindness. It is doubtful if even "some of the people" are fooled in major concerns "all of the time." Conversely, "intellectual" people, who are the least suggestible, whose critical apparatus always functions, cannot always keep their denials: expectancy is in them and promptings "work through," so that even Robert Ingersoll at his brother's grave confessed that he half felt the rustle of a wing and half saw the shining of a star.

Psychologists tell us that negative suggestions—"thou shalt not"—while undoubtedly having a place, are less effective than positive suggestions. Dr. Karl Ruf Stolz has said with penetration that the adverb "not" is the most uninteresting word in the language, and that "it tends to evaporate from prohibitions."[17] The old lady was not bereft of wisdom who disapproved of the Ten Commandments on the ground that "they put thoughts into your head." Psychologists further tell us that suggestions that are unintentional, such as the unconscious impact of a pure-minded man, are more effective

than hints that are deliberate—a fact that may some
day spell the merited death of the propagandist. They
further tell us that suggestions from persons penetrate
deeper than suggestions from stones, or even from bill-
boards. Apply these considerations to Jesus Christ. He
rarely said, "Thou shalt not": his plea was, "Happy are
they that." He was never coercive, but instead he kindled a light and asked, "Why even of yourselves judge
ye not what is right?"[18] He was, and is, no thunder
from a sky, no mere picture on a page, but a living
glory "full of grace and truth." Faith is not an inverted
memory image only, but a bestowal of expectancy upon
which the great world plays with many a prompting.
Even opposition can whet our faith, or throw it back on
prayer, as witness the oft-repeated portent of religious
revival during world-wide catastrophe. Meanwhile
God's beckonings do not fail. Thus are we guided by a
way we know not to a Home out of sight.

III

We return now to our original thesis: we cannot live
worthily without faith. *Self*-confidence, for example, is
a necessity. Imagine a man standing at the edge of a
crevasse wide enough to be dangerous but not too wide
to be jumped. If he should take counsel with his fears,
saying to himself, "I can't make it. I might slip. Just
look at that chasm!" he probably would slip if compelled to jump. But if he should say, "Of course I can
make it. I'll measure my distance—and here goes!" he
would probably overleap his danger. A man who has
lost his "nerve" is a pitiable figure of a man. The modern psychiatrist, when he has disclosed our trouble, proceeds to build up our confidence. He suggests that we
can leap our crevasses. He encourages us to self-
reliance. But he never quite succeeds. Why? For one
thing, we are subtly aware that self-confidence is never
enough. It is self-centered, loses love, becomes proud,
and thereby invites failure. For another thing, we know,
if we know anything, that we *cannot* master life in our
own strength. William E. Henley whose "Invictus"

made boast that he was "master of my fate" did not
master the tragic event that led to his death. We need
human help, and could not live without it. We need
more than human help, because all men are under defect of will and sentence of death. In such a world what
psychiatrist can build sufficient *self*-confidence? If we
have no better trust than self-trust we have no trust at
all: the crevasse swallows every man. Samuel Smiles'
Self-Help is thus sound doctrine—and quite unsound. Is
self-confidence ever enough? It is paradoxical: we cannot live without it; but if it stands alone, without some
deeper confidence, we cannot live with it.

Similarly, we need faith in our neighbors. Mutual
confidence among men or corporations is essential in
business, and mutual trust among nations is the necessary bond of world peace. The final guarantee of trade
is not in strong boxes, the Federal Reserve System, or
legal contracts: it is in widespread faith in the common
honesty of the common man. If we have no faith in the
driver of the car, we shall not travel; or, if we do, we
shall clutch the door handle, and develop hysterics. If
we have no faith in the doctor, he may cure us of our
physical ailment only to find that we have grown a neurosis in its place. If we have no faith in our children,
their future is not bright. If we have no faith in our
leaders in city or state, the pattern of our social life will
soon be a tangle. And yet, and yet, do we ever have
complete faith in one another, except under the wings
of a vaster faith? If our neighbor is to be regarded as
only a "small but boisterous bit of organic scum," if by
our *credo* there is no abiding value in him and none in
us, if there is no purpose behind his life and death, how
can there be any confidence? If truth is a whim and
conscience a convenience—or an inconvenience—how
can there be any faith? Then we may likely indulge in
mass murder—or be powerless to prevent it. How
cheap life becomes when our confidence is only in
man! Man's skill then is only a "trouble of ants," and
his science only a more cruel suicide! When we are intent on humanity alone, forgetting the Eternal Sky and

never inquiring after an Agelong Purpose, man's world becomes first a forlornness, then a dungeon, and finally an insanity of death. The doctrine of mutual trust is sound, and quite unsound. It is necessary, but in itself impossible.

All enduring faith is rooted in a radiant faith about our world. Dr. C. G. Jung therefore tells us that the problem of his patients is fundamentally a religious problem, and quotes their frequent comment: "If only I knew that my life had some meaning and purpose, then there would be no silly story about my nerves!"[19] Yet what a mass of contradictions, what a phantasmagoria of hasty skepticisms and adolescent notions, he himself proposes for a faith! We are creatures. Therefore true faith rests back on some faith in the Creation. If the cosmos is frustration and man only a midge-breed, self-confidence and mutual trust are a hollow farce. We cannot believe a man's word until we trust the man, and we cannot believe the man until we trust his world. That is a truism which of late we have chosen to ignore. In Sholem Asch's novel *The Nazarene,* a Greek skeptical philosopher says to a devout Jewish rabbi:

The gods were niggardly. In the deep darkness which is about us, they provided us with a single little light hung about our necks, and that is the light of reason. . . . . Reason casts its light the distance of a few footsteps, but beyond that the darkness still reigns. Rabbi, you would leap forward into the abyss of endless darkness . . . . and returning declare: "At the end of the night there is eternal day." How shall I know what lies there in the night, if I have never penetrated either with my eyes or with my other senses? And wherewith shall I seek to penetrate . . . . if not with the reason?

To whom the rabbi answers:

There is only one faculty which pierces the wall, the faculty of faith.

And the philosopher agrees, at least tentatively:

Perhaps that is indeed the way. Perhaps the truth is hidden from knowledge, and the secret can be reached only by a leap in the dark.[20]

It would be less pessimistic, and perhaps more true, to say, "Only by a leap into the Unknown." The Unknown is not utterly unknown, for it has its own beckonings, and the beckonings are strangely consonant with our deepest hope. But as for the leap, we cannot avoid it. Reason is not sufficient guide; for, despite our insistence that history repeats itself, it never does, unless with subtle differences. A new day, a new task, a new journey, a new friendship all demand of us a new venture. Paracelsus, in the Browning poem, asks Festus if there are not two moments in a pearl diver's life:

> One—when, a beggar, he prepares to plunge?
> One—when, a prince, he rises with his pearl?
> Festus, I plunge![21]

Every man, after his own fashion, is a pearl diver. He may judge life by its worst: "There are no pearls, and if there were they would not be worth the risk." Or he may judge life by its best: "The pearls are there to find, and the venture may find them." This latter judgment seems to be man's basic faith. Judged by its worst, life can be but a stoicism, or a desolation, and the best can never be explained. Judged by its best, life gathers serenity and power; and the worst then is at least partly explicable, if only as test and foil. This dual fact may not be ultimately determinate. Truth alone is determinate—or love, or God. If truth grants only a stoic courage, that must content us. But the pragmatic test driven inward, that is to say, applied to the integration and radiance of personality, is perchance more than pragmatic: it may be creative. Doubt builds no cathedrals, and sings no songs of praise. In any event, doubt and faith alike must make the venture; doubt judging life by the contradictions, and faith judging life by its sunstarts. For we travel always at the edge of the unknown. Would we have it otherwise? The world may be

round, but how can Columbus prove it? Only by an act
of faith:

> Columbus found a world, and had no chart,
>   Save one that faith deciphered in the skies;
>   To trust the soul's invincible surmise
> Was all his science and his only art.[22]

There may be rich prairie land beyond the New England hills, but how to prove it? Only by an act of faith:
prairie wagons began to roll. That wastrel may be ultimately worthy and lovable, but how to prove it? By loving him—ultimately! Cancer ought to be curable, but
how to prove it? Only by the expense, the long labor,
and the possible failure of research. If you should pluck
the sleeve of the research doctor and say, "Perhaps
there is no cure for cancer; and God, if there is a God,
may be laughing up His sleeve," what could the doctor
answer except, "I *do* believe"? One said long ago,
"Lord, I believe; help thou mine unbelief."[23] Would we
have it otherwise? Would we join the strange chorus of,
"Prove it to me," believing only when the mind has
been battered to a pulp by unanswerable arguments?
Such proof is not proof, but dark coercion; and the re-
sultant belief is not belief, but slavery. Faith grants life
its zest, its risk, its danger, its courage—and then, at
last, discovered oceans breaking on transfigured eyes.
Faith is a deeper gift than reason. It is not independent
of reason, or ever its enemy. In cancer research, faith is
clearly the *lifeblood* of reason: without faith that scientific quest would flag and fall. Faith plants the flag:
reason can only trudge down the path which faith has
blazed, and organize the land which faith has won.

IV

This description of faith itself appears to indicate a
necessity of prayer. *To pray is to expose oneself to the
promptings of God;* and, by the same token, *to become
less suggestible to the low persuasions of the world.* If
faith is the thrust of the self into the future in answer to

the suggestions of God, it is a vital matter to distinguish true signs from false. Perhaps that power to distinguish true from false was never so necessary as in an age of distraction and propaganda. Propaganda is a decoy of apparently worthy suggestions to tempt men to a false faith. The difference between propaganda and the propagation of the gospel is shown by the fact that propaganda is for selfish or merely partisan ends, offers a half truth as whole truth, and attempts to "use"—and therefore to dishonor—the people to whom it appeals. How to resist the lure of false suggestion? How to unmask it? How to be on the alert for the beckonings of God, and to recognize them when they flash? If prayer is a veritable Friendship, these questions are answered. When a human friend is by "adoption tried" and grappled to our "soul with hooks of steel," the whole world falls into the pattern of that friendship. "What would *he* think of this book?" we ask. "How can that journey be made to serve the friendship?" So with the higher Friendship. The world, for His sake, wears another aspect. Events have a different meaning. Doors open and opportunities beckon, to which, but for the Friendship, we might have been blind. The way of prayer is alive with such instances. Why should a visit in Joppa and a message from Cornelius mean that Peter should carry the Christian faith to the Gentiles, and thus deliver Christianity from a threatened nationalism?[24] Would that visit have received its correct interpretation as a sign from God if Peter had not prayed? So prayer exposes us to the appeals of God, and lowers our suggestibility to the poor persuasions of our world.

Again, prayer, if it be Christian prayer, *illumines and purifies faith.* Let us suppose a man has the wrong kind of trust—that, for instance, he regards life as a Klondike to be staked out and worked. His confidence is this: "Get there first and grab, and life will reward you." Much so-called faith is no nobler in its substance. *How to Win Friends and Influence People*[25] is a title with devastating undertones. *Why* win friends? To achieve some poor aim called "popularity" or "advancement"? *Why* the influence? For their real good or my

"God has some great purpose for us in and through death." I doubt if many folk affirm this. Death is the frame which surrounds

PRAYER, SUGGESTION, AND FAITH life   171

selfish ends? Almost any city and nation today needs political leaders who are ready to lose "friends" and alienate people; that all men may see with joy, years later perchance, some inrush of the Kingdom of God. Can a man of low faith pray before the face of Christ without being troubled and rebuked? Or suppose our faith is that by prayer we can undergird our army, other people who are praying for their army being left presumably uncomforted. Would that prayer stand for long unaltered before the face of Christ? Or suppose that our faith is worthier, namely, that God will grant deliverance from sickness. Such a prayer might be irrepressible because of love. But the praying man would remember, granted his silent fixing of the mind on Christ, that if every such prayer were answered no one would ever die, and that apparently God has some great purpose for us in and through death. The prayer would still be offered, but it would have its saving afterthought: "Nevertheless, not my will, but thine be done." Or suppose our faith is high-minded enough, but naïve, like that of the missionary in China who, when asked why he kept his young daughters with him during the Boxer Uprising, replied: "We gave our daughters to the Lord, and we are sure that He will permit them to suffer no harm." If that father prayed in sight of Christ he might remember that Mary gave *her* Son to the Lord, and that *he* died upon a cross with dust in his eyes and the sun's swords piercing him; yes, with mockery of men worse than dust, and treachery of men worse than swords. The father then might rethink both his action and his faith. Christian history, with its widening theology, and the Church's never-lost power of astringent self-criticism, seems to show that prayer purifies faith. "In Christ's name" is not a magic formula of faith: it is faith's redemption. "Name" means nature. "He leadeth me in the paths of righteousness for his name's sake,"[26] means, "He leads me in right tracks because that is his nature." "His name shall be in their foreheads,"[27] means, "His nature shall shine in their faces." When we end a prayer, as we should end it, "in Christ's name," we tell God that we judge His nature by the nature of

Christ, and that we ask for answer only as Christ's nature may be fulfilled in us. Thus, as often as we pray, faith is saved from credulity or selfishness, and made real.

Furthermore, *prayer grants faith the quiet surrender, the period of incubation,* which is needed *for a suggestion to become a confidence.* Psychologists are agreed that a "cue" for faith must sink into the subconscious by pondering, and by respite from the clamor of life. If the cue is accepted in expectancy, it summons the subsconscious to work for its fulfillment. "There exists in all intellectual endeavor," writes Dr. Joseph Jastrow, "a period of incubation, a process in great part subconscious, a slow concealed maturing through the absorption of suitable pabulum."[28] Thus prayer dwells on its truth: "God is like Christ. He has His own high purpose for my life. He will grant me strength. Life, by its opportunity and challenge and difficulty, will serve God's noble and friendly purpose for His world through me." Thus prayer, by its own brooding, enables the suggestion to develop in the soil of expectancy until it becomes a faith. Moreover, the quietness of prayer, its relief from struggle, dissolves hindrances. The effort to remember a name succeeds only when we forego the effort. The effort to overcome a falsity, fear, or hate succeeds only when we "surrender" to a Life greater than man's striving. Thus prayer seems essential in faith's evolution.

Again, *prayer reinforces faith.* These are the appropriate words:

> . . . . resolve
> Upbore him, and firm faith, and evermore
> Prayer from a living source within the will,
> And beating up thro' all the bitter world
> Like fountains of sweet waters in the sea,
> Kept him a living soul.[29]

Faith needs precisely the new strength, day by day, of some Fountain "beating up through all the bitter wastes" of earth. Bitter wastes cannot make themselves sweet: fountains must spring in sweetness from the ground of life. In an Atlantic City hotel there is a notice in each room advising that the water is drawn from deep artesian wells. Atlantic City is on a narrow sandy spit of land. On the east is the salty ocean, on the west a brackish tidal marsh. But shafts sunk deep enough yield pure water. When man, the creature, tries to be his own confidence, he tries to quench his thirst in salt. Faith may be mediated *through* the human, but it does not begin in our bitter wastes. Nothing is merely auto-suggestion: the light that strikes our eye comes from the Beyond. All our days are an adjustment to the Other-ness of the World. History is the long record of the cosmic shaping of life: "It is he that hath made us, and not we ourselves."[30] Admittedly we cannot live without faith in ourselves and in one another, but this faith is possible only as we first have faith in the whole Purpose of creation. We cannot flog ourselves into a total faith. We cannot for very long exhort one another into it. It can be caught, but not taught. Faith in its origin is a gift—a created well of water. Faith in its continuance is still a gift—from primal Springs beneath the bitter wastes. How can we receive it except in that waiting and acceptance called prayer?

> Into the woods my Master went,
>   Clean forspent, forspent. . . . .
> Out of the woods my Master came,
>   Content with death and shame. . . . . [31]

He came, not only content, but with faith renewed. He was not frantic now, but sure of himself. He was not despairing of others now, but sure of them: they were worth the sacrifice. He was not in doubt of God now: there was a Fountain in the bitter wastes.

V

We must write here an all-important postscript: *prayer itself is the central act of faith.* It has its own promptings—a tenderness on the world's edge, a sense of need, some home-yearning of the soul, a dim hearing

of Footsteps through the world. It is its own venture. It
tends to organize all our faith around itself—or around
the God whom prayer seeks or answers. Perhaps there
is no greater venture than to pray, saying to oneself: "I
cannot have faith in myself or in my neighbor unless I
have some faith in the Mystery from which—or
Whom—we come and to Whom we go. Perhaps the
Mystery has a mind to meet my mind's seeking. Perhaps
the provokings come from Him, so that my prayer is also
His prayer. Perhaps He has a heart to beat with my
heart. I will speak to Him in words, silence, and unut-
terable longing." Is there greater venture?

Speak to Him, thou! for He hears, and Spirit with spirit
    can meet,
Closer is He than breathing, and nearer than hands or
    feet.[32]

That is a greater hazard, in the realm of thought and
desire, than a rocket journey to the stars! The only
proof of prayer is—prayer. We can no more prove
prayer by argument than we can prove swimming by
diagrams on shore. We must pray. What other proof?
What more immediate or convincing verity of God?
Horace Bushnell tells us that his faith was so far spent
that once he believed nothing except vaguely and stubbornly that truth is better than lies, and that somehow
right is right. Therefore he prayed to something which
he addressed as "Right." He admits that it was a dreary
prayer, but declares that it was not unanswered. Another, in the same deep doubt, prayed, "O God, if there
be a God, save my soul, if I be a soul." That was an
interrogation mark or a misgiving rather than a prayer.
But he prayed it. He did not hug his doubts. He did not
splatter them on his neighbors, after our modern fashion. He sublimed them in the venture of prayer. It
would be wise for a minister, especially one given to
much argument, to recommend *that* method to the
skeptic. He might say to the doubter: "There may be a
God, and He may be essentially like Christ. If so, He
covets your friendship, and He has light for you. There

may be—or there may not. Let us not beg the question. But let us not shut the door. So, keep silence each night; and wait, without argument. Give Him a chance to speak—in His own language. Perhaps light will break." That proposal, if faithfully followed, would not be vain. Prayer itself is a venture which unifies all our faith.

Likewise prayer, being its own venture of faith, is itself faith in exercise. We know that body and brain grow weak through disuse, and strong through use; but we still assume that faith needs no exercise and no discipline. In a recent novel, a writer of modern outlook who has begun to suspect modernism discusses with his friend's wife the narrow religious zeal of the kitchen cook. They recognize the narrowness; but they are vaguely aware that it has, nevertheless, horizons and resource of which their culture is bereft. The writer remarks: "I myself have at very rare moments, which are not my worst ones, a strong inclination to faith—even to faith in the strict sense." Thereupon his friend's wife interrupts him: "Inclination! It is like having an inclination to be a singer. A person can possess a voice. That is a gift which comes from Heaven. But what are you going to do with your voice if you do not study and practice and work hard?"[33] Teta, the cook, had practiced her "inclination" of faith—by prayer and worship, however seemingly intolerant. The writer had let his faith atrophy: his "soul's surmise" was no longer an expectancy, but only a wistful doubt. Prayer is faith in exercise.

We have not said that prayer is the only duty. A man may pray, but prayer will not plow his field. Even so, the field will not be plowed in honor unless he prays. "Faith without works is dead,"[34] but not more dead than works without faith—and perhaps less evilly contagious. Likewise, faith without prayer is dead. We end where we began: we are lost without confidence. But true confidence lives in God, and prayer is friendship with God.

Chapter XI

PRAYER, INSTINCT, AND MOTIVE

I OUGHT TO know my own motives," says the man. The heat with which he says it is evidence that he does not know his own motives. The chances are that he knows as much about the moon. The man's name? Your name or my name. The insistent probing of Jesus to find the motive behind the deed wins our approval. Character ought to be judged by its inwardness. Then how may we know our real motives of which we are often amazingly ignorant? How may worthy motives become sovereign? How may unworthy motives be redeemed? We ask now if prayer has any answer to these questions.

I

What is a motive? The dictionary answers, "That within the individual, rather than without, which incites him to action." It is doubtful if *within* and *without* can thus be separated. The Latin verb *moto* means "to move," and the Latin noun *locus* means "place." So a "locomotive" moves us from place to place. A motive moves us: it is the steam in us. We use that word: we say of a neighbor, "He certainly got steamed up about it." Perhaps our instincts are the live coals, and perhaps the cold water poured in the boiler to make steam is some "attack" from the outer world. Thus the instinct of flight or fear would be aroused if Dracula appeared, and we would run. Some psychologists[1] have argued that we are afraid because we run, and others that we run because we are afraid. Both groups may be right.

Some hot coal of instinct—flight and fear—cold water in the coming of Dracula: the steam generated is a motive, which might be named in this instance the motive of self-preservation. But where do instincts originate? In native responses of the organism—in the random movements of a babe, and, ages earlier, in the blind response of protoplasm to the total environment. A reflex occurs when the doctor taps our knee with his little hammer, and the reflex is hard to control. Our resentment at being slighted is more complex and generalized both in stimulus and response, and can better be described as instinctive. The order of evolutionary life might roughly be drawn thus: blind response, random movement, conscious awareness of instinctive act, and motive. At any rate there is a gradation.

II

Motives develop, then, from the interplay between our instincts which we may broadly define as innate tendencies or inherited responses, and the prodding world. This description does not pretend to be accurate, let alone definitive. There is at present no such accuracy at our avail. Psychologists cannot agree even on a list of instincts, let alone on a judgment as to their essential nature. Dr. William E. Hocking has printed several lists of instincts from as many psychologists.[2] The layman gathers the impression that his own loose use of the word—the "fighting instinct," the "sex instinct," the "gregarious instinct," the "religious instinct"—is not inexpert. Some psychologists dismiss the word altogether, affirming that the basal traits of our species are now so overlaid by individual complexity and social constraint as to be lost. Nearly all psychologists tend to reduce the list of instincts to such primary urges as hunger, sex, fear, rage, self-assertion, gregariousness, and love. We must be content to accept this general guidance.

But there are facts about instinct on which the experts are substantially agreed. Instincts are *adaptive*.

They "meet" the environment, as when the thirst instinct finds a mountain stream. Instincts are *purposive*. They have a drive towards the completion of life. Thus the instinct to exercise or to rest preserves and enhances individual life, and the sex instinct or the parental instinct safeguards and fulfills the ongoing of the race. This fact has primary importance. It shows that even a "blind" instinct is invested with meaning, and carries a cosmic prophecy. Instincts are *inseparable*. They are mixed, or they coalesce. It might be more accurate to say that each is an aspect of the central urge to live. So even such an apparently sharp unit as the mating instinct is actually not alone. The youth in courtship is satisfying impulses of self-assertion, pride, love—and in dim foretaste perhaps of homebuilding and parenthood—as well as the urgings of sex. This fact of an apparent coalescence of instincts, even though the unity may be as yet potential rather than actual, is likewise rich in implications. It points to a kingdom of instincts in which each instinct may find itself, not by license, but in a "service which is perfect freedom." Is there, then, a principle of selection guiding all instincts? Is there a self embracing and governing them? Or a Self above the self? This signpost we shall soon follow.

One other leading fact about instinct should be noted. Instincts can be *modified* by experience. Experience is here a wide word. It includes all the pressures of the cosmos, its days and nights, storms and sunshine, ice ages and tropical ages in continued evolution, dangers and beckonings: our organism shapes, and is shaped by, its world. Experience, in its power to modify our instinctive life, includes also each man's own life of memory and reason. His instinct of hunger with its accompanying pleasure-on-satisfaction may clamor for Welsh rarebit at midnight; but a memory image reminds him that the last such indulgence was followed by a nightmare, and reason insists that nightmares are no proper prelude to the day's labor. So the hunger instinct is curbed and trained. Conscience, however we may choose to define it, also grants guidance, especially when instincts clash, as often they do clash. Conscience says to the acquisitive instinct, "Thou shalt not steal"; and adds, with wisdom to enlist higher wishes, "It is better to have self-respect and the regard of neighbors than to own that pocketbook."

That last phrase, "the regard of neighbors," indicates a still wider inclusion of the word experience. Social pressure shapes the instinctive self. The shaping is sometimes benign, sometimes deformed, but never relaxed. We are always by nature "members one of another." Illustrations are legion. Oliver Twist's instincts and motives were deformed by a society of thieves, and Nicholas Nickleby's by a coercive school. The influence of a home for weal or woe is almost beyond compute: the neuroses of midlife are traceable in a multiple of instances to the blindness or self-will of parents. If some nations and races are acquisitive or aggressive, the angularity may be due to long ages of persecution. Said one young Jew of fine character, incisively and with subtle implications, "You are a Christian. That is why I am a Jew." How motives are modified by competitive commerce, the drab poverty of slums, the recurrent tramplings of war, or the depersonalizing pressure of great cities! The social constraint has also its *saving* grace. A worthy home is a noble sculptor of humanity. Great music makes the spirit sing. When the Negro mammy said at the funeral of Lincoln, "Take a long look, honey; that man died for you," she confessed an agelong heroism by which the dross of motive becomes almost divine. Motives can be modified. Indeed, they can be *sublimated*. Anger can become righteous indignation. The sex instinct can turn into a passion of social service, or a devotion to the creative arts.

Thus from instinct and experience comes our gamut of motives—honor, shame, love, pride, fear, self-assertion. Make your own list. In the present stage of psychology you may not be wrong. Are motives more profoundly shaped by prayer? In a moral order prayer cannot indulgently erase vicious experience, or instantly compensate for our continuing social neglect. But prayer may have, nevertheless, its essential function in the realm of instinct and motive.

III

"But I ought to know my own motives," says the man bearing our name. Perhaps he ought to know, but he may not know. This the Bible has always understood: "The heart is deceitful above all things, and desperately wicked: who can know it?"[3] Why does the man vote Republican or Democrat? "Because I believe in the principles of the party," he says; "I ought to know my own motives." Evading the awkward question as to whether there is excess of principle in either party, the man, despite the fact that he thinks he knows his motives, may vote Republican in hope of lower taxes, or Democrat because the Democrats gave his nephew a job: "The heart is deceitful above all things." Why did he decline that dinner invitation? "Well, I was not feeling very well, for one thing; and, for another, I have been terribly busy." But the real reason may have been: "So-and-so will be sure to be there, and he gave me a raw deal. He may be brilliant, but he's conceited, and he needn't think I'm going to play second fiddle." Why is the man a pacifist? "Because war is a vicious circle, and because personality ought always to be treated as sacred: I ought to know my own motives." But, actually, the man may be a coward hiding from violence. Why did he enlist in the army? "Because I believe in fighting in my country's defense." But his real motive may have been the fear of being branded a coward. Why does the man speak so eloquently for that benevolent cause? "Because of compassion for the poor: I ought to know my own motives." But perhaps he likes to hear himself speak, or wishes other people to think him compassionate. Are these instances too pessimistic of human nature, and too damning? There are probably occasions when we interpret our motives for poorer than they are, as when a man says of a genuine pity, "It was the quickest way to get rid of him"; or of a genuine prayer, "It was only force of habit." There is an appealing instance in the story of the Emmaus Road. The two disciples besought Jesus: "Abide with us: for it is toward evening, and the day is far spent."[4] But they were not primarily concerned with either the clock or the courtesies. Life is a moving screen hiding a Mystery, and Jesus had thrust a hand through the screen to grant revealings. He had fringed their dusty road with Light. The deep in them had felt the pull of the Deep in him. For that reason, not for the reasons they offered, they wished him to stay. It is now an open secret of psychology that every man is likely to misconstrue his own motives.

This is a proper place to discuss the effect of complexes. The word "complex" is a modern cliché, carelessly used of almost any outstanding trait of personality. Its strict meaning may be illustrated in any clear instance of the inferiority complex. Imagine a child whose parents have frequently deplored the fact that he seems stupid. His pride is hurt. The disparagement first rankles, then is believed, and finally cankers self-respect. "I'm no use," the child says. He secretly reiterates the self-slander. The sense of inferiority becomes a complex. Karl Ruf Stolz has indicated three generally agreed upon marks of a complex: it is a dominant idea or system of ideas with dark emotional accompaniments; it is painfully at odds with the victim's standard of life; and its influences conduct unawares from below the threshold.[5] These marks are plain to see in our imagined instance of inferiority. That child, become a youth, finds his physical energies coiled around the idea that he is inferior. The nexus is painful, because he has set before himself a standard of capacity and achievement. Even when his mind is off guard, as when he suddenly finds a whole circle of friends listening to him, he will blush and stammer, being subconsciously held in thrall. Falling in love supplies a dominant idea; but its emotional involvements are not dark, it is not painful—save in exquisite joy and fear—and it is not necessarily at odds with a standard of life. It is a vortex of psychical energies, but not a forbidding vortex. Therefore it is not called a complex. Dr. J. A. Hadfield would name it a sentiment.[6] The complexes fall into typical groups. There is the Narcissus complex, so called after the

Greek youth who, being disappointed in love, fell in love with his own reflection in a pool. There is the Oedipus complex, which indicates excessive mother-dependence; and many others. No one is completely free from their influence. Usually they result from some sudden or long-drawn unhappy emotional experience, and sway us without our being aware. Thus a man who has avoided military service from fear may thereafter violently scorn patriotism, denounce war, and develop an antipathy for any kind of uniform or flag. We do not know our own motives. "The heart is deceitful above all things."

IV

Therefore we are tempted to "compensate" ourselves, as when a coward blusters; or to "transfer" our weakness, as when we criticize in others the very faults that are deep-set in ourselves; or to seek refuge in some other form of "rationalization." It is a comparatively new word in psychology, but not a new idea. We used to say, "He's kidding himself." Rationalizing is self-deceit. It is making "the worse appear the better reason."[7] The war has given us the word "camouflage": ships are painted with strange lines to make them seem like distant clouds, and tanks are decked with branches to resemble a tree. Rationalizing is camouflaging our motives—from ourselves. Thus we are "too tired" when the boresome caller is announced, or "Mrs. So-and-so lives too far away to make an acceptable secretary" when Mrs. So-and-so is becoming too popular for our own pride. Similarly we may excuse unruly conduct by saying, "A man loses his influence if he is peculiar or prudish"; or we may refuse to face the fact of our miserliness by insisting that, "A man ought to provide for the rainy day."

Most of these rationalizations are apparently not serious in their hurtfulness. There are hundreds of them in our language, nay hundreds in regard to death alone. Partly because of a well-nigh ineradicable hope, partly because we are unwilling to face a stark reality, we say

of death, "he has passed away," "he has gone west,"
"he has been translated." The very word "cemetery"
means in the original Greek "a sleeping room." A host
of words on other topics show a mild self-deceit. He is
not a thief, but merely "light-fingered." He is not lust-
ful, but merely "sowing his wild oats." Most of these
camouflages are trivial; but even these, if they become a
habit, can root the nature in dishonesty. Some have disastrous proportions, as in the case of the man who explained that the seriousness of his life of crime was always hidden by the jargon used: the victim was never
killed—the gang never faced that realism—but was
only "taken for a ride." National rationalizations are often tragic in their issue, both to the nations that harbor
them and to surrounding nations. Germany refused to
acknowledge wrong or defeat in the last war. The sense
of frustration that comes of defeat is hard for an American to understand, for we have never suffered a major
defeat. Suppose we had been conquered, how readily
would we admit the fact? So Germany was not wrong or
defeated: she was threatened with encirclement, she was
the victim of geography and blockade, and she was ambushed by an international Jewish plot. Thus rationalization may be vast enough to be disastrous, or an accu-
mulation of many small self-deceits may be disastrous.
When rationalization reaches the stage of pathology it is
called "paranoia." A complex may develop so cancer-
ously that it becomes almost an independent system and
causes dissociation of personality. For, be it noted, the
universe ultimately defeats rationalization. Thirst is not
quenched by an imagined glass of water, or by a lake
seen in mirage. At long last disease is not cured by
bread pills. The universe is invincible Truth.

V

Then what can prayer do? That is a false way of stat-
ing a question. It might be better to ask, "What can we
do for prayer?" For prayer is ultimately a friendship:
only base people cultivate a friendship in order to "use"
it. Mary Pickford's proposal, "Why not try God?"[8] is a

mild though unintentional blasphemy. God is not a kitchen gadget or a patent medicine. The question might rather run, "Why not let God try us?" though God, be it said, is too God-like to "use" or "abuse" our personality. Let us ask, rather, what is the issue of prayer in regard to instinct and motives.

Prayer is a fundamental honesty, and therefore grants us knowledge of our motives. Of course, prayer also can be made an "escape." But the fact that an endeavor can be perverted does not condemn it. Psychology itself can be made an escape: the modern mind is prone to evade the onset of a moral demand or a true emotion in a very amateur and cheaply skeptical psychoanalysis. The perversion of prayer is not easy when Christ is accepted as living clue to the nature of God. Dwight L. Moody once wrote in a man's Bible, "This Book will keep you from your sins, or your sins will keep you from this Book." Thus we might say, "Sincere prayer will keep you from self-deception, or self-deception will keep you from your prayers." For Christ is "the brave Son of Fact," and God conceived under the image of Christ is realism. He "needed not that any should testify of man: for he knew what was in man."[9] Others had said, "Thou shalt not kill," but he drove the issue back to the motive: "I say unto you, That whosoever is angry with his brother without a cause shall be in danger of the judgment."[10] How quickly he pierced our rationalizings! When the man came pleading his fair-mindedness, "Master, speak to my brother that he divide the inheritance with me," Jesus answered instantly, "Beware of covetousness!"[11] Always he answered, not merely the question, but the questioner. If Christ is the focus of our praying, if we remember that God is a Christlike God, prayer cannot be a self-coddling. So real was Christ that Peter fell back from his presence with a cry, "Depart from me; for I am a sinful man, O Lord";[12] so real, that when he saw women weeping for him sentimentally as he trod the Via Dolorosa, he would not let them take refuse in any mere emotionalism: "Weep not for me, but weep for yourselves, and for your children."[13] Christian prayer cannot easily be dishonest.

The task of the psychiatrist is to persuade people to be real. He says to the young woman: "You say that you must stay home to be with mother. *Is* that your motive? Perhaps you are afraid of the busy world with its responsibilities and demands." He tries to persuade her to talk herself out—with reality. John B. Watson, whose psychology certainly cannot be commended wholesale, has wisdom when he suggests that unconscious motives are those which have not become articulate. Psychiatrists therefore use this "talking cure." Words give the self an outlet, and sharpen self-searching into reality. But is the psychiatrist or counselor or minister or family friend the kind of man who quickens realism, and who can deal with it tenderly yet in truth? That is the misgiving which besets us concerning every human counselor. But God is Truth. We can *talk* to *Him:* "in thy light shall we see light."[14] Prayer is thus being honest with oneself—and with God. It is making articulate our half-conscious motives. It is the "talking cure" in the light of the Eternal. It is an exercise in reality.

VI

Prayer cleanses motives and sublimates them. We may well wonder where the sifting of motives will end. Easily it could go on and on. A man might suspect even his best intention, and say, "Perhaps I'm still being selfish in ways I have not guessed." Morbidity might easily be the issue. An inward turning mind feeds on itself and becomes hypochondriac, but prayer opens the door to the cleansing winds of God. There is an interesting instance in the life of Galileo, as described in a recent novel entitled *The Star-Gazer*.[15] Galileo knew the power attributed to the tomb of St. Anthony. If a man should walk around the altar, lay one hand on the lid of the Saint's tomb, repeat exactly thirteen times the wonder-working prayer, and then ask one wish at a time, the wish would be granted:

St. Anthony of Padua,
Who came from Padua,

And prayed God for thirteen favors,
And got them all;
Grant my request,
By the five wounds of Christ.

Galileo resolved to ask money for his urgent need, health for his children, and old age for his mother. But when he reached the tomb he reflected on the life of St. Anthony. What a "great thing to have been a saint, to have renounced with incredible strength the sweetness of life, not to have tasted the intoxication of wine and women, to shine high above the sins of every day." Then he placed his hand on the tomb, repeated the prayer exactly thirteen times, and found himself saying: "I beg you, St. Anthony, to plead with Jesus Christ for me that he should enlighten my mind and let me invent something very great to further human knowledge." So that was what he really longed for in his deepest heart! It was easier to read the stars than to read himself! He had intended to pray for an earthly boon, but the prayer itself cleansed the whole realm of motive. Thus a woman might discover in her prayers that her motives in visiting the sick are not as noble as she believed: she covets the title of "Lady Bountiful." But, if she is wise, she does not relinquish the chosen task: she continues it as unto Christ. Prayer is the ultimate honesty that clarifies motives, and the ultimate cleansing by which motives are both purified and directed to higher goals.

VII

Perhaps *prayer* may be *the* instinct, *the motivation that gathers and unifies all our motives*. Modern psychology was tempted to advise a few years ago, "Satisfy your instincts." It laid stress on the damage done by repression of instincts, the sex instinct being the favorite illustration. Now a wiser mind prevails. The sex instinct is powerful and valid. Victorian prudery darkened it and thwarted it, and forgot that no instinct can be killed in prison, but escapes somehow to work havoc. Even so, the fact remains that the sex instinct, given full rein, defeats its own biological purpose, which is, apparently, the ongoing of the race. Given full rein, it easily causes neuroses, and perhaps runs to perversions. Given full rein, it may trample other valid instincts, such as the maternal instinct, the creative instinct, and even the instinct of self-preservation. Repressions are dangerous, but instincts running amuck are more dangerous.

There is in man a conflict of instincts. Urgently he needs order and harmony in the turbulent realm. This prime fact the advocates of so-called liberty do not face. The "self-expression" philosophy of life has assumed grotesquely that each instinct lives in its own realm, like a row of animals in a zoo, each in its own cage. It has said of each animal, "Iron bars are not its proper habitat. Let it be set free, or it will turn into a neurosis." But our instinctive nature does not consist of a row of instincts, each of which may be loosed in turn for exercise. By that strategy the instinct may or may not be satisfied; but the man will daily grow more dissatisfied. The instinct of pugnacity, when gratified, does not leave the other instincts untouched. It may violate the gregarious instinct. Dr. William E. Hocking has rightly insisted, "To liberate human desires singly may result not in the liberation of human nature but in its disintegration."[16] Our nature is not a bundle of instincts: it could more accurately be described as a total instinctive self having many facets. According to Dr. Alexander Shand, the emotions themselves tend to gather into emotional systems. Love, for instance, ties into itself such apparent opposites as fear and hope, joy and sorrow.[17] Instincts coalesce. What our nature needs is indeed "self-expression"—if we have once determined the nature of the self:

Within my earthly temple there's a crowd.
There's one of us that's humble; one that's proud,
There's one that's broken-hearted for his sins,
And one who, unrepentant, sits and grins.
There's one who loves his neighbor as himself,
And one who cares for naught but fame and pelf.
From much corroding care would I be free
If once I could determine which is Me.[18]

As a wiser mind prevails, the word used is "sublimation." Even Freud would say that the sex instinct cannot be given rampant license. In instances, and as policy, it may have to be "sublimated"—diverted into a higher channel such as art. The acquisitive instinct may have to be sublimated into trusteeship, and the fear instinct into taking precautions for the safety of other people. But this is discipline, however often the word "sublimation" may be used. The tree must not be allowed to put out too much leaf here, or too much wood there: it must be trained, and made fruitful. Then *how* shall instincts be organized? How may we establish a harmonious realm of motivation? Which instinct shall be given rule—Sigmund Freud's sublimated sex instinct, or Alfred Adler's sublimated instinct of self-assertion, or W. Trotter's sublimated herd-instinct? Is there a central instinct—an ultimate stimulus and an ultimate response? Psychology alone can give no final answer to these questions. We cannot understand the meaning of an eye by medical dissection of an eyeball, or even by medical dissection of the whole body. The sun and its universe are involved. We cannot understand an instinct in its real meaning by scrutinizing the instinct. Can we understand even our whole self by concentrating on the self alone? If, as Dr. James A. Hadfield insists, there is in us an appetite for perfection—"the urge to completeness is the most compelling motive of life"[19]—how are we kept on that upward road? Is prayer the deepest instinct, the ultimate motive, the final sublimation—and itself prevision of the Goal? "Thou hast made us for thyself, and we can find no rest until we rest in thee."

VIII

Therefore prayer grants power. The words are deliberate. The power is a *grant*, not merely a self-quickening. It is true, of course, that any motive tends toward its fulfillment. It *is* a motive: it *moves*. One school of psychology, unconvincing but not empty of truth, argues that all mental life is incipient action; and there is indeed evidence, from actual physical test and measurement, that even abstruse ideas, such as the idea of beauty or rationality, are accompanied by imperceptible muscular movements. This fact need not surprise us: the flow of consciousness is through attention, perception, emotion, and thought—to action. Attention: the man sees water. Recognition: "That is a trout stream." Emotion: "How grand to be there!" Thought: "I wonder how my stock of trout flies survived last summer." Action: he goes to find his tackle box. Obviously a clear motive and one surcharged with feeling has greater "drive" than the mixed and cloudy motives in which we usually live. So if prayer clarifies a motive—if it unties the knots in our life of motivation, resolving, for example, a Narcissus complex—and if prayer purifies motive, and if it charges the motive with feelings of devotion to Christ, then, per se, the motive has greater power.

But we now write not of mere awakening, but of access of power. Psychiatry assumes that if only hidden motives can be brought to light, and the patient recognizes them for what they are, he has the power to set his own house in order. That is a vast assumption. It is partly true; for, as long as a man is responsible at all, he is not helpless. But it is not wholly true. Thus the psychiatrist finds sometimes that the patient has leaned so heavily on the counselor as to be almost incapable in himself. When Paul said, "The evil which I would not, that I do," he knew the wrong motive, but was still helpless: "Who shall deliver me from this body of death?"[20] In any realm of life we are dependent on a "beyond" power. We have eyes, but they are helpless without the sun's light. We have ears, but they are dependent on the great world of sound. In clarified motives we have inner eyes: is there a world of Light? We have inner ears: is there a world of Sound and Speech? We have hunger: is there Celestial Food? As for the whole organism of instinct: has it been created, unlike any other, without its satisfaction? The world about us is not passive. Obviously it is shaping man's ongoing life.

> Think you, 'mid all this mighty sum
> Of things forever speaking,
> That nothing of itself will come
> But we must still be seeking?[21]

Illustrations are hard to find, for there are no parallels for divine power. When the submarine "Squalus" was raised, human instruments were not enough. There is not much leverage on a tossing boat—or in a tossing self. Human arms and even man-constructed engines have only limited power. Floats were attached to the "Squalus" so that tides might do the work. Thus the moon, and all the interrelated powers of the sky, raised the "Squalus." Man only made the attachments. Paul found that he could make contact with "a Power beyond himself." Even so the martyrs were able to meet death, the saints and prophets gained wisdom, and Moses in the midst of tedium "endured, as seeing him who is invisible."[22] The psychiatrist knows that the patient must not "transfer" reliance from himself to the counselor. Does he know that the patient *cannot* stand alone? It is not that kind of world. In every realm of life power comes, not merely from within the man, but from beyond the man. In prayer, if prayer is not divorced from honest thought and life, we draw power.

The life of Francis is hardly explicable on a level merely human. The psychologist has the right to trace the psychological factors and processes which changed the gay youth of Assisi into "God's poor little man," just as a botanist has the right to dissect his flowers. But flowers are not explicable without sun, wind, rain, and soil. So St. Francis is an enigma unless we posit a Beyond. The saint was *not* merely the youth *psychologically* changed. He had power over even the proud Pope Innocent III,[23] who, after he met Francis, dreamed that he saw the Church of St. John Lateran falling until propped by a ragged pilgrim from Assisi. He had power over a church imprisoned in its own learning and officialdom. He had power over the quarreling bishop and mayor and reconciled them.[24] He had power even over the Saracen commander. He brought a new springtime to the world. This power is not what the world calls power, for the world's power only blasts. This power is real power. It lifts man to

> everlasting light,
> Above the howling senses' ebb and flow.[25]

He is now linked with all the correlated powers of the Sky.

Thus the Bible prayer concerning motives: "Search me, O God, and know my heart"—for man does not know his own heart. "Try me, and know my thoughts"—for man does not know his own thoughts. "And see if there be any wicked way in me"—for man needs cleansing and cannot cleanse himself. "And *lead* me in the way everlasting"[26]—for man is weak and cannot find the way or walk alone. Such a prayer is final wisdom about human motives. It is not unanswered.

Chapter XII

PRAYER, MEMORY, AND THE SUBCONSCIOUS

THE TERM "THE SUBCONSCIOUS" has won its place in everyday speech. Rightly, for we all have evidence of the *fact*. We try to remember the title of a book, and fail. Mild mental distress ensues: "I know it almost as well as I know my name." But we still fail. We cease trying, and are soon immersed in other interests. Three hours later, or next morning, we suddenly exclaim, "Oh, I know that book title." The knowledge came not through the conscious area of mind, but through the subconscious. There is the fact. Many people nowadays are half afraid of it. They think they are at the mercy of the subconscious, which they picture as a kind of cesspool beneath the floor of life, or a "vasty deep" whose ruinous upsurge is beyond their control. Matthew Arnold's lines, and the title of the poem from which they come, "The Buried Life," seem to them both fitting and ominous:

> From the soul's subterranean depth upborne
> As from an infinitely distant land,
> Come airs, and floating echoes, and convey
> A melancholy into all our day.

I

What *is* the subconscious? The psychologists cannot agree on a definition. Sigmund Freud says—we write in necessarily swift and general terms—that it is an area of repressions where thwarted "natural instincts," mainly infantile and sexual, find their outlet in dreams and phantasy. C. G. Jung, who broke with Freud, his great teacher, largely on this issue, maintains that the subconscious has two strands of population. One strand is the forgotten issue of our own past experience in its hopes, memories, desires, hates, loves, and fears. The other strand he calls the "collective unconscious": it consists of the "remnant of ancient humanity," our animal and cultural heritage, and inchoate impulse from past evolution. William E. Hocking holds that memory outside the lighted focus of present attention is the main and perhaps sole ingredient. He dismisses the doctrine of the collective subconscious as a "confused and fumbling theory."[1] He affirms that the subconscious is a memory deposit. Then he takes a further important step. He argues that our immediate life of sensation and action, being immersed in our present world, partakes of finitude; but our memory, being reflective, has intimations of eternity. That is to say, memory, since it is delivered from the bondage of the clamant "now," is in measure above time, and is therefore more likely to reveal the springs of selfhood. Our definition of the subconscious, where doctors disagree, is not necessary, even if it were possible. An amateur guess might suggest that both Jung and Hocking could be partly right. We turn, then, to a discussion of memory and prayer.

II

St. Augustine's burst of gratitude for the gift of memory is classic: "Great is the power of memory, exceeding great! An inner chamber large and boundless! . . . . Men go forth to wonder at the height of mountains, the huge waves of the sea, the broad flow of rivers, the extent of the ocean, the courses of the stars—and forget to wonder at themselves."[2] The description is accurate. Memory is not only an "inner chamber," but a "power"; not only a treasure store, but also a wand which, at the call of some new event or at the beckoning of the will, can summon a past experience to give it new life.

Forget to wonder at ourselves.

Knowledge depends on memory—not on memory alone, for memory is never alone, but on our selfhood's gift of memory. We speak of a "rope of sand" when we wish to indicate an altogether untrustworthy bond. A rope of sand is not possible: its particles cannot cohere. Knowledge seems to come to us in particles, through this book, that teacher, and the other happening. Knowledge might remain in particles, slipping away from us as soon as gained, if we had no memory to make it cohere. Similarly, *friendship* depends on memory. We may be absent from a friend for a year or ten years, but when we see him again we recognize at once the familiar voice, the handclasp, the little tricks of gesture. So memory guarantees and restores our friendships. Nay, memory in this realm confers an added boon: it enables us in the absence of a friend to see and know him more truly than when he is with us. For, though memory easily romances, heightening past joys, it has also a strange clear light denied to present experience. *Business* also, and the whole business of living, depend on memory. There are other ledgers than those on the desk or in the safe. Blunders and successes are recorded on an invisible page; together with ventures, methods, and decisions. Any businessman without that ledger of memory would land speedily in bankruptcy, or in the hospital. Memory has many talents: it can learn; it can retain knowledge; it can recall knowledge; it has those radiations which we call "recognitions"; and, over and above these competencies, it invests the self with that wisdom unawares which we call experience. A man suffering from amnesia is only half a man. Such a man, a shell-shocked war veteran, appeared on a public platform with the pathetic plea, "Can anyone tell me who I am?"

We cannot forbear the digression that memory seems to be the refutation of materialism. If thought is only a function of brain, as the mechanists maintain, and if brain, as the biologists make clear, decays and is renewed in its tissues every few years, why does not memory change as the brain changes? Even if we grant the unproved theory that memory "runs" on paths, made ever more smooth by use, in the neural system, the paths are still in the changing present while memory overleaps the present. When emotion has scored deep an experience—as, for example, a sorrow—the one bereaved will recite incidents of twenty years ago in their exact momentary sequence. If the memory be that of a traveler, he can in a flash recall events of thirty years ago in another land. Thus, for his experience, he can annihilate time and space. How can a function of matter conquer time and space? Since we are for a moment "off the main track," let us notice, and then resist, another bypath; namely, memory's intimations of immortality. In any sudden joy or sorrow we exclaim, on some fringe or in some depth of memory, "I have known you of old!" Thus also with a new friend: we met him just now, but in an instant accord we have known him for a thousand years. Perhaps this strange nostalgia is one reason why we assign Paradise to the long-lost past. This sense is too subtle and vague to justify a doctrine of reincarnation, but it is there, and Wordsworth has given it words appropriately deathless:

> Our birth is but a sleep and a forgetting:
> The Soul that rises with us, our life's Star,
>   Hath had elsewhere its setting,
>   And cometh from afar:
>   Not in entire forgetfulness,
>   And not in utter nakedness,
> But trailing clouds of glory do we come
> From God, who is our home.[a]

Furthermore, memory, when a friend has died, is the channel for our deeper understanding of his life. His faults are not denied or canceled, but they fall away; and we see as never before the splendors in his lowliness—the eternities in his humanity. These bypaths lead to a gate of mystery. We shall not now follow them. But they support Dr. Hocking's contention, above noted, that memory has seeds of immortality.

III

Memory tests and methods of memory training are interesting. They are set forth in any competent text-book of modern psychology.[4] We are concerned with them only as they relate to prayer and personality. Our present quarry is meanings rather than techniques. Memory, to serve our creative growth, cannot run wild or feed on itself. Memory is by nature selective, else it would perish of its own excess. Memory must be trained. Someone has suggested as a wise prayer: "Lord, teach me to forget what I ought to forget, and remember what I ought to remember." Constantly to re-hearse our successes would leave us with an obnoxious ego. Constantly to gloat over forbidden yet secretly practiced things would leave us with a rancid mind: fleshliness, says a character in a novel, "is like a recur-ring decimal."[5] Constantly to deplore our failures and sins would leave us with weights upon our wings. Con-stantly to revive real or fancied ills would leave us bitter and perhaps paranoiac. These are examples of memory gone wrong. But suppose we can choose right memo-ries—a mind richly stored with vows, quotations from kindled minds, and bright experiences; and suppose these were made daily more vivid by our attention to them, by the frequency and recency of their recall! Then would our memory become redemptive.

How is memory trained to remember? In simple terms, by attentiveness, frequency of impression, re-cency of impression, and by gathering the desired items into a system. As for attentiveness, a recent question-naire gave the respective slogans of certain much adver-tised products, and invited us to attach the correct name to each slogan. Some of us were lost because almost on principle we do not attend to advertising. We attend to books and people. So we cannot remember advertising, but we can often recognize poetry quotations and re-member conversations. As for frequency of impression, the Lincoln Memorial in Washington is set as a constant reminder; and in its own script it has an interesting illustration of its purpose. In its record of the Gettysburg speech there are these words: "The world will little note, nor long remember, what we say here, but it can never forget what they did here." But already the speech at Gettysburg is better remembered than the battle at Gettysburg, because of its intrinisic worth, but also because of frequency of impression—through Lincoln memorials. As for recency of impression, a telephone number used yesterday is remembered better, under ordinary circumstances, than a number used last year. As for the training of memory through the ordering of knowledge into systems, "memory systems" are sufficient evidence, or the astonishing memory of an astronomer concerning the stars. Another factor in remembering should here be noted: we tend, apparently by nature, to forget what is unpleasant and to recall what is congenial. How easy to forget our appointment with the dentist, and how easy to remember when we begin a vacation! This tendency may be good basically, and is certainly on the side of hope. But it can be overdone. It may lead to unreality, perhaps to repression, and even to outright dishonesty.

These facts themselves show, at least provisionally, the essential place of prayer in our life of memory. Christian prayer sets Christ in the center of the field of attention: we fix our thought on him, and his light judges and transfigures the whole land of recollection. Habitual prayer, by frequency and recency, drives deep the picture of Christ, on whom to look is not merely to contemplate a picture, but to invite a Friend. He becomes the center of reference in our "memory system": we recall naturally those facts that belong to him. We forget what we ought to forget, and remember what we ought to remember, yet without "repressions" or surrender of honesty. We are saved from the snares by which memory goes wrong. His image has expulsive power, until memory becomes his world. And yet—and yet— are we ever master of memory? Over conscious memory we may gain some mastery. But what of our subconscious—the memory thrust from awareness because it is dark or sinful,[6] or the distracting memory which some tiny event brings back almost despite us. The smell of a country lane can recapture some boyhood vividness, the name of a street some buried transgression. Even if these memories are not rearticulated, they rule us from "below the threshold." Perhaps we are beset by more than our own subconscious: perhaps we are swayed unawares by that inchoate world called by Dr. Jung "the collective unconscious." Our main problem is with the subconscious mind.

IV

The subconscious, however we may choose to define it—whether with Dr. Hocking as an "apperception mass" or memory deposit, or with Dr. Freud as a realm of infantile and sexual repressions, or with Dr. Jung as all these plus the "collective unconscious"—is that area of mind which influences the self from below the threshold of awareness. The psychologists, though they disagree about definitions, agree about the various ways in which the subconscious is revealed. It shows in *dreams,* like that in which the writer saw a victim of the Inquisition strapped back down on a rack with a drip-drip-drip of water falling relentlessly on his forehead. A week before I had been reading about the Inquisition and about that particular torture. While I slept a faucet was dripping in the near-by bathroom, and the bed itself was not very soft. But I was not then conscious of the memory of my reading, nor of hearing the steady drip of the faucet, nor of the hardness of the bed. My subconscious was at work, not merely recalling and receiving impressions, but organizing them. So the subconscious shows in dreams. It shows in *slips of speech and action,* like that of the bachelor escorting to a dance a married lady whom he had hoped to marry, and introducing her as "Mrs. So-and-so," giving her her maiden name;[7] or that of the professor who, going upstairs to dress for a dinner which he did not wish to attend, was startled to find himself in bed; or that of the minister who, rushing over without breakfast to his church to conduct early prayers, asked the blessing at table in-

stead of offering the invocation. The subconscious
shows also in *humor,* even more than in sober speech.
In humor the conventions are relaxed, and the hidden
mind is revealed. This we can admit without necessarily
agreeing with Freud that all humor is "letting the cat
out of the bag." Thus people falling in love disclose
their feelings in a gentle joshing, and people falling out
of love theirs in humorous jibes that have an "edge."
Thus a supposedly decorous man will surprise his
friends by telling a risqué story, and later surprise them
more by going morally to seed. Or a man may say of a
politician that he "has a glorious future behind him"
(Edwin B. Holt's illustration);[8] thus announcing, for
those who can hear, not only his sense of humor, but his
impatience with one politician and his resentment
against the whole tribe. In many such ways "the hidden
part" of the mind is revealed.

V

These illustrations are themselves enough evidence
that the subconscious is far vaster in extent than the
conscious mind. Our explicit awareness is like the lights
of New York City seen at night from an airplane:
"*There* is the Hudson, its blackness edged by diamonds;
and *there* is Radio City, and the Empire State Building;
and *there,* in lines, are the avenues and streets!" But
little is seen compared with what is not seen—myriad
folk in home and factory; myriad others walking, sleeping, dancing, or tossing in hospital; and, even below the
unseen folk, tubes and tunnels, rock deposits and sub-
terranean streams; and, encompassing all, the "vasty
deep" of the ocean. The conscious mind is but the few
points of light; the subconscious is the vast realm of the
unseen. In a recent book, Dr. Jung has written: "Conscious mind is based upon, and results from, an unconscious psyche which is prior to consciousness and continues to function together with, or despite, consciousness."[9]

Like the unseen city, the subconscious also is organized, and has power to organize. It "carries through"

the projects of the conscious. It is not merely a vast pit into which we pour our memories of events, loves, fears, longings, and strife. It is a secret kingdom which takes these guests, thrust out or wandered out from consciousness, and gathers them into a community. This hidden realm exercises its steady influence over the visible world of clear consciousness, an influence more powerful because it is not realized, almost as the New York unseen from an airplane may determine the points of light. This description probably goes too far: most psychologists agree that the organizing power of the subconscious is normally within limits, and that the limits are ultimately set by the conscious mind. But none would deny that the subconscious always strongly affects our articulated thought. A novelist working on a plot, or a scientist on an experiment, finds the solution when off guard: the subconscious has carried on at the point where the conscious left off, and though for the time unaided, has reached the goal. All of us, if we are wise, "sleep on" our difficult decisions: we deliberately or unwittingly enlist the help of the subconscious. Coleridge's poem "Kubla Khan" was given to him in a dream. Psychologists who have analyzed it declare that it represents in its structures and allusions twenty-five years of poetical labor. But it was not consciously wrought. Rouget de Lisle slept at his harp while composing "The Marseillaise." So the subconscious is organized, and in some sense creative, as well as vast.

A further comment should be made: the subconscious is not necessarily bad. Why should it be? Freud pioneered and left the world in debt to his discoveries. But certain of his overemphases, now being corrected, are no blessing. William McDougall once declared that Freud made of the subconscious "a mere fermenting dung-heap." That characterization was unfair, but not without some cause. Even Freud would have to allow that what becomes articulate in the mind is first there in some inchoate or inarticulate form. What he called the "ego-ideal," the better life towards which we strive, must first be hidden somewhere in our nature. Even if the subconscious holds only what we repress—though most authorities would agree that it holds much more— it holds the *good* we repress, as well as the bad. A psychologist might tell us that Paul's conversion came from long-repressed good memory, and not least from his repressed memory image of the transfigured face of martyred Stephen. If the subconscious is a mass of subliminal memories, the mass holds good memories as well as bad, even granting our perverse habit of forgetting what we would like to forget. Moreover, a subconscious that can organize a "Kubla Khan" is not a curse. Dr. George A. Coe tells[10] of a young woman who, when a man proposed to her, found herself saying "No" though she had opened her lips in the full intention of saying "yes." Probing her mind, she came on certain memories of reports about that man, and certain rightful scruples and fears, which now had organized themselves into a decision. In her *awareness* she wished to marry him, but in her unawareness had known she ought not to marry him. As later events proved, her subconscious decision, invading her focal mind, had saved her from unhappiness. So the subconscious is not necessarily bad or necessarily good. It is what we make it by God's help, and after that it may largely make us. At any rate, whatever is radiant in consciousness is first unconscious: it wells up into our focused life and light. Whence? How? That mystery no psychology has yet fathomed. If God is, then God Himself is at the deepest springs of mind and life.

VI

We have already suggested how prayer may be linked with the voluntary memory. Now we inquire about the influence of prayer on the subconscious area of the mind. It is a cardinal question if only because many people fear that they are, and must be, victims of subliminal forces. Dr. Jung, in his later writings, seems to encourage this fear: "The general aspect of unconscious manifestations is in the main chaotic and irrational, in spite of many symptoms of intelligence and purposiveness. The unconscious produces dreams, irrational fantasies, peculiar visions, primitive emotions, grotesque or fabulous ideas, and the like—exactly what one would expect of a dreaming person stirring in his sleep."[11] Are we, then, at the mercy of some cosmic dream—or nightmare? Such a description is not likely to win wide assent. But, even if it be but fractionally true—and we must recognize in it strands of truth—it makes clear man's need for some veritable control of the subconscious.

Prayer focuses the conscious mind on God made known in Jesus; and the conscious mind, however much influenced by the secret city, *still has wide dominance.* Freud and the psychoanalysts proceed on the assumption that if a man once understands the unconscious influences at work he can rule them. The "conscious rational," to use Freud's phrase, can govern or direct the "unconscious emotional" whenever the latter is brought from its hiding place and stripped of its disguise. We would add, "Yes, granted a genuine faith in the friendliness of the universe, and granted some venture in prayer and deed." A simple instance of this rule, though not one by which to buttress any hasty theory, is our power to wake at a determined hour in the morning. We say to our subconscious: "You and I have early journeyings: I trust you to rouse me at six o'clock." It is astonishing in such instances to find what an accurate and dependable alarm clock we carry inside us. The mind does not consist of two alien realms. It is apparently one organic mind. Therefore, this chapter has been careful to use the phrase "the subconscious area of the mind," rather than "the subconscious mind." For the subliminal is not separate, and to regard it with alarm would be surrender and finally chaos. Coué used to urge that we should say several times over, especially just before we sleep, "Day by day in every way I am getting better and better." Without some Christian faith, the faith that what is highest in spirit is deepest in nature, that formula is mere vaporing; but, granted the faith, a better formula thus used might be real resource. With Christian confidence for support, the technique is sound. Instead of saying, "You and I must wake at six o'clock," we may say, looking on Christ, "The Lord is my light and my salvation; whom shall I fear? The Lord is the strength of my life; of whom shall I be afraid?"[12] That, driven into the subconscious, or, better, allowed to fall into it, would shape and mold the secret city; whose influence then, in turn, would shape us. In the story of the temptation of Jesus, there is a striking instance of succor from the subconscious. He had brooded long in prayer over the great insights of his Bible. So, at each temptation, the proper words sprang to his lips, apparently without any searching for them: "Man shall not live by bread alone. . . . . Thou shalt not tempt the Lord thy God. . . . . Thou shalt worship the Lord thy God, and him only shalt thou serve."[13] Do not childhood prayers return in stress, even after a prayerless adulthood? Prayer can govern the conscious life, and the conscious life can direct the subconscious. Thereby the subconscious may become an attendant angel. Prayer focuses attention on Christ, and thus scores deep the memory image. Habitual prayer gives frequency of impression: "Every day will I bless thee."[14] Moreover, if a man be faithful in prayer, if he keep troth not only morning and night, but "in between times" in ejaculatory prayer, the impression on the conscious mind is always recent. Thus our awareness is shaped, and our awareness has priority and rule. The subconscious may even then rebel, but mainly with such weapons as the conscious self chooses to give; and often it will be a splendid ally.

Again, *prayer grants release and healing to our repressions.* Later we shall discuss our *unworthy* repressions. But this is a proper juncture to remind ourselves that not all repressions are unworthy. Some repressed fears are understandable and pitiable. Some repressed sorrows are a token of courage. Some repressed noblenesses are tragic in their waste. All schools of psychology are agreed that repressed tendencies are not destroyed: the prisoners always escape. If they cannot force the door, they dig tunnels of dream phantasies or neuroses. The nervous energy expended to keep them imprisoned leads to exhaustion, inability to concentrate, upbraiding, and perhaps to mental breakdown. So far Freud is right. A method has developed in psychiatry whereby a man is persuaded to relive, in conversation or in the hypnotic state, the tragic experience which he has locked up in the subconscious, thus to give it egress. The therapy has been widely used with shell-shocked soldiers. Apparently it has given few cures. Why should it cure? If an experience is so terrible that a man dare not face it, the mere repetition of the tragedy can hardly be expected to be redemptive. But if the experience can be relived *in a new climate,* in the light of the friendship of God, the rehearsing of the tragic past may then become very freedom. We must face our sorrows, but not in a mind merely sad: "In my Father's house are many homes."[15] We must face our fears, but not in a mind merely frantic: "There is no fear in love; but perfect love casteth out fear."[16] If the sorrows are offered as on an altar, they are turned to insight and calm. If the fears are brought to God, they are relived in a new world. When repressed good is granted channel in prayer, out it comes—that is why evangelists centralize a kneeling bench. Here is an instance, sufficiently disguised lest pastoral confidence should be broken, but not essentially changed, of liberation from fear through prayer. She had become afraid of death. The fear began in a terrifying happening in adolescence, and was hammered in by her later frequent engagement as organist at funerals. When the fear was thus described to her, and its origin and imprisonment thus traced, much of it was overcome. Then by prayer she learned to say: "God understands this much better than I. If He is like Christ, He does not wish me to live in fear. I need not strive. I will open my hand. He waits to give deliverance." The cure was not sudden except towards the end, but it was complete. Insomnia and its effects were definitely overcome. Thus repressions, blameworthy or merely unfortunate, are granted release by prayer. They are like buried oilfields. They may seep destructively into fertile fields. They may "break" like a "gusher," and spread ruin. Prayer, by constant drilling, gives them channel and turns them to constructive use.

Prayer grants a more positive boon: it gives the sub-conscious the relaxation necessary for its own best endeavors. Let us return for a moment to our scientist or dramatist whose problems and plots are solved when the mind is off guard. Sir William Rowan Hamilton tells us that he saw the quaternion calculus in a flash, when walking over the Irish hilltop.[17] To take a similar instance, James Watt discovered the secret of the steam condenser while watching his mother's teakettle. In all such "Flashes" two elements are constant. There is, first, a long prior study and labor. Hamilton and Watt had worked on their respective problems for years. The quaternion calculus would never surprise a mind unversed and undisciplined in mathematics. Second, there is a period of relaxation, a time of incubation, during which the subconscious mind is secretly busy with the problem in its own laboratories; a quiet time, when there is no conflict between the clamant will and the subliminal forces. As in the sudden remembering of a name, the subconscious brings the answer. Hamilton and Watt both asserted, "It came to me in a flash." In a recent article in the *Journal of Chemical Education,* Washington Platt and Ross A. Baker give the following description of a hunch:

A scientific hunch is a unifying or clarifying idea which springs into consciousness suddenly as a solution to a problem in which we are intensely interested. In typical cases, it follows a long study but comes into consciousness at a time when we are not consciously working on the problem. A hunch springs from a wide knowledge of facts but is essentially a leap of the imagination, in that it goes beyond a mere necessary conclusion which any reasonable man must draw from the data at hand. It is a process of creative thought.[18]

Thus with prayer and our more vital questions: "How may I find God? How may I overcome my fears? How may I be reconciled with an enemy? How shall peace come among men? How may I learn to live like Christ?" We shall not gain an answer without prior la-

bor in life and thought, and we shall find small help in
an individual life or a social order that is delivered to
selfishness. Therein is the shallowness of some doctrines
of prayer guidance. God does not guide us *without* our
thinking or *despite* our thinking, but *through* our thinking: we cannot turn the mind into a blank page or into
a cheap ouija board. Always there is need of rigorous
thought and action. But these do not suffice: the mind
must be given respite, rest, quietness, and creative silence. The clever, too-busy conscious mind must be
stilled. What better relaxation than brooding on the
eternities of God? That quietness is the ultimate crea-
tiveness. When the mind is freed from the clamorous
world, when it is at home in God, answers flash—more
important answers than the quaternion calculus or the
steam engine. The world cannot solve its problems of
daily life or warring nations without this resource of
prayer. Perhaps that is the deep reason why in times of
stress people betake themselves again to the Church. A
return to prayer is the necessary prelude both of creative selfhood and a creative society. The life of Jesus is
replete with instances of insights which flashed on him
because he was willing to be still: "My soul, wait thou
only upon God; for my expectation is from him."[19]

VII

But is there not in the "Kubla Khan" something more
than Coleridge's twenty-five years of reading and labor,
more even than can be attributed to the organizing of
his subconscious? Is there not also something called in
our language "inspiration"?[20] Is there not in the discovery of the quaternion calculus, or in Hosea's insight
into the patient love of the Eternal, a *new* element, an
increment of truth and grace? Psychology dismisses the
question—and is still troubled. Karl Ruf Stolz advises
that "esoteric and mystical qualities and effects should
not be postulated of the subconscious. . . . . It is not
a gate through which occult entities or forces with
which awareness may have no intercourse invade human life."[21] But the leading words in this statement are

wide words, and our question remains unanswered. Dr. Jung, in wistful surmise, and strange inconsistency with his comment above quoted, says: "It is obvious that the center of a transcendental consciousness"—which he links in hypothesis with the unconscious—"cannot be the human ego, since the ego has neither a hand in producing such experiences nor the necessary intelligence to understand them. It can only be their victim—or the receiver of divine grace."[22] Our question touches the fringe of mystery. What is the *added* gift granted by the hidden areas of the mind? If the ground of life is an Eternal Spirit, that gift receives its name. Then prayer would be a Friendship of joy and light. The reflective self, says Hocking, "is immersed in the being of time."[23] The Bible says, "The Lord is my light and my salvation."[24] Prayer would then go even deeper than the subconscious. It would open up at the very depths of the mind the incalculable springs of God. "And in the hidden part thou shalt make me to know wisdom."[25]

Chapter XIII

PRAYER, IMAGINATION, AND THOUGHT

WHAT HAS PRAYER to do with thought? "Nothing," our skeptical world might answer, "nothing, except to curdle thought by make-believe and false emotion." In philosophy and science we disparage prayer, for it pleases us to pretend that thought can be "purely objective," as though it were not *our* thought. But, however the scientist may squirm, he cannot shake himself free from the scientist. Sinbad the sailor finally flung off the Old Man of the Sea, but how shall the scientist rid himself of himself? His "natural laws" are still infected by his mind, and his mind is borne along on the destined purpose-stream of his whole nature. Suppose prayer were the integration of his nature, and therefore the illumination of his thought!

Milton feared his imagination would be brackish and his mind dark, unless by prayer he invited Light:

> And chiefly Thou, O Spirit, that dost prefer
> Before all temples the upright heart and pure,
> Instruct me, for thou know'st. . . . .
> What in me is dark
> Illumine; what is low raise and support;
> That, to the heighth of this great argument
> I may assert Eternal Providence,
> And justify the ways of God to men.[1]

Many another poet has sought "the Muse" in felt dependence on the Beyond. Prayer did not curdle the mind of the Old Testament prophets. As men of imagi-

nation, as thinkers, they read national destiny and
planned national action with acute wisdom; while secular minds, called "gifted," plunged headlong into folly.
As for Jesus, his flame of intellect redeems our night.
Did prayer paralyze *his* mind? He would tell us that
prayer is the safeguard, quickening, and deeper wisdom
of all thought. Here, then, is a central and fascinating
issue: What is the function of prayer in imagination and
reason?

I

Imagination is the ward of experience. We can picture only what we have directly or indirectly known.
Imagination is under the prompting and duress of the
world, and our loveliest fancies are still those of creaturehood. Imagination may *combine* elements to make a
strange creature with a man's head, mazda horns, a
sheep's body, and seaweed for a tail; but each element
is still drawn from experience. We cannot imagine
heaven, but only a heaven-on-earth such as would banish our known sadness and multiply our known joy. The
items of vision are always given: our only power is in
their new association. Even that power is not fully free.
For imagination is imprisoned within time and space,
which it can amazingly foreshorten or extend, as in
dreams, but which it cannot escape. We cannot project
a new note of music, or a new dimension. In the mind's
picturing we are pensioners of the universe, both for our
colors and our canvas.

But this power to separate and recombine is still a creative gift. Old strains become in Dvořák's mind and
hand a *New World Symphony*. We can picture a star
once seen, though all is now dark; and we can see it,
moreover, as the star of Bethlehem, its beams shaped
like a cross. Thus imagination is more than an intricate
pattern of remembrance: it is in measure creative. It
fashions both the world and the man. As for the world,
every journey or means of journeying is first imagined,
any building is fancy frozen into stone, and any music is
a dream caught in a net of sounds. As for the man,

every crime is first imagined, and every heroism. Francis Thompson insists that Shelley's genius is entangled with his gift of make-believe: "The universe is his box of toys. He dabbles his fingers in the day-fall. He is gold-dusty with tumbling among the stars. He makes bright mischief with the moon. . . . . He teases into growling the kenneled thunder, and laughs at the shaking of its fiery chain. He dances in and out of the gates of heaven; its floor is littered with his broken fancies. . . . ."[2] Perhaps all genius, whether of master-criminal or saint, is likewise entangled with make-believe. That is to say, imagination is almost as momentous to character as a seed is to a flower. No man goes wrong *suddenly:* he falls slowly through a series of unworthy thoughts. A boy does not *run* away to sea; the haste is only in his neighbors' eyes: he slowly moves to sea, drawn through a thousand secret pictures of the dustless roads of ocean. No man is *instantly* a hero: "The soul," said Marcus Aurelius, "is dyed in the color of its thoughts." Even the most severely conceptual thought is dependent on imagination. A scientist canvassing various possible hypotheses is drawing by his fancy on all his experience through life and books. The fancies may not be full-orbed. They may be by currency instead of by barter. An incipient movement of the lips or a shred of a word may serve as token of some complete mental picture. Nevertheless, in imagination, inchoate or clear, he is artist and dreamer, not a drab creature of cold reason. His hypotheses originate like Robert Burns's poems:

> E'en then a wish (I mind its power)
> A wish that to my latest hour
>   Shall strongly heave my breast—
> That I, for poor auld Scotland's sake,
> Some usefu' plan or beuk could make,
>   Or sing a sang at least.[3]

Burns *did* make a book and sing a song, because he imagined it and because a wish has power. If only men "would mind its power"! Consciousness is dynamic:

thought runs out in action, and action is the fulfillment of thought.

II

If we can first trace the necessity of prayer in our life of imagination, we shall move toward an understanding of the function of prayer in the whole life of reason. Does prayer safeguard and illumine the *passive* imagination? We know how dreams, reverie, and brooding can color life. An evil dream may shadow a new day, reverie may bless or steal day's active hours, and brooding may make life vengeful or divine. Habitual prayer, especially prayer before sleep, holds cardinal value; for our dreams reproduce—in what strange forms!—recent happenings and oft-repeated longings. If our last waking thought has been on God vivified in Christ, our dreams are under high governance. Our secret longings then are laid open and healed, our grudges are canceled, and our best visions are driven by the act of prayer towards their completion. It is thus possible to subdue and redeem even the horrendous dreams which afflict anesthesia. Is prayer the ground control of the seeming waywardness of passive imagination?

Does prayer guide the *active* imagination? Passive imagination helps creative work, since flashes of light come when the mind is off guard, but it is only smaller brother to the active imagination. Waking thought has more creative power than dreams of day or night. This active imagination is native. In some kind and measure it is the gift of all men. It can be called excellent when it serves the health of personality. Thus Shelley's imagination in "The Cloud" is excellent: the sequence of similes, the glint of minor pictures, the turn of phrase, the momentum of the poem all serve the poet's theme; and the kindled theme serves the more gracious life of man. Dr. O. H. Ammann's imagination is excellent in the plans he drew for the George Washington Bridge. The lay mind can partly conceive the questions he asked himself. If the bridge should be built here or here, what of the foundations, the approaches, the danger from storm? What of the possible strain, the War Department requirements, and the cost in comparison with agreed-upon expenditures? The questions were multitudinous, and each levied a toll on the imagination. The engineer dissected past knowledge and experience, chose, discarded, and combined. He made past failure a warning, and past success a cheer. Similarly, if our lifetime imagination is to be excellent it also must be dedicate to some bridgespan, a Life Purpose regnant over every minor task. It must have some ultimate wisdom to dissect past experience, and to combine its elements in new patterns of beauty and compassion. It must have ultimate hope to change failure from futile regret into friendly warning, and success from foolish pride into sober cheer. Is prayer this wisdom? Is prayer this hope? Does prayer enthrone Christ as the regnant purpose of all life, thus giving imagination its lighted focus? Does it provide in Christ a criterion of selection by which experience and knowledge become our guide and not our chain? Does it thus purge failure or morbid regret and make it a precious discipline? Does it thus save success from human conceit and change it into a wayside spring? The dexterity of the imagination can defeat baleful visionings while these are still at the mind's threshold. Then is Christ an instant Presence, instantly found in crisis prayer? Is he constant Presence—the mind's vital ground? Our modernisms may scoff or wonder: the testimony of the saints abides.

There is an even more crucial question concerning prayer and imagination: does prayer resolve *imagination's pain?* Inherent in our fancies is a certain anguish, like that exquisite wounding which sensitive spirits suffer when they hear great music. The "Andante Cantabile" of Tschaikowsky resolves the discords of earth, but still reflects them. It allays earth-noises, only to make us more distressfully conscious of them. All imagination is thus tinctured with longing. Imagination pain is like the tension in which poets live, that straining bond between the drab actual and the shining ideal. Sometimes on this bridge of tension the poet is nearer the lighted end. Then he writes:

And though the mutterer laughs and church bells toll,
Death brings another April to the soul.[4]

But sometimes his mood is nearer the dark end. Then
he, the same poet, darkly tells us:

Not for us are content, and quiet, and peace of mind,
For we go seeking a city that we shall never find.[5]

Imagination causes tension. We say of a boy longing for
a boat, "His heart is set on it." Vital desire is now *there*,
in imagination; but his actual living must be *here*, where
as yet there is no boat. The incorrigible sainthood in
every man similarly suffers. Perfection is *there* in the
imagination—"That I may know him, and the power of
his resurrection, and the fellowship of his sufferings";[6]
but imperfection is *here* in present life—"Who shall deliver me from this body of death?"[7] The mind is cut,
and bleeds. Nor is the pain attendant only on what
might be: it besets also the imagination of what has
been—"A sorrow's crown of sorrow is remembering
happier things."[8] The psychologist may have to revise
his dictum that imagination can only combine elements
of experience, or else may have to admit that all experience has its fringe of eternity; as, for instance, in the
word "finite," which contrastively implies some awareness of "infinite." For imagination, sometimes at its
center, sometimes at its edge, has always a flash of perfection, which, seen against the shadows of earth, brings
pain, as morning light vexes sleep-bound eyes. All pain
lacerates. Surgical pain may spell health. But any unre-
solved pain is finally fatal. Does prayer resolve this exquisite pain of imagination? Does it bring men into the
presence of God? Does it give them assurance by showing them that Perfection *is*, that it is the encompassing
Reality of our tumultuous earth, and that men may here
and now breathe its air and live in its light? Does prayer
thus fortify a man to return to the tasks of earth with
patience, a higher realism, and an unquenchable resolve?

The saints do not ask these questions. With radiant

face they speak their quiet credo. Prayer for them is a
veritable communion with God, not a mere soliloquy or
a psychological tinkering. These pages have pleaded
that God takes us unawares and must be assumed, by
the very constitution of man's nature, as freedom must
be assumed.[9] We cannot prove truth by logic, for inevitably we assume truth in order to integrate logic. We
cannot prove God by man, for He is the axiom by
which alone men can live. The saints prove God by the
adventure of prayer. In God their imagination is both
quickened and redeemed. But let this answer about
prayer and imagination be provisional, at least until we
have confirmed it by examination of prayer's function
in the wider life of thought. To that wider country we
now journey.

III

What is thought? Its mystery, despite psychological
probing, has not been dispelled. Is thought a *process of
imagery?* No, though imagery is in some part involved.
When a man thinks, "I had better use a typewriter," he
does not recall in *full* image every experience with pen
and typewriter. The mind could not be burdened thus:
it would die of its own weight of treasure. The thinking
man usually trades, not with the actual goods of the imagination, but with a convenient coinage. The thought,
"I had better use a typewriter," employs the veriest tag
ends of images, vague word pictures, or throat movements anticipating the spoken resolve.[10] Then is
thought an *imageless* exercise? Probably not; for though
our thinking may seem as remotè from full-orbed imag-
inings as astronomical formulae are remote from the
stars, yet, just as the formulae refer back to the stars, so
our thought coinage would be worthless without experience held in memory and imagination. Then is thought
merely *incipient action,* the imperceptible response of
nerve and muscle to outer stimuli?[11] Again, probably
not. It would be foolish to suppose that thought moves
in some ethereal isolation. Man is spirit in flesh. However the words *spirit* and *flesh* may be interpreted,

whether as dualism or monism, man cannot in this world escape his body. The most abstruse thought demands outlet in some kind of gesture, and would suffocate without release. A lesson taught is clearer than a lesson merely thought. That fact is enough proof that thought, although not itself incipient action, certainly requires action for fulfillment. The river of consciousness flows through sensation, percept, thought, desire, into motivation and deed. These elements are not elements: they fuse. Nor are they in strict sequence: the river has eddies. But there is some indication of flow. Thus thought could be described as incipient action, just as instinct could be described perchance as incipient thought. But the description would be superficial, for thought is essentially concerned with *meanings*. "This means" is apparently the motto and hallmark of all thinking.

Therefore thought remains a mystery. For what at innermost is the power of light which enables us so to harvest experience that we say of each new event, "This means"? The savage at the mouth of his cave said of the storm, "This means—" Theology, philosophy, and science through the ages are but the steady revision and clarification of meanings. These meanings must be at first hints from the universe. Then they are the answering ventures of man's mind. "This means" links each man instantly with his whole world. It makes him citizen of the skies.[12] A fisherman wades a trout stream, and sees on the stream's surface an oily circle near a dark rock. He says to himself, "This means a feeding trout." Experience, memory image, desire, hope, and incipient action are all entangled in that attributed meaning. The fisherman's thought continues: "This means that a fly cast over the trout may hook it." Thus the acquisitive instinct of the fisherman, the combative instinct, the hunger instinct, and the creative-skill instinct—if they are ever separable—may all be satisfied. Life finds its temporary fulfillment.

Sometimes the world beyond our eyes directly provokes our thought: a red glow in the west catches us, and we say, "This means that day is done." Sometimes the provocation is indirect, coming apparently from within: we feel hungry and say, "This means it is time to eat dinner." But always "this means" links us with our whole universe. We can no more give account of thirst without reference to the world than explain "left" without reference to "right," or "dark" without reference to "light," or "relative" without reference to "absolute." Thus whenever psychology strives to walk alone it blunders into prison: it examines the term "hunger" without benefit of the term "food." Thought is always more than a memory-imagination deposit: it is also a world deposit. Thought is a gateway of mystery: its "this means" gives us passport to the beyond, and makes us potentially friends with the universe. The challenge sometimes comes straight from the event, as in an earthquake; and sometimes indirectly through the needs of the observer.[13] A handkerchief, if a finger is cut and bleeding, may suddenly mean "bandage." Then what does each human instinct *mean* in its ultimate demand? What does the coalescence of instincts *mean* in this strange, almost defenseless, creature called man? What does our whole nature *mean?* Hunger means food, even as food means hunger. Then the universe means—? and man means—? Without some answer we cannot live. Without some answer, however inchoate, we do not live. Religious faith attributes radiant meaning to man and his world, and so grants sanity and soundness to our days. Augustine was thinker as well as praying man: "Thou hast made us for Thyself, and we can find no rest until we rest in Thee."

If we accept the initial mystery of "this means," we can give some further description of the nature of thought. Meaning enables us to go from the known to the implied, as in the solving of crime: "*This* footprint *means* that the man wore a size ten shoe." Meaning enables us to establish comparisons and contrasts: "*These* similar facts in physiology *mean* that both creatures are mammals"; and thus it leads to those universals which are the splendid wealth of science. Meaning enables us to trace the sequence called causality, and to adapt means to ends, as in the diagnosis and healing of disease: "*This* pain *means,* with its history of nausea, and its accompaniment of irregular pulse and high temperature, that the patient has an infected appendix." Thus thought is more than a relationship between man and his world: it weaves a net around the world to help us comprehend it. The strands of that net are legion: How?—thus! Why?—because! If?—therefore! and many another strand. Is the net actually "out there" as well as "in here"? The mystery deepens. Let us be content to say that man, in his power of thought, seems to be subtly but definitely different from lower creatures, and in wonderful rapport with his world. Is thought man's best harmony with the universe? Nay, thought must be fulfilled in action or it dies; and thought itself is a flung faith sharpened by desire. Man is more than a lonely thinker returning with baffled mind from the mysterious immensities of the beyond: he is yearning, hope, and brave venture. We draw near to our central question: What of prayer and thought?

IV

For convenience we adopt Dr. John Dewey's now classic instance and analysis of the process of thought.[14] He was in downtown New York at 12:30 P.M. when he realized that he was due at 124th Street at one o'clock. He canvassed in his mind the various ways of travel, decided in favor of the subway express, and reached his destination before the appointed hour. His analysis of his thought process in its successive stages is roughly as follows: *first,* felt difficulty, "I am in danger of being late"; *second,* clearer definition of the difficulty, "How can I get there in time?"; *third,* a study of alternatives while judgment was suspended, "Shall I go this way or this or this?"; *fourth,* decision, "I will go by the Broadway subway"; *fifth,* action, "I go." These stages are each capable of further differentiation. The felt difficulty, for instance, might begin as a shock on reading a telegram, and continue as a problem. The stages might differ in emphasis under different circumstances. In case of a sudden fire there could be no long canvassing of alternatives, whereas in a basic problem in physics suspended judgment could fill a lifetime. Two or more stages might seem to fuse in swift thought. But this sketch of thought process, with whatever necessary modifications, does provide some norm and guidance. Let us take two instances of our own, one from the realm of theory, the other from our social contacts. The first might concern the wire obtruding from the road opposite the toll booth at the Henry Hudson Bridge in New York City. The stages of the thought process are clear: *first,* a felt difficulty, "That wire is strange"; *second,* definition of the difficulty, "Why is it there?"; *third,* study of alternatives in suspended judgment, "Is it a wire carelessly dropped? Or set there for guidance? Or to register by contact the number of cars crossing the bridge? Or a device for grounding the electricity from friction which otherwise the pay clerk and passenger would receive as shock when the coin is passed?"; *fourth,* decision, "It is a device against electric shock"; *fifth,* action, "I am grateful, and now drive with confidence." The other instance might be the thought process following the receipt of a venomous letter. The stages are again roughly in accord with our accepted pattern: *first,* a problem, "He hates me"; *second,* clearer definition of the problem, "What shall be my response?"; *third,* study of alternatives in suspended judgment, "Shall I write a more venomous reply? Or ignore the letter? Or enlist the indignation of my friends in opposition? Or admit the partial truth of the letter, and seek the writer in hope of reconciliation?"; *fourth,* decision, "I ought to heal the cleft"; *fifth,* action, "I go to his house."

Of these three instances, the first and third are more critical for personality. Under ordinary circumstances a man could live honorably without knowing why a wire projects from the road opposite the toll booth of a bridge. But Dr. Dewey's desire to go in half an hour from downtown New York to Columbia University, presumably for a classroom appointment, held deeper issues. In the case of the venomous letter also, loyalties are involved. Any process of thought implies a problem to be met or a mental conflict to be resolved, but the major problems concern both thought and conduct. They are affairs, not of theory alone, but of motives and people. They are crucial questions. Whom shall I marry? What work shall I choose? How shall I spend my money and meet my debts? How can I face surgery with courage and calmness? What shall be my attitude to poverty, war, and death? But whether the problem be a pleasant curiosity or a tortured spirit, thought begins when the impact of events bids us stand to the challenge. "What does this mean?" the universe says to us. Then begins the mental process which ends in, "This means"; for rightly ascribed meaning is the signature of intelligence and the root of character.

Then what of thought and prayer? We have traced the stages of thought process. At each stage the praying man finds in prayer a sun and shield. When the challenge sounds—when, let us suppose, a telegram comes with news of a friend's death—he is not frantic: he has affirmed his faith in a Christlike universe, and by prayer and sturdy deeds has won confidence. When he defines the problem, he works with a quick and quiet mind: "I must meet this issue both in thought and act. What shall I think, and what shall I do?" When he studies alternative courses, meanwhile suspending judgment, prayer gives his mind a wise delay: the issue is pendant in Light. Low alternatives are thrust aside: "I will not evade the issue called death. I will not send a merely formal reply, nor leave sorrowing folk to care for themselves. I will not shrink from the trouble and expense of a journey." His mind is still: he waits, and listens. When he reaches decision, it is a decision in the mood of Christian prayer: "I will send a wire in such-and-such friendliness. I will return at once to help. I will cleave to my faith, striving by speech or silence to impart its comfort and courage." When he acts on his decision, his energy needs no self-flogging, no neighbor's exhortation: he is empowered by an Unseen Grace: "This I now do by Thy help!" In some problems these stages of thought and their accompanying prayers fill years: the problem of life conscripts us at birth and gives discharge only at death. In other instances, such as the stress of an accident or an electric shock of joy, there may be no time to pray: all the stages of thought are then one flash and flame. But even then, when challenge and decision are too swift for full-formed prayer, prior prayer is "very heaven." Is there not a story of Dwight L. Moody to the effect that everybody on shipboard was frantically praying during a violent storm, while he, supposedly the man of prayer, seemed unconcerned? He was reproached, "Why are you not praying?" "I'm all prayed up," he said.

V

Following the steps in thought process as they are suggested by Dr. Dewey, we can show more clearly that at each step prayer is a necessary ally. Dr. Dewey would be horrified; but there is a deeper "functionalism" than his brave mind has dreamed. *Prayer gives thought its poise.* How striking is the fact that thought is provoked by crisis, that the meaning of life is drawn from insistent challenge! That fact holds a profound philosophy of experience. How shall we meet the onset? Not in fear or frenzy, but in assurance and calmness of mind. Anger roils thought: we need sunlight and sand to clear the muddy stream. Pride inflates thought in folly: we need some Ineffable Will before whom we may bow in lowliness, as astronomers are lowly in sight of stars. Worry frets thought: we need some final Certitude. Selfishness makes thought cross-eyed: we need the Horizon. So we say to the man distraught, "Calm yourself." But only partly can he calm himself.

> Father, in Thy mysterious Presence kneeling,
>   Fain would our souls feel all Thy kindling love;
> For we are weak, and need some deep revealing
>   Of trust and strength and calmness from above.[15]

It is no accident that the great thinkers in any realm have been men of simple goodness who have lived in a mood akin to reverence.

Prayer gives a faith-norm by which the problem may be rightly defined. Thus it governs the second step in Dr. Dewey's description of the thought process. Dr. Dewey, finding himself downtown at 12:30 P.M. when he was under honorable necessity of being at Columbia University at 1:00 P.M., might have given his problem a different definition. Instead of asking himself, "How can I arrive in time?" he might have asked, "What excuse can I invent for avoiding the appointment?" His statement of the problem was really determined by a faith—the faith, namely, that a man must act in honor. Without some faith in the universe we could not live. Science itself would flag without its positive avowals. The scientist seems to disavow assumptions. Scientific honor requires that he shall not jump to conclusions, nor allow truth's white light to be stained by hasty wishes. Yet the scientist makes no move without a credo. He accepts certain axioms, and must, or every move in science would be blocked. He assumes, in tremendous faith, that the cosmos is orderly, trustworthy, and accordant with our mind. These assumptions are inevitable. They are science's necessary faith. But the scientist is also a man, and the assumptions of his manhood are more deeply essential than the axioms of his science. The old story of Manoah and his wife[16] shows the alternatives of faith and doubt. Manoah judged life by its terror: "We shall surely die." His wife judged life by its joys: "If the Lord were pleased to kill us, he would not have . . . . shewed us all these things." Our recent skeptical humanism, now almost in eclipse, follows Manoah: it judges life by nature's seeming impassivity, vowing that we are born on a bleak rock and on a bleak rock must perish. In opposite faith, the Christian judges life by Christ. By sure surmise, or by intuition, or by logic traveling too swiftly to reveal its steps, or by instant response to a Beckoning, the Christian says, "Christ is the clue, and the revealing, and the destiny." These are perennial alternatives: we judge life by its worst or by its best, by its static or its music. Moreover, doubt, in the root meaning of the word, implies wavering. We properly call it *mis*-giving. It is alien from our nature. If we judge life by the worst, the best becomes inexplicable except as cosmic mockery: our breath then is dusty death, science is a mild insanity, right is wrong or whatever ruthless power may wish to make it, and the hopeless years echo in violence. From such *mis*-giving we recoil in a proper, involuntary, and final shudder of soul. But if we interpret life by its best, the worst can be explained, not fully, but with sufficient light for living: it becomes the darker choice which makes our freedom real, the challenge to courage, the brave odds of faith, and a token of the Mystery which provokes our awe and worship. Just as science would collapse without its light-filled axioms, so the scientist would fall, and all men with him, in lack of cardinal faith. Prayer affirms that the highest in life, namely Jesus Christ, is deepest in nature; and prayer flings itself on that faith as a swimmer on the sea. Only such faith can keep life whole, rational, and worthy. Only such encompassing faith can give meaning and correct statement to the problems we confront. Prayer at its truest is not curdling of thought: it is the life-blood of thought. Without prayer, thought would bleed to death.

Prayer gives light for suspended judgment, and thus governs the third step in thought process. Wise thought *does* canvass alternatives: "Look before you leap." Decisions should be objective—freed from prejudice and false emotion. A woman takes a piece of cloth to the store window. A daylight lamp is not enough: it is still surrounded by the yellow light of other lamps. Only the sky's light can give true color. And there's a parable. It is wisdom to say, "I'll sleep on it." It is deeper wisdom to say, "I'll pray on it." That judgment shall be suspended is not enough: it must be suspended in light. Without some respite from the world our judgment cannot mature, and without light judgment is still blind. A mother, not knowing to which of two schools to send her boy, prayed for guidance. She did not forgo her mind: God gave it for use. But the strain of thought was now abandoned; the clamorous desire found rest. New factors shone clear, and known factors took a different proportion. Suddenly, as if a voice had spoken, the hint

came, "Consult So-and-so." It developed, whether by
unconscious memory or outright guidance, that the man
in question had studied at one of the schools.[17] The
conference which followed pointed to a wise decision.
Psychology can describe the incident in terms of
"lapsed remembrance" and "reversed effort," and the
description gives clearer understanding of mental processes. But it is a *description,* not an *explanation.* Even if
no specific "leading" had come from that prayer, the
mother would have been of clearer and purer mind to
make judgment, because she canvassed alternatives in a
whiter Light than earth can give.

Prayer gives thought its "inspirations" for decision,
thus governing the fourth stage in thought process. That
word "inspiration" is a bugbear to psychology. Thus Dr.
Edward S. Robinson looks askance at William Blake's
contention that his poems are a gift beyond his own
poor gift. He describes the claim as an "extreme case of
so-called inspirational" writing, and remarks in a mild
condescension that "we ourselves should hardly fall
back upon such an explanation."[18] The instance is
Blake's striking account of the poem, "Jerusalem":
"I have written this Poem from immediate dictation
. . . . without premeditation and even against my
will. . . . . I dare not pretend to be any other than the
secretary; the authors are in Eternity."[19] The psychologist's additional comment is this: "But there are certain
important facts which indicate the inspiration is no more
supernatural than any other form of imagination."[18]
Elsewhere the same psychologist writes similarly. "Because the movement of thought takes place so unex-
pectedly as to astonish the thinker himself, there is
likely to be the feeling that it is determined by mysterious forces. This is correct, if we mean by mysterious
forces, unconscious factors. . . . . Such sudden inte-
grations are wonderful. They are wonderful just as the
sprouting of the seed and the revolving of the earth are
wonderful. But they are not unique phenomena."[20]
These gainsayings seem impressive, but there are easy
to puncture. Scrutinize them. The real issue is not
whether sudden inspiration is "more supernatural"

than any other form; for all imagination, swift or
slow, has its "Beyond" as well as its "within." Moreover, to eqaute "mysterious forces" with "unconscious
factors" is a blithe begging of the whole question.
Again, to compare the "sudden integration" of the im-
aginative mind with the wonder of a "sprouting seed" is
by analogy a complete surrender of the case so blithely
begged. Here, if ever, is an instance of the "psychological fallacy." A seed does not sprout of itself: it sprouts
because there are "mysterious forces" *beyond* the
seed—sun, wind, rain, and the whole economy of the
universe—playing upon mysterious life *within* the seed.
An oculist may properly assume, for purposes of study,
that light is in the eye; but light is not in the eye, except
as the instigation of light in the sky. The psychologist
may properly assume, for purposes of study, that the
mind is alone "in its own place"; but the mind is in its
world. It is a seed quickened by the sky, an eye visited
by light. William Blake looked at life whole—the "Beyond" as well as the "within." There is no reason to
assume, other factors being equal, that his own account
of his writings is mistaken while the psychologist's account of them is true. Blake described his mind in its
universe: psychology describes it only "in its own place."
To erect fences is doubtless necessary for the convenience of study, but to assume thereafter that there is
nothing over the fence is huggermugger. Musicians,
poets, scientists, inventors, in instance after instance,
are in substantial agreement with Blake's account of
"inspiration." They agree with the psychologist that
"flashes" do not come to a lazy or unversed mind. They
agree also that unconscious factors are involved. They
would not deny that the psychological account is valid
within psychology's appointed bounds. But they insist
that discovery is "given," that it "comes," that it is
"sent." They know, in short, that man's mind is not
alone, but is visited and enriched. Actually there is no
such phenomenon as spontaneous combustion: fire
comes from the sun. The saints insist that men may cultivate the Beyond by labor of mind, by labor of hand,
and by prayer in the mood of Christ. They tell us in

accents of deep certitude that such prayer invites, not vainly,

> the gleam,
> The light that never was, on sea or land,
> The consecration, and the Poet's dream.[21]

Such is the wisdom of the saints. The psychological fallacy can never confound them.

VI

Decision having been reached, does prayer empower a man to act on it? Is prayer thus the clinching by deeds of the whole thought process? Jesus in Gethsemane confronted a problem both for thought and conduct. It was no wire in the road, no mere appointment uptown, no tiny venom. He faced the ultimate derision. He who deserved our best was now victim of our worst. The land he loved disowned him. The fellowship of Israelitish faith, to which he brought a holy zeal, upbraided him and plotted his death. The state, whose sword he met only with the Spirit's sword, hurried him to his cross. His dearest friends forsook him. Now death approached—bitter, mocking, and foul with man's selfishness. That was the black gauntlet flung. *First, he met the onset* with calm mind, being schooled in prayer, and his last words are still a gentle daybreak. *Next, he defined the crucial issue* worthily: "How can I best fulfill God's purpose?" *Then, in suspended judgment,* hour after hour, he prayed, scrutinizing each alternative, staunchly rejecting each base proposal. Should he bring down earthy judgment on his foes? Should he seek a poor escape? Should he strike a bargain with Pilate and Caiaphas? Should he go elsewhere to teach, the world being in sore need of God? Should he accept death with stoicism? Or should he appropriate death in daring and creative faith? *Then by prayer he made his choice,* but found the prospect still so black that he must cry, "O Father, if it be possible, let this cup pass from me: nevertheless not as I will, but as thou wilt."[22] *Finally, by prayer he gained power* for the last great deed. There was no denunciation of the foes who soon would kill him, or of the friends who had slept while his agony had been drops of blood. There was no wavering and no fear. "Rise, let us be going."[23] Prayer faced the shock, defined the issue, pondered alternatives, made the decision, and carried resolve into the deed of Calvary. Rashness doubly rash could hardly deny that prayer illumined his thought and energized it—by whose white vigil we are saved.

Chapter XIV

PRAYER AND CONSCIENCE

THE FOLLOWING IS a dispatch printed in the *New York Times*: "Many Germans in occupied Poland appeared to be conscience-stricken by the country's devastation and the sufferings inflicted on the Polish people. In collection boxes in several damaged churches in Warsaw German coins and banknotes are frequently found—obviously conscience money. . . . ."[1] That reported incident confronts us with a vexed but fascinating issue—man's conscience.

I

What is this thing called a conscience? In the index pages of most books of psychology the word is not even listed. Dr. E. L. Thorndike in his book *The Original Nature of Man* says bluntly, "No innate difference of response to 'right' from 'wrong' acts is listed here, in spite of the opinions of a majority of students of ethics."[2] "Right" and "wrong" he prints in quotation marks. This viewpoint is in one sense neither surprising nor particularly blameworthy. The doctor in his diagnosis of disease does not often use the word "conscience." He is concerned with the sickness and health of the body, and the psychologist is concerned with the sickness and health of the mind. Ethics is not his major study. In another sense this dealing with the words "right" and "wrong" as though they were merely fictions is staggering. For the body-doctor knows that coddling wealthy hypochondriacs for fat fees is shady medi-

cal ethic, and the psychologist knows he ought not to
steal the pocketbook of his patient. He knows too that
the patient, in the vast majority of instances, accepts the
words "right" and "wrong," and finds within their
meaning much of his peace and misery. Dr. Thorndike,
indeed, having printed "right" and "wrong" in quotation marks, reminds us that Lloyd Morgan and others
hold a different conviction, and quotes him as follows:
"Among civilized people conscience is innate. Intuitions
of right and wrong are a part of that moral nature
which we have inherited from our forefathers."

Our modern emphasis on psychology has given credence to certain definitions of conscience which, though
widely accepted today, do not bear careful investigation.
Definition of conscience or of any personality force is
obviously difficult, but we can still see when definitions
are mistaken. Conscience is *not* merely ancient custom
or merely present social pressure. Nor is it, despite the
Freudians, identification with, and consequent fear of,
our parents—the vestige or residue of infantile dread.
Conscience may be mediated through custom or parental injunction. Conscience may be quickened or dulled,
especially in a child, by social pressures; and the fact
that juvenile delinquency varies directly with poverty
and congestion should give pause to our too hasty con-
demnations. But we are still confronted with the question of why some customs should be accepted as "better," and why enlarging conscience should rebelliously
break other customs which it deems outgrown. The con-
scientious objector to war is required by *his* conscience—whether he is justified or treasonable is not here
the issue—to oppose both custom and social pressure.
How shall we explain him? If conscience had not been
at odds with social custom would any progress have
been possible? Dr. William E. Hocking rightly maintains that the "you ought" spoken by the home or the
tribe lacks authority until it is answered in agreement by
each man's "I ought," and that home and state wait
anxiously for that accordant response.[3] We may register
another exception to popular theory: conscience is *not*
merely an "inferiority complex" resulting from thwarted

power impulses, as an Adlerian might propose. For a complex dwells in the subconscious mind and is unhealthy; while conscience, however we may define it, is in the conscious mind and is usually recognized as potentially healthy and indeed necessary. We would have scant regard for a man without conscience. Moreover, conscience finds us, not so much when we have been thwarted in our power impulse and feel inferior, as when we have *fulfilled* our power impulse by making force our right. So King Claudius found:

> But, O, what form of prayer
> Can serve my turn? "Forgive me my foul murder"?
> That cannot be; since I am still possess'd
> Of those effects for which I did the murder,
> My crown, mine own ambition, and my queen.
> May one be pardon'd and retain the offence?
> In the corrupted currents of this world
> Offence's gilded hand may shove by justice,
> And oft 'tis seen the wicked prize itself
> Buys out the law: but 'tis not so above;
> There is no shuffling, there the action lies
> In his true nature; and we ourselves compell'd
> Even to the teeth and forehead of our faults,
> To give in evidence.[4]

There are other exceptions. Conscience is *not* merely "the voice of the repressed good," despite Dr. J. A. Hadfield;[5] for a repression becomes subconscious, while this inward monitor is by nature conscious; and a repression is pathological, while a good conscience *is* good. Conscience is *not* merely "an awareness of the success or failure of . . . . life in maintaining its status and its growth,"[6] despite so wise an investigator as Dr. Hocking. For conscience is always more than awareness. It is not merely a thermometer or a measuring rod: it has judgments and penal fires and radiance of approval. Conscience is *not* the admiration we have for great and good men, for *we* do the admiring and our admiration has a positive ring: it is more than a reflex or rebound. Conscience is *in us* toward great men, as well as also doubtless from them to us. It is not a mutual admiration society: it has a throne set and books opened and balances brought for a verdict. Conscience is *not* an instinct, for it stands apart as mentor of the instincts. Conscience is *not* merely hereditary bias, for it approves or disapproves our native bestowals; and it knows that, whatever measure of allowance may properly be made for the "taint in the blood," a man cannot justly blame his misdeeds on his great-grandfather.

How we squirm to escape the axiomatic in our conscience, and how we fail! We try to make even the new astronomy our scapegoat: "In so vast a universe what are right and wrong?" The answer is, they are still right and wrong, as hundreds of words of praise or condemnation in our language clearly show. There is something primal about conscience—like our assumption of freedom or the faithfulness of the universe. That conscience is mediated through social custom may be due to the fact that it is the nature of conscience to exalt certain social loyalties. That conscience raises individual rebellion may be due to some Right which "whispers each man i' the ear." We are accustomed to describe our "ought" as the pilot on the bridge of the ship. It is a poor description, for this pilot is somehow joined with the nature of the stars by which he steers, and therefore praises and blames both the passengers and the crew—memories, thoughts, motives, appeals, and deeds. Perhaps Dr. Hocking is right: "It might appear, then, that conscience is not in itself any part of the will—certainly not an instinct—but something outside of all these, like self-consciousness pure and simple."[7] When all our discussion of "maladjusted personalities" has received its due weight—and it *has* weight—there is still a chasm of difference between Cain's evasive eyes and Abel's dying eyes. The word conscience means "knowing with." Is it a knowing with God—the impact on our self-consciousness of His apprehended Good? When we say a course of conduct is "better" we imply, however dimly, a far-off "best." How far can we say of conscience, "O Lord, thou hast searched me, and known me"?[8]

II

Conscience grows, since growth is a mark of all man's life. Fanatics imprison conscience by false stringencies; libertines spoil it by false freedoms; and the intelligentsia choke it in a fog. Every man's conscience is fallible and far from perfect. Conscience is a quest, with milestones to mark the journey, like the scientist's truth or the artist's beauty. The world has a just quarrel with a Church which has often tried to equate its conscience with heaven's whole light. The world has known well that some brands of church conscience have been far from heaven-blest. Conscience may rationalize and become *deceitful:* Adam blamed the wrong on Eve, and Eve blamed it on the serpent, and that old story is as modern as the next heartbeat. Conscience may be *sadly mixed* with selfishness: the above-quoted *New York Times* dispatch about conscience money in Warsaw churches said further that some Germans, after helping the Poles, asked for a "certificate" testifying to their sympathy, because they might need the certificate if the enemy ultimately triumphed. Conscience may be *narrow,* and that fact needs to be scored deep: the "Puritan conscience" is not an empty gibe, even though its historical warrant may be disputed. Conscience may *be out of balance,* having a false scale of sins and virtues: the churchmen in Christ's day bitterly condemned carnal sins, and had no conscience about their own hypocrisy and pride; and our world has not yet come to terms with Christ's catalogue of virtues and transgressions. Pride is still in our eyes only a defect, whereas to him it was a deadly sin. Conscience may be *repressive.* It is possibly on this score, more than on any other, that the intelligent world takes issue with the conscience of the Church. A really good conscience does not repress, for what is repressed becomes a repression and eventually finds secret and unhealthy outlet. A poor conscience has often practiced for itself, and required in others, the repression of the sex instinct instead of its worthy fulfillment or its disciplined sublimation. That repression has issued in censorious criticism of the "fallen," and in secret pruriency. True conscience does not hold basic impulses in irons in the cellar, but grants them radiant satisfactions and sets them to constructive tasks. Conscience may be *morbid,* feeding upon itself: every minister is beset by the gloomy soul who comes accusing himself of having committed the unpardonable sin. As further illustration of morbidity, the usually gladsome St. Francis would have been even more a saint if he had not injured his eyesight by excessive weeping for his real or fancied transgressions. Deceitful, mixed, narrow, out of balance, repressive, morbid: such are the disfigurements on conscience. It is a heavy "bill of particulars." Even if there were no distortions or failures, we would still have to admit that the best man's conscience is only partial and in process of growth. What is right today we may recognize as wrong tomorrow. In what a strange dilemma of conscience a man would find himself if he had been a deserter through acknowledged cowardice in one war, and in some new war found himself for conscience' sake a pacifist! On the Peary expedition to the North Pole were three men among the others: Professor Ross G. Marvin, an American, and Kudlooktoo and Harrigan, two Eskimos. They were on a difficult trek with Marvin in command. Harrigan refused to obey orders, at risk of life to all three. So Marvin bade him begone—in that white, hopeless waste. Thereupon Kudlooktoo shot Marvin to save his countryman.[9] At the time he thought he was doing right, but later he confessed in agony that he had done wrong.

So conscience is both defective and adolescent. It may become blind and crippled. In most men it is far from true adulthood. In only a few has it the light of genius. It needs correcting, like a faulty compass. But how do we know the shortcomings of conscience, even of conscience better than our own? There is a question! Is it because of a Conscience above our conscience, or because of some brooding Ideal? Our conscience at its best, even though definitions may still elude us, is the cutting edge of life, a creative "divide," a "knowing with" the Knower in whom all goodness coheres.

III

If conscience needs to be trained, it needs still more to be *healed*. What flippancies we offer about a bad conscience! We say, "The past is past," whereas in truth the past is always present. The New England hurricane is not past: the woods are littered with broken branches, trees once healthy struggle with infirmity, and the landscape carries still the marks of the storm. While memory endures in man his past is always present. We say, "Let bygones be bygones"—as if we could! There are no bygones, for whatever we have done wrong is *in* us, possibly as repression and fetter, assuredly as mark and strain. We say, "No use crying over spilt milk," though that weeping might actually be of much use. It might forearm us against repetition of the blunder. Besides, though split milk is presumably an accident, theft or false testimony is not an accident. Life that dishonors conscience is not spilt milk: it is injected poison. A man of insight exclaimed, "Take my influence and bury it with me!" He probably knew that it could not be done. Another sensitive spirit exclaimed of our human nature, "The whole head is sick, and the whole heart faint. . . . . There is no soundness in it; but wounds, and bruises, and putrifying sores."[10]

What is to be done about our dark memories, the wounds of conscience? At a banquet at which Queen Wilhelmina and President Roosevelt both spoke by radio, the whole audience spontaneously cheered the appearance of the Polish envoy and the Chinese envoy, whose countries have been recently ravaged. The applause registered a moral judgment: we recognize wrong as wrong when we see it. Our relativisms vanish in such a moment. Relativisms always vanish. Some shrewd commentator has suggested that the Ten Commandments favor the rich. He has evidence for support: "Thou shalt not covet thy neighbor's house, ... nor his manservant, nor his maidservant, nor his ox, nor his ass, nor anything that is thy neighbor's."[11] He insists, therefore, that the Ten Commandments are merely relative. But if he is right in his criticism of the Decalogue, he is judging it by a higher standard; and "higher" implies "highest." Thus no command of conscience is *merely* relative. We know wrong when we see it: we are aware of our own inward Polands, our own broken decalogues. What shall we do with that wound? Shall we be satisfied to admit it to ourselves, and to go on admitting it? That is our common practice. We inwardly admit the wrong, and make the admission a poor substitute for a genuinely remedial attitude and act. But such an admission is only an irritation of the wound, and may lead to hypochondria in the realm of morals. We may end by subtly enjoying our own remorse—in a mild psychological masochism. Then what to do? Shall we try to forget the wrong, and repress the memory as often as it returns? That resolve would plaster the wound and seal it: the poison would spread deviously and find outlet through other sicknesses apparently not connected with the repression—through nervousness, anxiety, violent criticism of others, failure to concentrate, and a disintegrated life. Psychology has made us doubly sure that a repressed memory cannot ultimately be repressed. "Murder will out"—even of slain memories. Human nature is so constituted that it cannot keep a secret: "For there is nothing covered, that shall not be revealed; neither hid, that shall not be known."[12] That word is not a threat. It is simple fact. For honest minds it is the token of an honest universe. There is little use in tickling a wound to keep it irritated, and less use in sealing it so that the pus is driven into the bloodstream. The doctor usually lances an infected wound so that it may heal from its base outward to the scar.

IV

Now we may be better prepared to consider the necessary linking of conscience and prayer. *Prayer trains the conscience.* It is a cardinal fact that we are creatures, creaturely dependent on the vast encompassing Mystery of the world. We eat and drink, but only as the world supplies food. We see, but only as the sun gives light. So with food and light for our crippled and feebled conscience. They are not merely "in here," but "out there" in the Spirit who "impels all thinking things, all objects of all thought." "Open thou mine eyes" is an agelong petition not unanswered. If we take a watch to a jeweler, he may test it and say, "You have been too near a dynamo." Then, with his own magnet, token of a cosmic Magnetism, he may draw out the bias. Then he may set the watch by the sun and stars—by time in the sky. It is a parable. In prayer we bring our conscience to God. We are always too near the distractions of the world. We contract an earthy bias. If then we try to take our spiritual time from one another, chaos comes upon us. There has been too long one time of Congress, another of business, another of professional life, another of our pleasures, and still another of our homes. Chaos is not resolved until by the pleading of prayer we set our watches once more by the Sky.

It is no accident that men who have learned to pray have become the world's conscience, nor is it strange that their prayers should again and again break in confession: "Remember not the sins of my youth, nor my transgressions: according to thy mercy remember thou me for thy goodness' sake, O Lord"; "Wash me thoroughly from mine iniquity, and cleanse me from my sin."[13] Such prayers—granted they are part of a proportioned prayer life in which thanksgiving, adoration, and devotion also have their due place—give integration to personality. That fact is their vindication, as indeed it is the vindication of all prayer. Only the Real can grant serenity and wholeness. Prayer is in many forms. In communion with nature's vastness a man prays, or in solemn gratitude for life's blessings, or before the image of the cross. We shall soon discuss ways of praying. Here and now we are concerned to urge that genuinely Christian prayer, in whatever form, is a corrective and an education of the conscience. No man could look long on Christ in prayer without growing a new conscience about widespread poverty, war, or our individual unworthiness. Indeed, genuine prayer would leave us so ill at ease concerning unemployment and the war system that we would be tortured by the sense of difference between what is and what ought to be, and would lay resolute and redemptive hands on all our twisted schemes to shape them to a fairer pattern.

V

Prayer does more than train and correct conscience. In surgical compassion *prayer lances the infected wound which our self-will has healed.* How? By confession. Mr. P. C. Wren has a story called *Coward of the Legion.* A book by Dr. Clifford E. Barbour recalls it.[14] The hero or villain of the story, Jean Dubonnet, had risked his life for a wounded officer, and was to receive a medal for bravery. Being congratulated, he broke into self-denunciation and confessed himself coward. He refused to be comforted, and insisted on baring his story. He had loved a woman in the Paris underworld, not knowing she was married. They agreed to die in a suicide pact before her husband could return. She drank the poison, but his nerve failed. His Apache friends reviled him, and branded on his breast the words, "Liar and Coward." Over his tunic there would soon be the Croix de Guerre, and under his tunic there was the branded condemnation. That contradiction was intolerable. He could not forget, and to confess the guilt was in itself no full release. A friend had a solution for the strange dilemma: he would burn out the charge as it had been burned in—with an iron. Nor would he grant an anesthetic: he knew that for such a man as Jean Dubonnet only pain could burn out the wound of soul. Years later, when "the coward of the Legion" was killed in battle, his colonel testified, "I have lost my bravest soldier."

Cauterizing steel is no general panacea for a guilty conscience. But the story gives us a clue. The record of our sins must be burned out by the inward fire of confession. For most people some human confession is a helpful, and perhaps almost an essential, release. The Roman Catholic confessional is not fallacious as a confessional. Our serious and proper misgivings arise on other grounds. The Roman confessional is compulsory. It is sometimes psychologically shallow or crassly perfunctory. Its imposition of penalties has often been arbitrary and unwise. It has been known to teach that penance can in itself somehow balance the moral books. These are the facts which provoke our misgiving. A forced confession is a violation of personality. Only a mind sensitive as light and deeply compassionate can minister to a bruised conscience. Penalties may be a coercion; and, in any event, merit is from man to man, not from man to God. But the right kind of confessional meets a deep need, and Protestantism's failure to provide creative opportunity for confession has driven many of its people to the inadequate resources of psychiatry. Group confession, for reasons already sketched, is of dubious worth. It is questionable if confession can ever be made wisely to a group. Certainly it cannot be made wisely to a group of naïve and perhaps curious people. In most instances, though not necessarily in all, confession should be made to the one most injured, especially if that one has any shepherding grace. Or it should be made to some worthy man or woman who understands the cure of souls, and who can represent by good character and tender though rigorous understanding the whole humanity against whom sin has been committed. In any event, whether confession to human ears is wise or unwise, confession should be made to God. For, inasmuch as we are creatures, our deepest sin is against the Creative Life. Only He who has made us can fully understand us; only He is pure; only He can forgive.

To these high matters we shall return. Our present plea is that prayers of confession are the lancing of the sealed wounds of conscience, and the path to spiritual health. The confession should be full and free. One grain of sand can clog delicate mechanism, and one cherished grudge unconfessed can spoil a prayer. Confession prayer is not easy. It is like a cauterizing needle. But we shall be wise not to ask any anesthetic. Then the wound is opened, and it heals from its base—from the very ground of our nature. To admit our wrongdoing to ourselves, and to do no more, only irritates the wound. To try to forget, to laugh and drink and labor, refusing to look at what we have done, is to seal the wound and to spread the poison. To confess to wise human ears and to God's ears, making full acknowledgment, is to lance the wound. Prayer is thus the beginning of healing.

VI

Again, prayer carries through the process of healing, and *grants us a new conscience*. Even full confession is not enough. Medical records are full of cases of men who, cured of a culpable sickness, promptly repeat the offense. Our unruliness is such that, once made clean, we again besmirch ourselves. What we need is newness of nature. How may such a miracle be wrought? Conscience itself hints at a basic integrity in the scheme of things. A man may sin in a secrecy which defies all human search. His sin may have no traceable effect on any neighbor, as, for instance, in the case of a scientist hiding new truth. That sin would be unknown, but conscience—the "knowing *with*"—would tell him that it is not unknown: the universe has eyes and ears. The sin, being sin against the scientist's own mind, would be deeper sin against the Creative Spirit. "If I ascend up into heaven" of a dearly bought success, "thou art there." "If I make my bed in Sheol" of some self-abandonment, "thou art there." "If I take the wings of the morning" in some attempted oblivion, "thou art there." "If I say, Surely the darkness" of the subconscious "shall cover me, behold the night shineth as the day. Whither shall I go from thy spirit? or whither shall I flee from thy presence?"[19] That was the reason, perhaps, why German soldiers left their conscience money in a church: the sky had been gashed. That was why Kudlooktoo reached the conviction that he ought not to have slain Marvin: he had no right to usurp the throne of Justice. The essence of sin is the attempt to make ourselves God. Is this righteous Universe also compas-

sionately concerned with my trouble of conscience? Is
He not only just, but grieving and loving? A coldly
righteous Scheme might leave us angry and in despair.
An indulgent Scheme which dismissed our guilt with a
wave of the hand, "Oh, forget it!" might leave us scorn-
ful and bereft. Only an Order of Holy Love can grant
us newness of life.

Thus this requickening of conscience should hold
some veritable pledge of forgiveness. The evil issue of
our sin must somehow be canceled both in ourselves
and in our world. We cannot forget a bad conscience,
for a fraction of a second is enough to disinter all the
past; and, even if we could forget, the repression would
find unhappy outlet. Nor is confession enough: the
damage must be repaired, and the task is beyond our
skill and dubious purity. George Bernard Shaw is re-
puted to have said, "Forgiveness is a beggar's refuge: a
man must pay his debts." The playwright gives no guidance to that solvency. The social stain of a diseased
conscience is not easily traced: it is like black dye
poured in a stream. Who has wit to trace that dark de-
filement? Who has power to cancel it? We cannot pay
that debt, nor can we borrow from our neighbors; for
we are all "in the same condemnation." The ancient
Jewish Day of Atonement showed deep insight. The
high priest laid aside his official robes on that day, because he also was a needy suppliant. He brought a "sin
offering," first for himself and the priesthood, and then
for the people. He sought atonement, not only for the
nation, but also for the Temple and the Altar. No man
can say, "I forgive you." He can say only, "I forgive
you, as I ought, within the measure of my power." That
measure is not wide—no wider than his own dim righteousness and love, no wider than his own poor power to
trace and cancel the black legacy of his own transgression. If any leader, even the high priest, should shout,
"I hereby cleanse your conscience of dead works," we
would answer at least silently, "Who, then, will cleanse
you? We have all gashed the living canvas of Beauty.
Can you speak for Dawn and Dayfall? We have all tres-
passed on a living Right. Can you act as Ultimate and

Creative Goodness?" The judge in John Masefield's poem had deep wisdom. He sentenced the murdered man, and then prayed in secret:

> O God, Thou knowest I'm as blind as he,
> As blind, as frantic, not so single, worse,
> Only Thy pity spared me from the curse.[16]

So newness of life involves a theology—a profounder faith by far than any mere philosophy. Not even prayer can safely be illiterate or unversed. The doctrine of the Cross, whereby the death of Christ, as well as the life of Christ, is apprehended as the focal revelation of God, is still man's ultimate insight. Calvary is *the* solving word. There God is seen as Grief as well as Justice, as Love as well as Righteousness—in whom grief, justice, love, and righteousness are one Flame. There God is seen pronouncing forgiveness, who alone is able to forgive. There God is seen transmuting man's evil, changing the curse into a promise by alchemy of creative love, so that even Golgotha becomes the world's door of hope!

> If in that secret place
> Where thou hast cherished it, there yet is lying
> Thy dearest bitterness, thy fondest sin,
> Though thou hast guarded it with hurt and crying
> Lift now thy face
> Unlock the bolted door and let God in
> And lay it in his holy hands to take:
>
> How such an evil gift can please Him so
> I do not know,
> But, keeping it for wages, he shall make
> Thy foul room sweet for thee with blowing wind
> (He is so serviceable and so kind)
> And set sweet water for thy thirst's distress
> Instead of what thou hadst of bitterness;
> And he shall bend and spread
> Green balsam boughs to make a springing bed
> Where thine own thorns pricked in;
>
> Who would not pay away his dearest sin
> To let such service in?[17]

Prayer must be informed and irradiated by this faith, but the faith cannot become potent save by prayer. There is no counsel for a broken conscience except to say, "Fling yourselves by prayer on the unseen Mercy." The psychiatrist cannot save us, nor the preacher. He also is only a man, and himself wounded in conscience. He, the creature, has no wit to play the Creator. He cannot make or remake the soul. Only Life, grieving and just, loving and holy, can perform the miracle of renewal; and the old prayer, rightly construed, is man's only but sufficient resource:

> Nothing in my hand I bring,
> Simply to Thy cross I cling.[18]

That faith is proved only in venture of prayer. Without prayer conscience is blind, infected, and hopeless. Newness of life comes by friendship with the Giver of life.

Even in modern psychiatry the patient makes, and must make, some kind of a "transfer." He lays on the mind-doctor his burden of sickness. So in prayer we lay on God revealed in Christ the burden of a darkened conscience. The ancient theology of substitution thus returns in new guise. The psychiatrist "gives back" a more realistic mind to the patient whom he must not make "dependent." God "gives back" to man a conscience "cleansed of dead works." The effects of wrong may remain, but only as reminder of grace. The punishment becomes a precious discipline. We are now self-dependent and yet not self-dependent: "I live; yet not I, but Christ liveth in me: and the life which I now live in the flesh I live by the faith of the Son of God, who loved me, and gave himself for me."[19] For Christ is not a picture on the wall of history, and the Cross is not merely a dark happening set in ancient time. Christ is a living Spirit, and the Cross is God's eternal travail. When we pray we do more than contemplate a portrait: we invite a Friend.

This attempt to trace the issue of prayer in our personality has been only an exploratory journey. Others

must cultivate and organize the land into which we have
ventured. Attention, faith, motive, memory, thought,
the subconscious, and the conscience are primal energies; but they do not exhaust the treasures or potencies
of the self. No sufficient account, but only an implied
account, has here been given of prayer and the
pleasure-pain impact of our life, for instance; or of
prayer and our will. But our exploration may have
traced main contours, watersheds, rivers, and lakes.
Enough may have been written to show the necessity
and joy of the Friendship called prayer. We shall turn
now to a discussion of prayer in its major modes, and
inquire concerning the personality value of prayer's various forms. Then we shall try to trace the influence of
corporate prayer. Then we shall perhaps be ready for
our final venture—the attempt to state in straightforward terms a *way* of prayer both for private devotion
and for corporate worship.

experience. Vocation, faith, motive, memory, thought,
the subconscious, and the conscience are primal energies: but they do not exhaust the meaning of personal-
ness.

Chapter XV

PERSONALITY AND PRAYER'S MOODS

THE MOODS OF prayer are as varied as the moods of
men. They form and reform like waves of ocean. They
are the weather which makes fertile the land of man's
deepest Friendship. Sometimes they are as dark as
thunderclouds, or as sudden in joy as a sunburst. They
are as changing as humors and tempers of any soul. We
speak of thanksgiving, confession or intercession. These
differ, or we would not use the different words. Yet they
are the same—one landscape of prayer, one melody of
Friendship in different keys, one white light broken into
spectrum bands. Any mood of prayer trying to stand
alone is poor and weak. Thus confession without
thanksgiving is morbid; contemplation without intercession is selfish; and any prayer without its consecration is
under threat of earthiness. Just as light becomes a richer
gift when prismed into play of color, and music has
wider power through its varying tempos and its major
and minor keys, so prayer through its various moods
leads life to fulfillment. " 'Tis a consummation devoutly
to be wish'd,"[1] a better consummation than Hamlet's
sleep-in-death, and worth our more devout desires. For
this consummation is life-in-Life.

I

Praise means a "breaking out" in spontaneous sound.
To ask why men should feel thankful in face of earth
and sky, and should "break out" in prayers of gratitude,
is like asking why birds should sing: it is their nature.

Birds cannot—and men should not—deny their nature. Complaint is unnatural. Misanthropy is a perversion, as, indeed, we instinctively feel whenever we meet a man like Scrooge.[2] But thanksgiving is normal and "comely." Katherine Mansfield, at a time when she was rejoicing in the tonic mountain air of Switzerland, but lacked religious faith, wrote to a friend, "If only one could make some small grasshoppery sound of praise to someone—thanks to someone. But who?"[3] She dimly knew the answer, or she would not have asked the question. Life is good, despite its tragedy—perhaps because of its tragedy—and we feel, like Katherine Mansfield, that we must sing praise and offer thanks.

How good is man's life, the mere living! how fit to employ
All the heart and the soul and the senses for ever in joy![4]

Praise is man's instinctive celebration of the goodness of life. This gratitude to the Universe is a personal reaction, and therefore testifies of itself to the fact and presence of God.

The Bible's pages are jeweled with thanksgivings as a spring meadow with flowers, and in like beauty. The "Hallelujah Chorus" raises no doubts except in a sour mind. The questions may properly recur at other moments. But that moment is beyond argument. When praise to God breaks thus in waves of exaltation, human nature finds in foretaste its far-off goal. Such laud is man's highest art and richest gift; and it is ultimate, a quintessence of life, an "end of the road." We know then that the forest harp and ocean's multitudinous roar are nature's praise to God, and we surmise that at the creation "the morning stars sang together, and all the sons of God shouted for joy."[5] The witness of Jesus would have been incomplete if at the Last Supper he had not praised God, in heartbreak of courage and faith: "O give thanks unto the Lord: for he is good: because his mercy endureth for ever. It is better to trust in the Lord than to put confidence in man."[6] That song was always sung at the Passover. Sung by Jesus at *that*

Passover and crisis, it was indeed a "sacrifice of praise."

The issues of thanksgiving in personality are not hard to trace, for they flow in light. We are delivered from the curse of ingratitude. Resignation—another proper mood in prayer—is saved from gloominess: it has its counterpart of joy. Wonder is quickened, and wonder is the fountain of discovery. When wonder dies—when we imagine that our sunlamps rival the sun, and that life in its terror and gladness is only drab and "scientific"— the springs of new truth fail. But when we are baffled, silenced, and exalted by the majesty of stars or the gentle glory of Christ, and we give thanks, our whole nature goes questing and new revelations await the quest. Praise likewise gives the outlet to a primal impulse of our nature. Thus it prevents "repression," and grants that glad health which always attends the true release of our nature's energy. The stream of life is not thwarted, to spread destructively as in the ingrate, but goes singing to the Sea. Sorrows then are seen in true proportion: they have their corresponding credit entry in joy. Corporate praise, as in our national Thanksgiving Day, is the antidote of social bitterness. Whenever that fine anniversary is genuinely kept, it quickens a comradely sharing and a resolve to use God's gifts for His sake who gave them. John Masefield's counsel then has deeper tones:

> Best trust the happy moments. What they gave
> Makes man less fearful of the certain grave,
> And gives his work compassion and new eyes.
> The days that make us happy make us wise.[7]

For the profound wisdom of individual or corporate praise is its acknowledgement of a Personal relationship. An exploited earth betrays us, and a possessive human nature turns to dusty death, for earth and man alike belong to God. To glorify God in "wonder, love, and praise" is the foregleam of eternal life.

II

The value of the mood of *confession* has been so tested and verified age on age that prayers of penitence are in every liturgy. In any event, confession would be found in life, for by nature a pent-up power breaks its bounds. True strategy provides a true outlet: "Confession is good for the soul." We have discussed how such prayer lances a festering conscience, and invites true healing. The evil memory is no longer buried to spread its poison underground. It no longer seeps to make wide marshes of anxiety, spitefulness, self-distrust, inability to concentrate, and many another dark neurosis. It has now its open channel. The infection is drained away, and "of the Most High cometh healing."[8] Personality is "square with the world," and, granted some genuine will to make wise reparation, can again meet life with firm step and honest face.

We should here note that confession involves more than wrongdoing. It unburdens fears also, disappointments, and sorrows. Fear is perhaps a primary instinct. It finds us in childhood when we cower beneath bedclothes, follows us in midlife through our dread of poverty or failure or sickness, and overtakes us at last in the vague apprehension of death. When fear is under control and directed to right ends, as when the driver of an automobile fears to "pass on a hilltop," it is our friend. But when it turns to cowardice it is a blackmailing foe: we pay and pay, and still must pay, until we are destitute. The New Testament rightly says, "Fear hath torment."[9] Any psychologist knows that fears must be faced. We cannot forget them, leaving them behind us, for the breath of the pursuing fear is still hot upon us. When fears are faced they may prove unreal. If they are real, they always shrink when honorably faced, and can be conquered. The psychologists are likewise agreed that our fears, once faced, must "come out" in some clear-cut action. Fear of sickness should consult a doctor, and an airplane pilot after a crash should "take off" again soon before fear wins mastery. There is a further prescription on which mind-doctors agree: the facing of fear and the liberating act avail us only when they are held in a basic faith—the faith, namely, that life means well, and that we are intended to prevail over all our frantic fears. Psychology then must turn to religion—or else try, as all too often, to whip up faith by exhortation. This cure applies also to disappointments and sorrows. The healing items are realism, action, and faith:

> Give sorrow words: the grief that does not speak
> Whispers the o'er-fraught heart and bids it break.[10]

The personality value of confession is thus trebly evident. Prayer *is* facing the fact, and asks, when poverty or pain threatens, "Need I fear poverty or affliction? Many a greatheart has been poor, and pain has often become insight." Prayer *is* itself an act, earth's ultimate deed, and it energizes our daily life: "I have spoken my sorrow, and now will find release by sharing in active love my neighbor's grief." Prayer *is* itself faith: it trusts to no mere human exhortation, but flings itself on God and finds that "underneath are the everlasting arms."[11] The New Testament affirms with psychological verity, "There is no fear in love; but perfect love casteth out fear."[12]

At this point a roadside danger sign should be erected. When confession becomes the dominant mood in prayer, and sins and sorrows are endlessly disinterred, prayer becomes morbidly unsound. Prayer should usually be composed in a major key. It should dwell in light, not in shadow. Confession fails unless in the very confession it turns to a prayer of resolve and faith. The Greek word for "repent" implies a rightabout-face. It looks on sin to deplore and confess, but then swings round sharply with resolute will to tread a new path. God does not wish us to remember what He is willing to forget. Yet confession is an essential mood in prayer. Possibly no mood has more instant blessing.

III

The grace of *petitionary prayer* has rarely been understood and almost never acknowledged. Of late it has been flatly denied. For, since the day when we were first bemused by the reiterated incantation of "natural law," petitionary prayer has been granted no place. Its alleged selfishness has been condemned, and its practitioners have been dismissed as childish folk beguiled by magic. This book has pleaded that petitionary prayer springs from crisis. We have said that it is inevitable in our creaturehood, and implicit in all prayer. We have affirmed also that such prayer, though often unanswered, has sometimes, on occasions signal in experience, "turned the event" in a surprise of joy termed heretofore "special Providence." We have further pleaded, in deliberate emphasis, that the description of our world as a realm of natural law is an account so fractional as almost to be false, and that spontaneity is a more characteristic trait of life than regularity. We have suggested that "law" is but the keyboard, whereas the unpredictable play of event and personality is the music. If these judgments are true, as this book unequivocally maintains, and if we do not refuse the revolution in thinking thereby required, petitionary prayer is no longer in disgrace of exile. It returns home to a place of honor.

The particular virtue of petition should have been apparent. We should have seen, when the blight of a misconstrued "natural law" first threatened us, that if man can change nothing by his prayers—if the Friendship on its human side is quite helpless in purposing and planning—man's freehold is lost. A friendship in which one party is always helpless or in prison is hardly worth the name. Our misconstrued "natural law" left both parties in prison. Religion must now openly challenge the misconstruction. Petitionary prayer underscores man's dignity as a man. It saves prayer, and therefore life, from idle stargazing. It keeps prayer's feet on the ground, and sets its hands and hopes to practical tasks. It gives the petition, "Thy will be done," a trumpet sound: it is now a crusade, not merely a sigh of resignation. Petitionary prayer, because it is often a very wrestling with God, is the safeguard of other prayer moods. For instance, mystic communion without the forthrightness and practicality of petition, might become by "absorption into the Infinite" both an escape from the demands of earth and a surrender of the birthright of personality. Friedrich Heiler may be mistaken in claiming for "prophetic prayer" a virtual monopoly, and in dismissing "mystical prayer" as a snare. That verdict seems harsh, for the mystics have spoken with authentic voice; and they have labored in many instances with serviceable zeal. A "both-and" appraisal would have been a truer judgment, it seems, than an "either-or" demand. But Fernand Ménégoz wins assent when he warns that mysticism is always in danger of subtle self-indulgence: it may forget both its own humanity and the practical needs of neighbors, and thus barter its freehold for a cloud of ecstasy. Of course, petitionary prayer also may become selfish, if it is not consecrate to the Kingdom of God. But, when licensed, it saves life from absorption: it maintains man's selfhood under God. Ménégoz writes:

Thus Christian prayer, by pleading before all else for the accomplishment of God's work of redemption, definitely overcomes the gross eudaemonism of primitive religions. And it is doubly great in winning this victory without losing contact with the natural life which, though its positive value is only relative, is, nevertheless, good and approved by God.[13]

Again, and even more incisively, he writes:

Evangelical prayer never destroys the reality of the movement of action and interaction between God and man. At no time does it allow, in the issue of religious faith, the subject to be absorbed in the object or the object in the subject. Prayer always remains a true give-and-take, a real traffic, even sometimes a real combat, between man and the Almighty God. Far from etherealizing itself in a contemplation basically inward-turning, antisocial, passive, and at bottom pessimistic, it breaks forth as a force, at once potent and pure, which raises and regenerates the world."[14]

Petitionary prayer grants to the whole life of prayer a realism and a practicality. Its vision is sound: God is not vague Goodwill, but Active Grace "setting in at single points." Its assumption of human freedom is sound: the freedom is limited, but, if God is man's friend, the freedom is real. Petitionary prayer safeguards man's essential dignity—that birthright of individual spirit which not even prayer may steal. It is therefore a worthy Friendship—a Comradeship in planning, in labor, and in communion—and not merely a "cloud of mystic light." Such a mood in prayer has manifest dangers. It needs the company and counsel of other moods: it is like Peter among the apostles. But it is an essential mood. It has its own essential blessing both for prayer and life.

IV

How is personality enhanced by prayer's mood of *intercession?* Many of our intercessions are petitionary: they pray God to turn the shadow from our neighbor's door, or to prosper him on his journeyings. So if our recent distrust of petition is invalid, our misgivings about intercession are also dispelled. Conversely, the peculiar grace that attends petition awaits also on intercession. But the urgency of human love in prayer, which urgency is intercession's mark, has its *distinctive* gifts. All life is under threat of selfishness. Prayer is not immune. One wonders if Simeon Stylites was deeply concerned for the people of Antioch. He wrote numerous epistles of advice on issues of the day to emperors, bishops, and councils. But these may have been a subtle self-glorifying, just as his pillar forty cubits high and his iron collar may have been exhibitionism or a bid for heaven's special favor. How much did he love the crowds who gathered at rumor of his dying? Did he die for them, for God, or for himself? Did he yearn in compassion over the city which loved him, and honored his very corpse as a "sacred body to be our wall and bulwark"? Or was he cursed by an inward-turning eye? We cannot know. Some of the epistles recommended intolerance.[15] That fact accords more closely with self-righteousness than with love. But we dare not draw judgment, especially adverse judgment, from our ignorance. He may have been a saint in truth, and must have been a saint within measure. If we have misgivings, they should turn from him to ourselves, as reminder that even prayer can become a self-indulgence and a self-assertion. In this realm also we gain life only by losing it.

We need not seek far for the grace which intercession sends on the intercessor. It is the more evident because he may neither know nor covet it. An unruly young artist, noting the change in his mother's face, asked her the reason. She said, "Your mother has prayed much for you." He answered, "Well, it makes fine lines." She neither knew the lines, nor desired them. Nevertheless prayer drew them in nobility and insight. Selfishness, whether of miser or worldling, is a prison; but love, whether of philanthropist or parent, is a gracious liberty. Love-in-prayer has vaster bounds: it is caught up into the eternity of God, for God is love. Is this the ultimate sublimation of those deep and varied urges which Freud categorized under the name "sex"? Is this the true "will to power" which Adler maintained is man's distinctive mark—self-assertion being fulfilled paradoxically by love's self-denial? When the hard counsel is obeyed, "Love thyself last: cherish those hearts that hate thee,"[16] and intercession is offered for an enemy, tolerance comes with understanding, and the breach may be healed. When friends are the object of love-in-prayer, their needs and virtues are more acutely read: friendship becomes more serviceable, and the bonds of human devotion are made stronger because they are woven now into the bonds of a Higher Love. Meanwhile the intercessor finds release. The clamant self no longer has dominion. The stagnant pool finds outflow. Sorrows are assuaged in concern for others'

sorrows, and joys made radiant by joy in others' joy.
"And the Lord turned the captivity of Job, when he
prayed for his friends."[17] When our country or our fellow men are our theme in prayer, wisdom deepens: we
see mankind, if not as Jesus saw them from his cross,
then at least with eyes cleansed by a divine compassion.
The richest gain remains: intercession is the very intensity of the true Friendship: for "he that dwelleth in
love dwelleth in God, and God in him."[18]

V

Contemplation is not characteristic of our age, much
less *contemplative and meditative prayer*. Perhaps that
is why our age is arid and violent. Because we are creatures, the fundamental tone both of prayer and life must
be receptiveness. This the scientist knows: he listens as
a little child: only so can he enter the Kingdom. This
the artist knows: he studies the masters as a suppliant,
and, even then, is not made strong until he kneels again
and again to drink at Nature's well. We prefer active
thought and trenchant deeds to contemplation. So
thought is often blind, and deeds are often cruel. Likewise we prefer realism to wonder and awe. So realism
becomes only earthiness, and we rightly guess that a
book described as "realistic" is likely to be sordid.

Prayer does not reckon its profits, for prayer is a
Communion. But there are gains in friendship—
provided we do not surrender the friendship in coveting
the gains. We have claimed that prayer's quietness stills
the busy mind, and gives the subconscious its opportunity to grant "flashes," or to carry through to completion the processes of conscious thought. That claim is
pertinent to contemplative prayer. Contemplation is the
gateway of truth, as any scientist or artist knows; and of
awe, as all the saints can testify. Truth and awe are
their own treasure. In this connection Fernand
Ménégoz quotes a striking comment of Maurice Maeterlinck:

To think is often to deceive oneself, and the thinker who has lost his way has frequent need, before he can find it again, to return to the place where those who hardly think at all have remained faithfully seated round a silent but necessary truth. They guard the fire of the tribe; and others carry the torches, and, when the torch begins to flicker in too thin air, must wisely come back to the fire. A world where there were only thinkers might perhaps lose the guiding idea of more than one indispensable truth. Actually, the thinker continues to think justly only as he does not lose contact with those who do not think at all.[19]

The distinction thus drawn is perhaps too drastic: those who guard the fire have need also to carry the torches, lest they should drowse or be lost in a mystic ecstasy. The contemplators must also be thinkers. But Maeterlinck is deeply right: the thinkers must ever and again become contemplators. Truth comes of a "wise passiveness," and beauty flows from nature's springs. We cannot be coerced; but, when a man looks long in silence on the mystery of the world and the deeper mystery of the Cross of Christ, it falls gently on the mind like dew upon a thirsty field.

Sometimes the contemplation gathers such light and fire as to become a mystic rapture—"the flight of the alone to the the Alone." This height of prayer has its psychological price; as, for instance, in that trough of the spirit called by the mystics "the dark night of the soul."[20] There are moral dangers also, as we have hinted. This rapture may so exalt a man that he forgets earth and flesh, which are still the ordained terms of our mortal adventure, the challenge and instrument of our spirit. It may so beguile him that he loses compassion, and ignores the workaday needs of his neighbors. It may tempt him even to barter his patrimony of individual selfhood. But if mystic communion is kept in comradeship with other moods of prayer, if it is trained to appreciate "brother body" and "sister earth," if rapture is accepted when it comes rather than covetously sought at all times, mystic communion is life's solving moment. Then the burden of the flesh is lifted. Then earth becomes God's shadow, and time His tread. Then assurance is sealed that "everything matters, nothing matters," since all is held in the love of God.

VI

We have singled only a few striking colors in prayer's spectrum. Many an intermediate shade we have ignored. But we would err in grievous disproportion if we should fail to mark one dominant band—call it the infrared, if you will—that of *adoration and consecration.* The final mood of prayer is, "Holy, holy, holy, Lord." For we are creatures, and He is God "before whom angels veil their faces." All true prayer is worship—the ascription of worth to the Eternal. Without adoration, thanksgiving may become a miserliness, petition a selfish clamor, intercession a currying of special favors for our friends, and even contemplation may turn into a refined indulgence.

The mood of prayer into which all other moods resolve is a consecration: "Nevertheless not my will, but thine, be done."[21] Thanksgiving is a rightful mood, but it is spoiled unless the gifts for which we are grateful are made an oblation. Confession is necessary, demanded alike by integrity of conscience and by our pent-up fears and sorrows; but our sins in their consequence must be left finally in God's kind discipline, and our fears and sorrows must be offered as a sacrifice to His will. Petition is valid, a title deed of man's freehold, but every freehold belongs to the Creator, and our clamant desire must still do homage to His light and love. Contemplation, by its very nature, fails unless it becomes an acceptance. Christ's prayer in Gethsemane was a petition: "O my Father, if it be possible, let this cup pass from me."[22] But he, who wore our human flesh, recognized a Purpose higher than human—"if it be possible" —and therefore kept the petition within the bonds of consecration: "Nevertheless not my will, but thine." The exiled and fugitive David, stricken by fever, in the loneliness of his mountain cave, longed in his delirium for a cooling drink from "the well of Bethlehem," the scene of his boyhood's happiness. But when heroic followers risked life to bring the cup, he would not drink it: "Nevertheless he would not drink thereof, but poured it out unto the Lord. And he said, be it far from me, O Lord, that I should do this: is not this the blood of the men that went in jeopardy of their lives? therefore he would not drink it."[23] The word translated "poured it out" is that used of an oblation. It describes the act of a priest at an altar. Prayer at long last is an altar and oblation. All life, its treasure of earth, its bitterness of sorrow, its shame of sin, even joys coveted as dearly as David longed for "water from the well of Bethlehem," are poured out in consecration. By this surrender prayer finds a "service which is perfect freedom." In this loss prayer wins its richest gain.

Chapter XVI

PERSONALITY AND PRAYER'S FORMS

LET MY PRAYER be set forth before thee as incense; and the lifting up of my hands as the evening sacrifice."[1] That petition grows, like Prince Ahmed's tent, to cover all the forms of prayer. Incense, rising to the sky to please the nostrils of God, is any altar or church. The lifted hands of the throng in the Temple Court betoken all prayer's gestures. The evening sacrifice symbolizes the whole gamut of religious services. Why this complicated structure of prayer? It would seem that a Friendship so elemental should need no elaborate fashion and deportment. Do not forms stifle the intimacy and artlessness which prayer requires? Forms are unyielding, while friendship and God's spirit are free. Forms are ostentatious, while communion with God is quiet and hidden. Why should prayer be swathed, and perhaps smothered, in ceremonial? Is personality thereby enriched? The issue is as wide as life, as vivid, and as vital. We shall not expect to find any rule of thumb. But we have need to find some rule of head and heart.

I

Forms seem inevitable in our world. We are not disembodied spirits: we are *bodied* spirits. Every invisible is made articulate in our life by a visible. Patriotism has its flag, and the marriage vow its ring. Even ghosts we represent as white shrouds with clanking chains. Perhaps body and spirit are at essence one—matter has now been resolved into radioactive energies—but to our

dim sight they are two in one: the body is at once the
limitation and expression of the spirit. So gladness takes
form in smiles or dancing; grief, with us, in black gar-
ments and tears. Even thought has its external fashion:
Rodin's "Thinker" sits with arm resting on knee, chin
cupped in hand, and eyes intently fixed. Every mood.
not least the profoundest mood called prayer, has its instinctive gestures and gathers its appropriate symbols.
There is little use in asking why:

> Why grass is green, or why our blood is red,
> Are mysteries that none have reach'd unto.[2]

Why body and soul are "marvelously compact together" is part of the ultimate enigma of creation.

Man's primal faith is that God himself accepts the
terms of earth. He is Spirit made known through flesh.
By this faith every visible thing is a word, and the whole
creation the vast sign language of God. So men are
prompted to read the stars, in times past by astrology
and in our time by astronomy; and to inquire for the
meaning of events in "the signs of the times." Do we
not constantly exclaim, as people touched by a mystery,
"How strange it should have happened so"? Does not
the Bible say grandly, "For the invisible things of him
from the creation of the world are clearly seen, being
understood by the things that are made"?[3] Thus Milton
wrote,

> What if Earth
> Be but the shadow of Heaven, and things therein
> Each to the other like, more than on Earth is thought![4]

Man's bravest and sublimest creed is that Christ is the
Eternal "Word made flesh." In such a world prayer
cannot be formless. The Quakers do not escape ritual:
they escape only elaborate ritual. Their plain room, the
long bench on which elders sit facing the congregation,
the cult of silence, the punctuation of silence by the
words of those whom the Spirit has moved, the distinctive vocabulary—the "thee" and "thou," the "concern"

and the "opening"—and the handclasp between the
presiding elder and his neighbor to indicate the close of
worship—these are all a symbolism. Forms are inevitable in a world where a man draws a distinction between
"me" and "my body"; and the plea, "I do not believe in
forms of prayer," will gather sense instead of nonsense
only when the pleader can walk instantly through a con-
crete wall.

A shallow skepticism dismisses all present religious
forms as the vestigia of primitive magic. It would be as
wise to repudiate medicine because it was once sorcery.
In any event, both the magic and the sorcery testified to
realities, and prophesied a better wisdom. Mario Puglisi
writes: "For primitive mentalities, which are essentially
realistic and materialist, the image of anything is equivalent to the reality which it represents. . . . . Hence
the origin of ritual dramas, mimetic rites, rites of initia-
tion, by means of which primitive man considers that he
can subject the world to his will." But he promptly re-
treats from this generalization, asking, "Can it really be
proved, with convincing arguments, that in the beginning man, in order to obtain release from the evils that
threatened him and the mastery over hostile powers,
made use exclusively of exorcisms and incantations, and
was altogether ignorant of prayer?"[5] and proceeds to
give examples of primitive prayers so pure in motive as
almost to put to shame our modern liturgies. Spirit and
form are the dual aspect of man's life. Forms evolve as
man evolves. They should improve, but they cannot be
refused. Even skepticism must find form in word and
writing. It has even its jargon and its incantations.
Forms can be destroyed, but not form. Spirit and form
are joined together for this life. No iconoclasm can ever
divide them.

II

Then which forms of prayer are best? Let answer be
postponed until the truth is underscored that any form
can be a threat. The danger of a form is idolatry, the

ignoring of the Reality for the image. Perhaps all idolatry, ancient or modern, comes in part of selfishness—self-idolatry. If God is only in the form, He need not be in the conduct. If God is only in our shrine, He is our possession and other folk are outcast. If God is only in the temple, He is safely imprisoned: the weekdays are ours, the streets are ours, and we need not change our ways: we are spared the mental venture and ethical devotion demanded by a God who is Holy Love everywhere and for all men. It is easy to offer only an image-ritual. The incense and the lifted hands are a very convenient escape. It is pleasant to be free in our own devices. Small wonder that the Bible at its noblest inveighs against idolatry, and warns us against formalism as against the curse! The commandments enjoin us: "Thou shalt not make unto thee any graven image, or any likeness of any thing. . . . . Thou shalt not bow down thyself to them, nor serve them."[6] Hezekiah smashed the "brasen serpent that Moses had made," the prized symbol of Israelitish redemption, because his people were offering incense to it; and he called it with saving realism, "Nehushtan"—"It is only brass!"[7] Micah thundered with mountain voice against a religion that had become a solemn farce, the ceremonial substitute for honest living: "What doth the Lord require of thee, but to do justly, and to love mercy, and to walk humbly with thy God?"[8] And Jesus said in acid words, "Ye make clean the outside of the cup and of the platter, but within they are full of extortion and excess."[9]

Sometimes idolatry may be pitiable rather than blamable—the token of our fear to trust the soul's surmise, the sign of our pathetic dependence on the visible. Sometimes idolatry may seem almost noble in its blind devotion. Then it is even more pathetic, as Evelyn Underhill's poem makes clear:

> I dreamed I was an Idol, still and grave;
> Too cold to comfort, and too weak to save.
> Sad angels watched me, and before my face
> One kneeling worshipper implored my grace.

No gift he asked, no favor did entreat
But this—to live for ever at my feet;
There, rapt in selfless ecstasy, to raise
Anthems of longing, litanies of praise.

So I sat dreaming, whilst through endless years
His psalm and his devotion reached my ears;
And grieving angels cried unceasingly,
"He, who so worships, should the Idol be."[10]

But almost always idolatry is admixed with self-idolatry. If countenanced, it kills the spirit, buries it in the form, and worships the grave. Its final issue is materialism— as if a betrothed girl should value her engagement ring not for what it represents, but for its gold and diamonds; or as if a man should attend Communion Service for the taste of the wine. Our heart's desire, if only we could read it, is God. But often we hide some low desire, which we think is heart's desire, under the forms of worship. Thus we deceive ourselves, and perhaps even try to deceive God. It is a sobering fact that whenever religious ritual has flourished, gathering its cult and its priesthood in ostentation, ethic and prayer alike have suffered eclipse. It is an equally sobering fact that every religious revival has broken the shackles of forms. So dangerous is this incrustation of custom, whether in life or prayer, that age after age revolutions have smashed our images as ruthlessly as Hezekiah smashed the serpent of brass. John Milton arraigned even the Episcopal Prayer Book and its oft-repeated collects, declaring with scorn that they were "cuckoo-notes."[11] John Bunyan and George Fox likewise warned men against the peril of printed prayers and worship by rote. The Independents in England rejected even the Lord's Prayer in public worship: they saw, whatever else they may have missed, that repetition easily becomes what Jesus called "vain repetition," a mere self-hypnotism. Tennyson significantly describes a church "in which he scarce could spy the Christ for Saints."[12] Every form is a potential danger.

III

But despite the iconoclasts—the destroyers of icons—we shall never escape forms. With each revolution new forms emerge, and when the tumult has subsided old forms return in new guise. Micah condemns ritual, but Ezekiel is called to restore a broken altar. Some *practices* of prayer seem to have great survival value. Telling the beads of the rosary will occur to mind as an instance. According to the Roman Church, the rosary had a miraculous origin: St. Dominic received it in a vision from the Virgin, carried it to a church to which the people had been mysteriously summoned, and persuaded them to its use—his plea being prospered by a violent thunderstorm in which the image of the Virgin moved her finger and pointed to heaven. Actually the rosary had early Asiatic origin, and may have been used first by ancient Buddhists. It has obvious dangers, but it could not have endured if it were bereft of value. The fact should be noted that the Roman Church recognizes the dangers. It is emphatic in teaching that the rosary has value only if the devotee is attentive in prayer, thoughtful in meditation, and sincere in motive. Certain *spoken forms* of prayer have likewise lasted through the centuries. The word "Amen"—"So let it be"—is an instance. Another is the antiphon beginning in the words of the minister, "The Lord be with thee," and continuing in the response of the congregation, "And with thy spirit." That form has been used since earliest Christian days, as has also the ancient ascription, "Holy, Holy, Holy, Lord God of Hosts." Certain *rites and ceremonies* accompanying prayer have endured, notably baptism in various forms, and the celebration of the sacrament of the Lord's Supper. This persistence of forms is not due mainly to ingrained conservatism. Religious observance can and does become perfunctory. But there has always been a nucleus in the Church to whom these forms have been the gateway to life; and, in any event, genuine prayer is never formless. Forms persist because they enrich life.

Then what *is* the value of a form? An initial answer, not deep-probing but not without point, might show that a form has the value of any good habit. When daily life is ordered on wise custom we are saved the necessity of constant minor decisions, and the mind is released to higher tasks. When we learn to walk by habit, the habit sets us free to think and talk while we walk. A writer, an artist, and a scientist each has his "chapel," his desk or studio or laboratory, and his "ritual." These speed his labor. Forms grant to the praying man a similar "cue" and liberation.

But there are deeper blessings. Let us try to state them in sharp phrase. A form provides a *focus,* like a lens catching and uniting the scattered rays of the sun. It gives concentration to the vague moods of the worshiper, and thus provides an opening for the Invisible before whom he bows. Human nature needs this focus. That child had more than a child's wisdom who, when her mother assured her that God is everywhere, answered emphatically, "But I need a God who is somewhere." In an old story, God allowed Naaman to carry back to his city of Damascus "two mules' burden of earth" from the Israelitish soil on which he had been healed.[13] When the soil was placed in the pagan temple, "the house of Rimmon," Naaman could worship the true God on God's own ground! That permission was a concession to Naaman's weakness. The concession was necessary. In some degree, it is always necessary. Incense curling to the sky verifies for man the Mystery "whom the heaven of heavens cannot contain." The unison lifting up of hands in the Temple Court, as the knights of King Arthur were wont to lift the hilt of the sword in token of the cross, gathers restless bodies into a resolve, and restless wills into obedience to the Will. The stated time of worship—"the evening sacrifice"—and the sacrifice itself may banish alien thoughts, and shape man's spirit to a spear thrust of desire and dedication. In every realm man is a maker of symbols. Patriotism, politics, trade, the home, and especially religion, are beset with them. In prayer the symbol is the meeting point of God and man. On one side of it God's "everywhere" becomes by His grace "there"—as on one side of an arch—and on the other side the paths of man's nature converge. The Invisible is there made near and poignant, as in a crucifix or chancel window, and man's divided self is focused in devotion. Small wonder that our various "icons" have become dear: the inconoclast can never utterly destroy them.

Forms have another value; they *unite* men in holiest bond. To sing a hymn, to join in scriptural response, or to pray together audibly the words of some great prayer may weld a congregation into one life. The visible token, the sacrament of the Lord's Supper for instance, doubtless asks from each worshiper some surrender of individual preference; but it gives him as compensation the enthusiasm of a sacred cause. The surrender of personal idiosyncrasies is a price wisely paid for the gains of a worthy commonalty. In this instance the price is not too exacting, for it is a merit of forms that they have no sharp coercion. A creed may divide men. It should not, for a great creed should be sung rather than debated. It is a banner unfurled to quicken our loyalty and hope: *credo* means in its core, "I trust and pledge my soul to." But we have made our creeds excursions into theology; and, because they are thus in the climate of argument rather than of fealty, they often set men at variance. But a symbol unites, for a symbol is in the atmosphere of worship. Moreover, because it is *one* symbol it unites men, while it still permits each worshiper to pour into it his individual faith. Therein is the value of a church of fine architecture: negatively it delivers us from the distractions of the everyday world, and positively it provides a symbol which unites worshipers without laying them under bondage. The shadowed depth of the chancel betokens Mystery; the cross on the altar focuses all eyes on the symbol of the Mystery made flesh; and the *Sanctus* meanwhile welds all who hear it in one holy life.

One other value of forms, among many values yet unmentioned, may here be noted: they *recapture* the

holy vows and ecstacies of other days. They recreate for
us

> Those hours of life that were a bursting fount,
> Sparkling the dusty heart with living springs.[14]

Once as we rode in an automobile there came over the
radio the voices of a choir singing the hymn, "Now the
Day Is Over."[15] That is always the closing hymn at
vespers at the lakeside where we spend the summer.
Even though we were now in the midst of city traffic,
the calmness and the sense of a Presence of those ves-
per hours came back instantly at the beckoning of a
prayer form. The *Mass in B Minor* of Bach gives at the
sixth hearing not only the inspiration of that particular
experience, but also echoes of five other times of insight. Clasped hands and bowed head may be enough to
turn the key in the treasury door of all our past prayers.
Thus a ritual or liturgy is both a spring and reservoir: it
grants new gifts and stores up earlier benedictions. The
oftener it is used, other factors being constant, the more
wealth it holds. We need not be surprised that forms
persist. They are a *focus* both for the Mystery vaguely
apprehended and for man's distracted self; they are a
bond uniting men in worship; and they are a *memento*
and *treasury* of past benedictions. Yet their danger remains. The focus may still become a dead end, the bond
a prison, and the treasury a fatal conservatism.

IV

Then which forms of prayer are best? There is no
rule of thumb, for the reason that every thumbprint is
different and distinct. Some *habit* of prayer is clearly
wise, for all life is built on habit; but the habit should be
under frequent scrutiny lest it harden into a confining
shell. Some *gesture* of prayer is wise. Here also there
can be no general prescription. Men have knelt, stood
with face upturned, sat haunched with eyes closely focused, and lain prostrate. They have prayed with hands
raised to the sky—the early Christians misconstrued the

history of that gesture, and adopted it because it seemed
to imitate the sufferings of Jesus on the cross—with
hands covering the face, with hands bearing gifts,
with hands clapping in rhythm, with hands clasped, and
with hands close-fisted beating on the breast.[16] These
facts warn us against dogmatism, but they testify to the
value of *some* gesture-accompaniment in prayer. "Un-
clasp your fists, and your anger will go," said a wise old
counsel. It is too optimistic, but has its truth. "Fold
your hands in prayer, or lift them to the sky, and reverence will come," is also, within limits, sage guidance.
That is to say, a gesture releases the random energies of
the body, and cuts a physical channel through which the
spirit may flow. Audible speech has this power in unu-
sual measure: words clarify the vague resolve and
themselves carry it into the deed. Again, some *rhythm*
in prayer's forms is wise. Hence our "orders of worship" with their changing moods and energies. Speech
and silence should both have place, for one is active and
the other receptive. Repetition gives deeper and deeper
imprint to a prayer, but becomes mere rote unless bal-
anced by newness. So liturgy and "free prayer" each
claim place and bestow a mutual good. All prayer's
moods, as we have seen, should find their due expression. Rhythm gives that relaxation and "reversed effort"
by which thoughts mature and wise practice is ingrained.

These suggestions need not be multiplied: we shall
venture some specific guidance in later chapters. But we
shall be guilty of grievous omission if we fail to study
Jesus' practice of prayer. He best can "sift like wheat"
the judgments we have passed on the necessity, danger,
and value of prayer's forms. He would warn us that his
practice should be our clue, not our chain.

"Time makes ancient good uncouth."[17]

And God fulfills himself in many ways,
Lest one good custom should corrupt the world."[18]

But in any age Jesus' practice gives light. Then what
were *his* forms of prayer? He prayed in the synagogue

and the Temple. Despite his protest against the blindness of the scribes and the greed of the priests, he found
grace in the commonly accepted ritual, and kept the
bond of worship with his neighbors. He prayed also in
the little group of the disciples. He prayed alone on the
mountainside by night, and in the evening quiet of the
fields.[19] He recommended the "inner chamber" and
the "shut door"—some wonted retreat of prayer. He
taught the Lord's Prayer, if not as a form, then certainly
as a norm. He approved also, by example or direct injunction, certain rites and sacraments. He used the ritual
of the "laying on of hands" to vivify the coming of God's
spirit to bless and heal.[20] He accepted baptism. For himself it was apparently a sign that he made common cause
with human need;[21] for other men it betokened the renunciation and cleansing away of an old life, and the
incoming and resolute acceptance of a new life. He instituted the Lord's Supper as a vigil of "remembrance" of
his life and death in all their profound meaning; and he
thus made, as we must later describe,[22] a Holy of holies
for Christian prayer. That form is at once our *Eucharist*
in thanksgiving, our *Communion* with God and our
neighbors, and a *Sacrament* (a Holy Ordinance) in very
truth. He instituted another form now forgotten, so Dr.
John Oman[23] maintains: he bade his disciples shake off
from their feet the dust of the village that would not receive them—for symbol that they could not dilute their
message, and for token that they must leave in God's
hands their success or failure. Dr. Oman calls this form
"The Sacrament of Failure." Perhaps he is right: in our
world we need such a ritual! It is clear that Jesus used
forms in worship and commended them, even while he
warned against their danger.

V

Can we now fashion some guidance for our prayer
forms? Forms of prayer are inevitable, dangerous, and
precious. Wise folk will come to terms with these three
facts. They will not despise forms, for forms are inescapable in our life of earth and flesh. They will not suc-

cumb to forms: "For the letter killeth, but the spirit giveth life."[24] They will choose and use the forms which
best focus God's mystery and the self's pure resolve,
best unite them with their neighbors, and best enshrine
the spiritual treasure of past days. Here the conservative
and the liberal each has truth. The liberal sees the dangers; the conservative sees the values. The liberal insists: "But man is a spiritual being, ever making forms
and ever breaking them. He must break them, or they
will imprison him. At best they are only his home, and
homes decay: they are not his life." The conservative
insists: "But forms *are* life, for here on earth spirit is
unknown and unexpressed save through the flesh. Without forms God is everywhere but not somewhere. Without forms man's life lacks concentration and resolve.
Without forms man is alien from his neighbor, and the
treasure of the past goes to waste. Forms must abide if
they would serve us: they should be honored in their
abiding." To both liberal and conservative the onlooker
may reply in gratitude to both: "But it is still true that
forms are necessary, dangerous, and precious. Formless
prayer would be as empty and homeless as the stratosphere, and merely formalistic prayer as gross as earth
without the sky."

So, in the nature of the case, only general counsel can
be given. In private prayer those forms are best which
best help a man to realize the presence of God made
known in Christ. Some people pray better walking or
standing, others better kneeling. In our Western world
kneeling seems to suit best both the supplication of man
and the majesty of God. Some people are helped in
prayer by the closing of the eyes, for the world is clamant; others by gazing on some picture or image of
Christ. Most people find it wise to have a quiet corner
in the home or a retreat on the hillside where a chapel
of habit may be built. Most people find it wise to pray
audibly, for words are the cleansing and the spear thrust
of the spirit; but silence also should have wide place,
since prayer is receptiveness, contemplation, awe, and
the communion which asks no words. Most people need
guidance and stimulus from the great prayers of the past

and from the Book of books. Most people find that the
beginning and end of the day are best times for prayer,
and would be helped if between times they sought some
church for quiet meditation. There is no rule of thumb,
but there is this straight word of warning: our generation knows the folly and unworthiness of empty forms,
but our generation is not yet wise enough to know that
worthy prayer can never be either formless or haphaz-
ard.

As for corporate prayer, in matters of taste and temperament there is no dispute. People are not *theologi-
cally* Roman Catholic or Quaker: they are *tempera-
mentally* Roman Catholic or Quaker. The theology
enters and it is important as an issue of intellectual honesty; but temperament largely determines the value of a
form. An elaborate ritual has dangers: it leads easily to
a mild or more vicious idolatry. But the attempt to outlaw all ritual has dangers: it may leave prayer inarticulate and therefore poor, and it may alienate us from the
host of neighbors who cannot worship without some
symbolism. "The golden mean" would seem the wise
rule. There should be some simplicity of family prayer,
some hallowing of highest friendship by group prayer,
some congregational celebration of our common life before the Unseen Face of God. The congregational
prayer should provide a worthy setting in visible symbols, in litanies and liturgies, in "free prayer" and silence. Individual need must be the index of elaboration
in the ritual—provided always that the individual worshiper does not exalt his tastes unduly or insist on his
own individual temple, but gladly makes partial surrender of preference for the sake of a common life held in
God. Pageantry has its place, perhaps more wisely as an
occasion than as a custom. There is no rule; but broad
human need and the test of time are probably best met
by an order of corporate worship which combines simplicity with reverence: the symbolism should be enough,
but not too much, to fulfill the prayer aspirations of that
uncommon spirit called "the common man." Perhaps in
coming days a large and vigorous church will include in
its range of worship all those major forms which have

proved through the years a "means of grace"—from Roman liturgy through Methodist liberty to Quaker silence. Perhaps, even then, its most constant prayer will be, "Lord, that this form may be a door, not an idol. Lord, that my worship may be my guide, and not my chain."

Chapter XVII

PERSONALITY AND CORPORATE PRAYER

CAN'T A MAN pray without belonging to a church?" The order of the word implies a question, but the tone of voice spells impatience and revolt. Our world has little use for corporate prayer. Even in many churches the prayer meeting is defunct. The "cause of death" was not single: there were many ailments, and praying folk were not blameless. But one major cause was the failure to see any necessity for corporate prayer. Sincerely religious people say, "But prayer in its very nature is private—a direct and secret dealing with God." The only answer is, "Yes and no." If we must choose one word or be shot at sunrise, the answer then is, "No." Prayer is private, but not altogether private. It could be altogether private only if our life were altogether individual. It will demand corporate expression as long as life is held within the corporate bond. A man can be an athlete alone, but he is a finer athlete within the team experience: in baseball the spectators and players alike look askance at "the individual performer" who nurses his batting average. A man can be a musician alone, forever playing solos, but he is an impoverished musician until he knows choral and symphonic music. A man can pray alone, and should, but his prayer also is incomplete without its comradeship.

I

In strict fact no man is alone. This the Middle Ages knew, with whatever blind spots elsewhere, and looked for a kingdom of God on earth. But succeeding ages proposed an individualism, and so, by paradox, lost the man in the mass. The exploration and exploitation of the planet fell prey to greed, and greed destroys the comradeship. The cult of goods blinds men to the common good and to the Good. Despite our knowledge and skills, wiser times may look back on these latter centuries, earth-centered and man-centered, with their trade scramble and mass bloodshed, as an age of eclipse. Are we on the edge of deeper darkness, or in the morning twilight? The daybreak, when it comes, will rediscover the oneness of mankind. No man is alone. In athletics even the discus thrower is not alone: he is indebted to his neighbors both for example and for the discus. A musician shut off from the world, playing his solos, is still not alone; for others made the violin, composed the music, taught the art, and printed the score. A hermit is not born a hermit: he is born a son. He is nurtured in family loyalty and social resource. He can live as a recluse only by the bestowals of our common life. A tiny child will put food into his mother's mouth, perhaps because his awareness is still so dim that he and his mother seem still one life. Then comes *self*-realization—a difference of action and perhaps a conflict of wills. The child learns to say, "They—I." But he could not realize the "I" without the "they." How in such a world can prayer endure without its corporate form? The "old-fashioned prayer meeting" may have invited banishment by intolerance and hypocrisy. The mood and method may have been wrong. But the need and impulse were not wrong: *they* are in man's constitution "from the foundation of the world."

Our *work,* however individual, is a togetherness. A machine civilization is like great hands drawing mankind into closer neighborhood. An oxcart may have been to some extent an individual venture: one man can make and drive an oxcart. But one man cannot make and drive a Boeing plane: he needs the miner, the inventor, the mechanic, the radio expert; and in our passenger airlines there must be four men on the ground for every pilot in the air. Rampant individualism is

doomed. Its present chaos is token of its impending
death: it is like the devil in Revelation, "having great
wrath, because he knoweth that he hath but a short
time."[1] Not in toil only, but in every mood and action,
men are held in community. We *sorrow* alone and together: "The heart knoweth his own bitterness,"[2] but,
"Misery loves company," and, "A trouble shared is a
trouble halved." We *rejoice* alone and together: joy is
an incommunicable secret, but the shepherd who finds a
lost sheep "calleth together his friends and neighbors,
saying unto them, Rejoice with me."[3] We *think* alone
and together: poetry is a lonely venture, but what a kindling of mutual minds when poets meet! We need not
belabor instances. The word of T. S. Eliot gathers all
instances:

> What life have you if you have not life together?
> There is no life that is not in community,
> And no community not lived in praise of GOD.[4]

The last sentence anticipates our progress. Our present
concern is to underscore a forgotten truth: "alone" and
"together" are the two sides of one shield.

II

How shall we group and measure the enchantments
that come through the common life? "Crowd psychology" is in ill repute, as though crowd influence were of
necessity debasing and violent. The very words "crowd
psychology" bring pictures of a destructive and murder-
ous mob. But there are as many kinds of crowd, good
and bad, as there are kinds of crowd-purpose. The
lynching crowd, a smudge on our national life, appeals
to blood lust and sends a man home "sunk i' the scale."
The demagogic crowd sometimes calls for self-surrender
to a cause represented as noble, but its gains are small
and its degradations great; for it appeals not to wide
love in noble dedication, but to hatred and the narrow
gods of class, nation, or race.[5] The football crowd is
worthier: some onlookers are pleased and others disap-

pointed, but most applaud: they know that "The game's the thing" in sportsmanship. The spectator or player in such a crowd returns home weary but with inward accord. The symphony concert crowd has still higher claims. There "crowd psychology" is under no suspicion. This is no mob ravaged by blood lust. This togetherness inflicts on nobody the sting of hate or defeat: it lives by its appreciations. The crowd almost makes the occasion: the musician gathers incentive from the commonalty and the hearer finds treasures never found in an empty concert hall. Meanwhile the music fashions the crowd into fineness, as gold is wrought in some genial fire. Each listener is cleansed as by a river which quickens even while it cleanses. He is illumined, and lifted high above the

> fretful stir
> Unprofitable, and the fever of the world.[6]

Who could condemn such a crowd? It does not debase the individual, but raises him, sometimes to "the seventh heaven." Then what of the prayer crowd? When the prayer is worthy, it is highest in the whole order of crowds. It enlists architecture, art, music, and liturgy for the contemplation of God made known in Christ. It celebrates all life before the Unseen Eyes. The worshiper returns home with a glow on the mind. He is now one with his fellows at their best: his prison of self is broken: he is proud of the pageant and pilgrimage of earth. He is now one with God: there is light above all clouds, land below all tossing oceans: cloud and ocean, earth and man, are held in the Everlasting Arms. This togetherness is the fulfillment of life.

So crowd psychology is good or bad according as its purpose and leadership are good or bad. Group influence has been so marked in religion that some thinkers have assumed, mistakenly but credibly, that religion is only social passion and God only a vague personalization of the common life.[7] We cannot classify or measure this increment in personality. It is more than increment: it is the quickening and completion of our whole nature. Even physical health is served. Team play strengthens the body, not merely through the muscle exercise involved, but through the spirit of comradeship. Enthusiasm for a cause in the joy of commonalty enables the watchers and marchers of a parade, or even a football crowd, to brave ill weather almost with impunity. If the flesh is thus blessed, what of mind and heart? The treasure is manifold and beyond measure. The imagination is quickened: lovers become poets. Thought is prompted: after great music or the meeting of some "Johnsonian Circle" the individual has ideas better than he knew. Motives are purified: the petty fears of introspection are dispelled, and windows are thrown open to a summer air. The lonely soul is no longer lonely: he has found friendship and the wide horizon.

The dangers of a low crowd psychology are as real as an epidemic. They would be sharply decreased if our commercial greed had not condemned multitudes of folk to a constant struggle, with its accompanying insecurity and bitterness, and thereby made them the easy prey of the demagogue. That fact should be scored. It is easy to use "crowd psychology" as scapegoat for our social ills. To imagine that a Hitler is merely "a thug loose in the world's street" is an almost childish simplification. A Hitler in Germany or a Huey Long in America is, of course, a responsible cause; and as such may not be minimized. But he is also a symptom and result. Germs are a cause, but they are dangerous only when the debilitation of the body grants them license. Some day we may be wise enough to provide good housing instead of asylums, hospitals, and jails. Some day we may defend people at small cost against insecurity, instead of defending them at vast cost from the demagogue become war lord. The threat of crowd psychology, whether of frenzied mob or subversive group, might almost be cancelled, and would certainly be blunted, by social righteousness. Worthy community is genuine wealth: base community is a plague. One or the other we must have, for togetherness is "by nature." The radio cannot become a substitute for political rallies, much less for public worship: neighborhood is in man's constitution. Togetherness cannot be denied; but it may be, and so must be, redeemed. When redeemed, it is more than mere asset: it is self-completion. The "I," as Dr. Fritz Kunkel might say, is nourished in the "We."[8]

III

Personality gathers unique and essential treasure from the prayer crowd. Those adjectives are sober: *unique* and *essential*. Should they seem wild, let this prime fact be pondered: though the individual is nourished by community, every community *on earth* fails him. He is then left lonely. Unless he can then find some higher Community, he becomes self-centered. Becoming self-centered he is under death warrant, like a leaf without a tree. The family is a clear illustration of this life-and-death sequence. At first the child is nourished by the mother's body. Later he is guided by family wisdom, and upheld by family love. In the shared experience of the home he comes to self-awareness and self-assurance. Then the nest is torn. Perhaps the break comes harshly, through divorce, or through parental pride or anger. Psychiatric records cry aloud against the wrong inflicted thus by parents on children. No parent is perfect: the breach appears: that is the crisis of adolescence. Thus Dr. Kunkel writes:

There is theoretically always a possibility of solving even the most difficult problem of this kind, but the solution of every problem pre-supposes a degree of patience, productivity, and love on the part of the mother which cannot be found on our earth. She would have to be as capable as an angel of unadulterated We-feeling, and we know that no human being can be so. Therefore, we say that, regardless of theory, in practice every child and every mother must come to the Breach-of-the-We. . . . . The moment that she becomes impatient, helpless, angry, or even hopeless the We is broken, whether she wishes it to be or not, and she cannot conceal that fact.[9]

Even if the home were always a blessing, it would still be broken—by time's erosion, by the impelling of nature which drives the grown child to build his own home, or by inescapable death. Then the individual is alone—in grim aloneness. He must find another community for his devotion and enrichment—some comradeship of work, play, politics, marriage, church—or else build a shell of egotism and slowly die. But every community of earth finally betrays him, both by failure and by the fact of death.

Therein is a strange dilemma of personality: we are nourished by the community, but every human community finally breaks to leave us bereft. The home fails us. The political or national fellowship fails us: worthy men are homeless in political faith, or else must choose between poor alternatives. The comradeship of toil fails us: there also we are involved in endless compromise. The world community is torn asunder, its uneasy peace hardly better than its violent war. When the breach is made in any community, the individual may try to live as an individual; but he never succeeds. He withers like a branch torn from a tree. Individualism becomes blind with pride, or anarchistic, or inwardly torn. Whether bravado is worse than nervous breakdown who can tell? The "We" and the "I" cannot live apart. The worthy man, when community fails him, will join some new community: he will extend the bounds of his nature by enlistment in good causes until he becomes "a citizen of the world." That is manifest wisdom, but it is not enough: every group breaks, and the worthy man, despite all his altruism, is still forlorn unless he can find the Beloved Community. His "I" must find lodgment, sustenance, and the opportunity for self-giving in a "We" that is above the threat of anger, greed, and time "Outside the Church there is no salvation." That dogmatism, properly understood, is not dogmatic but profoundly true. For though the Church also is seamed with chasms, many of them wicked and some of them inevitable, the Church is not mere frail humanity: it lifts its hands to God. It gathers the individual into a Community above the earth. It saves him from both broken community and fatal egocentricity, and nourishes him in the Eternal. That is why corporate prayer grants to personality a unique and essential treasure:

> What life have you if you have not life together?
> There is no life that is not in community,
> And no community not lived in praise of GOD.[4]

C. E. Montague has a story of a man,[10] by vocation a merchant and by avocation a mountain climber, who confronted the breach in community. His wife had died: he heard the news as he was recovering from a gas attack in the war. His son and daughter, disillusioned in that age of disillusion, had each contracted a loveless marriage. They deemed their father passé and provincial. He woke one morning aware that he had suffered a slight stroke. Why live? He would not kill himself, but resolved instead to climb an Alpine ice slope never yet climbed. If he succeeded, all right. If not, it was a good way to die, especially when there was no zest to live. He almost succeeded. But he could not cut the last few steps: his strength had gone. He waited. Death might come to him, or he might slip and go to death: it mattered not, and he felt no rebellion. Then he heard a woman's voice. She was in fear and danger somewhere just above him. He called to reassure her, and—it was a kind of miracle—his strength returned. In strange access of power he cut the steps, reached her, took her weight as she dangled, and thus saved both her and the husband who had grimly held the rope. The essayist makes a shrewd comment: the hero, he says, had been two men, one climbing and the other watching the climb; but the cry of need made him one man in service, and so his strength was doubled.

The story has other implications. In it are the overtones and undertones of *community*. The marriage bond had failed the man through death. The family bond had failed him through the shabby mind of son and daughter. His nation and generation had failed him through war. He was too noble to become merely egocentric. So he arranged to die. Then he was joined again to the comradeship by a cry of peril: he forgot himself in a neighbor's need and life gathered both meaning and power. But a question remains, not as a criticism of an enkindling story but as a statement of a deep dilemma in our nature: what was that man's objective when he returned to the inn in the valley? How could he heal the breach in further disappointment, or when a second stroke occurred? Even if there were no human failure, community on earth would still be mocked by death— unless there is a Fellowship transcending all failure and all death. Corporate prayer is that Fellowship: it saves the individual from both the forlornness of broken community and the worse desolation of an egocentric life.

IV

These truths find illustration in any of the dominant moods of prayer. Group prayer not only completes private prayer in the joy of togetherness, but saves togetherness from its own internal strains. Because blessings spring from our common life, like flowers and fruit from the earth, corporate *praise* is as inevitable in normal life as individual praise. True thanksgiving is like that of the oratorio *The Messiah*. There are solos of praise such as "Rejoice Greatly," and choruses of praise such as "Hallelujah!" Together we celebrate the bounty of the world, for together we are blessed, and the blessing comes through common toil. Together we celebrate the beauty of the earth, for the sense of beauty also is quickened by community, through artist, sculptor, poet, and musician. Recently we saw a patch of woodland where the owner had planted one hundred thousand jonquil bulbs. He wrought a loveliness, but he was only an undergardener: he could not make the bulbs; he could only receive them from One who said, "Let the earth bring forth grass, the herb yielding seed, and the fruit tree yielding fruit after his kind, whose seed is in itself, upon the earth: and it was so."[11] Together we celebrate the faithfulness of human toil. There are many lazy folk, but many more who are industrious. The trains run, the mail is delivered, the books are printed, and a million amenities of daily life fail not, because our days are girded by obscure work well done. Together we celebrate the comradeships of family, toil, play, education, and friendship by which our separate lives are nourished, adoring One whose will and wisdom sustains them all in love. Together we celebrate "greatness passing by," the insight and heroism whereby our liberties are dearly bought. Because each of us is daily enriched, each should pray "in secret." Because all are enriched, and each through all, we should pray in corporate praise.

But this praise would halt, and might turn even to misgiving or mockery, if there were no higher praise. For how can we be thankful if the breach in community is irreparable, and we are condemned to loneliness? Forlornness and egocentricity know no praise. Therefore corporate Christian praise has always focused on Jesus: he is the disclosure of God's nature and purpose; his Cross is the weapon and eternal sign of man's redemption; and in him is the warranty of the New Commonwealth. Thus the community on earth gives highest praise for the healing of its brokenness, and celebrates with gladdest songs a Fellowship above the threat of time. It is no accident, but fulfillment of deepest need, that the Roman missal gives the prayer for Whitsuntide as follows:

Truly worthy and right, just and salutary is it, that we thank Thee ever and at all times, Holy Lord, Almighty Father, Eternal God, through Christ our Lord; who ascended above all Heavens and sitting at Thy right hand poured forth the Holy Spirit of promise upon men adopted as children. Therefore, the whole of mankind on the earth exults with a common joy; but also the Powers above and angelic Principalities sing a Hymn of Praise to Thy glory, and cry without end. . . . [13]

Such hymns as "Jerusalem the Golden" are not sticky sentimentality. Doubtless they can be used as "escape." But, rightly used, they testify to our profoundest lack—

the lack of an enduring comradeship on earth—and to
our profoundest joy—the joy of a discovered Community:

> They stand, those halls of Zion,
>   All jubilant with song,
> And bright with many an angel,
>   And all the martyr throng:
> The Prince is ever in them;
>   The daylight is serene;
> The pastures of the blessed
>   Are decked in glorious sheen.[13]

That is the acme of praise—the fellowship on earth
thanking God that the breach in our comradeships is
healed in the love of Christ, and hailing the Community
which has

> A forted residence 'gainst the tooth of time
> And razure of oblivion.[14]

The same basic need of personality is met in corporate prayer of *confession*. If it is true, as we have urged,
that egocentricity comes partly from failure of the group
to nourish individual life, then there is demand indeed
for group penitence. Without corporate confession our
individual contritions leave us still imprisoned. Our
blessings are mediated through the common life, but so
is our hurt in wickedness. Each man is *socially* guilty by
deed or consent. His individual transgression comes
from the climate of the times, and flows back like a
rivulet into the broad river of public wrong. His private
angers swell mob violence: his private greeds feed a
gross commercialism. The shame of city streets and the
shadow of city slums make every man accountable, and
no man is sound in health until he has made joint confession with his neighbors. It is strange indeed that we
should speak so often about a man's duty to the state,
and so rarely about the state's duty to the man. How the
breach in the comradeship threatens and despoils personal life! A recent novel[15] portrays a Russian family

of the landed group who have been driven into China
by the Revolution. Peter was too young then to understand the social struggle. He was in no sense culprit, but
only pathetic victim. As a young man in China he is
again driven from city to city by the Japanese invasion.
No community is permanent: he has no certain place in
the comradeship of toil or education or city or nation.
The family, his only haven, is inevitably broken by failure and death. Then? Then he must become anarchistic
in character, and so perish; or he must find a new community for his nurture and devotion. The book, with a
stab of insight, shows him at the last recrossing the Russian border at risk of death to join the Communists, not
because he believes their cause, but because he cannot
live without community. But they also failed him, as
any sequel to that story could have shown. Then? Then
he must live in religious faith or cease to live. He must
be caught up into the indissoluble Community, and confess before God the failures of the human comradeship.
How many homes are broken, openly or secretly, to be-
tray the children! How the city fails us, its pall of
smoke symbolizing its blight! How government betrays
the citizen across all the world! How education falters
in its attempt to educe the hidden splendor! How the
church on earth, by its unseemly strife or division, by its
pettiness or cowardice, makes homeless even the man
upon his knees! But *his* prayer is not to the church, but
to God. There is a Church above the church, cailed in
the great liturgies, "angels and archangels," "the spirits
of just men made perfect," "the communion of saints,"
"the fellowship of the prophets," "the noble army of
martyrs." In confession, individual and corporate, we
are joined with that bright company. Our judgment on
human groups is sharpened and cleansed, even while
our consecration to them is renewed. The inevitable or
sinful breach is healed. The preaching of the "social
gospel" seems gauche and earthy, not mainly because it
is clumsy and entangled with some "ism"—though that
blunder is all too evident—but because it stands alone:
there are too few great hymns of social passion to support it, and, more especially, too few great prayers of

corporate penitence. By such prayer the man and the community alike recover health.

Clearly the prayer of *intercession* is not complete, either as prayer or as fulfillment of our human nature, until it is also *joint* intercession. Just as clearly our togetherness fails us without such prayer. When intercession is private it may be its own mockery: it prays for *all* but prays *alone*. It is complete only as it becomes itself an act of love, a corporate venture.

> For all are brethren, far and wide,
> Since Thou, O Lord, for all hast died;
> Then teach us, whatsoe'er betide,
>   To love them all in Thee.[16]

How can the breach in community be healed until the community pleads with God for all its members? How otherwise can private selfishness be delivered from its prison? The warnings of modern psychology against "introversion" mean that every man must pour his life in love into the commonwealth. His little causes must ever widen their bounds until he is citizen and lover of mankind. Nay, he must push back the limits of earth and sky, and be joined with a Community above change and threat. The Church is prophetic of that Higher Comradeship; for the Church, even though it may have faults as thick as dust, worships God. Corporate intercession for the poor, if it were worthy and constant, would leave us stricken with such discontent that we would banish needless poverty. Corporate intercession for peace would keep bonds of love across the chasms of war, and end war as a grotesque relic of a bygone age. The German cook, applying in wartime for a position in an American home, and fearing lest her nationality might disqualify her, said simply and poignantly, "We weep the same tears, madam." Corporate intercession breaks down the barriers between rich and poor, young and old, and keeps the comradeship in that objectivity of love which is the only sure foundation of peace. Without that prayer no civilization would be worth defense. In such togetherness our egocentric mind is delivered from itself, and is provoked by its own prayers to serve the whole community of mankind. Meanwhile the prayers themselves have power over events and men, and "create new situations." We shall not find any commonwealth on earth until we have first found it in our united intercession.

"Can't a man pray without belonging to a church?" He cannot pray well or fully until he is a member of some fellowship of prayer. "But isn't prayer in its nature private?" No, nothing is in its nature wholly private: it is both private and corporate. Jesus advised us to pray in secret in an inner chamber with the door shut. That counsel remains, for every man's heart is still a moated castle. But Jesus taught also a group worship: "Where two or three are gathered together in my name"—or two or three hundred—"there am I in the midst of them."[17] He said the Temple should be "called of all nations the house of prayer."[18] That counsel also remains, for the moated castle of man's heart draws its stones from common ground, and its moat-water comes from a common river of life. Corporate prayer is not a process of addition—one added to one added to one until every worshiper is counted. It is a process of *multiplication:* a divine electricity flashes from every life: there are endless "commutations" of the Spirit. Corporate prayer is not an aggregate: it is a symphony. "Where nine or ten are gathered in holiness," said an old Jewish proverb, "there is the majesty of God." So Jesus prayed on the mountainside all night alone. But he prayed also in the synagogue and Temple, and in the little group of his disciples. We need community. When an earthly group betrays us, we must build new communities of home, toil, art, nationhood, and the world. Perchance no age was ever more clearly summoned than our age to the task of rebuilding community. In these new commonwealths we must live and love, lest the paralysis of egocentricity should slay us. But, because every community is "devoured by Time's devouring hand," we must be joined to a Higher Community, "where neither moth nor rust doth corrupt, and where thieves do not break through nor steal."[10] The fulfillment of our nature is in corporate prayer.

Part Four

A WAY OF PRAYER

Chapter XVIII

A WAY OF PRIVATE PRAYER

THE DISCIPLES OF Jesus tracked down his empowering secret, and found it in his prayers. Then they asked instruction in their prayers: "And it came to pass, that, as he was praying in a certain place, when he ceased, one of his disciples said unto him, Lord, teach us to pray, as John also taught his disciples."[1] Jesus gave the instruction: "After this manner . . . . pray ye."[2] He taught men *how* to pray—a duty in which his Church is remiss. The Church exhorts people to pray, but rarely gives them specific guidance. This failure strains credence unless we assign it, as perhaps we must, to the Church's own doubt of prayer's influence. There is a cruel story of a bishop who resolved to practice what he had so often preached: he would speak to God in direct simplicity. He spoke. A Voice, gentle but holy, answered him, "Yes, what is it?" The bishop was found dead on the chancel steps.

We have affirmed in these pages that prayer can turn the event, change the person, and give access of life in highest Friendship. If these claims are even half true—we believe they are fully true—prayer is the vital act. Bluntly, what do we most need? We need Someone to thank for life's glory and danger. We need forgiveness—the assurance that the folly of our sins is forgotten, their wretchedness canceled, and their cruelty turned to man's ultimate gain. We need zest, "another April to the soul." We need freedom from the pursuit of fears and the prison of hate. We need reinforcement—not merely our human resource, which at best can only point the prow and set the sails, but the sea wind and the sea tide to speed our stranded ventures. We need, in short, nothing less than friendship with God. "The Spirit itself beareth witness with our spirit, that we are the children of God."[3] We need that clear testimony of the Spirit, the brooding and breathing of another World, the known presence of "the Ideal Companion." Jesus said we could gain it through prayer. A little thing, this stilling of the mind to reverence, this schooling of the will? A little thing to bring so vast a boon? The optic nerve is a little thing, but it gives us sun, stars, and all the wonder of the earth.[4] Prayer is the optic nerve of the soul. Why do we cut the nerve?

We now attempt some clear and detailed guidance in private prayer. There can be no rules, certainly no binding rules, but only hints. Yet no man need travel an unmarked path. The saints are our teachers; and other men, versed in prayer, who would be aghast to be called saints. Jesus himself is *the* Teacher. Prayer is friendship with God. Friendship is not formal, but it is not formless: it has its cultivation, its behavor, its obligations, even its disciplines; and the casual mind kills it. So we here offer, as guide-map not as chain, a simple regimen of private prayer.

I

Where shall we pray? In a *quiet and private place.* That was the bidding of Jesus: "But thou, when thou prayest, enter into thy inner chamber, and when thou hast shut thy door, pray to thy Father which is in secret."[5] The counsel is specific: the room should be remote from distractions, the door shut against noise, and the prayer so free from posturing that it is "secret." Jesus himself, intent on quietness and sincerity, sometimes prayed on a mountainside, far into the night, or "rising up a great while before day . . . . departed into a solitary place, and there prayed."[6] Our age is restless and noisy: it is harder to find stillness now than in pioneer or rural days. City congestion and distraction war against the soul. A wiser civilization will disperse our

teeming masses into friendly communities open to the
fields and sky. As for sincerity, it is perhaps both more
difficult in our age and more important than quietness;
for it is our modern fashion to posture in the glare of
publicity. Amid tumult and glare we must do the best
we can: in some quiet corner of home or church, free
from prying or approving eyes, we must make sanctuary. "Be still, and know that I am God."[7] In the din
of traffic we may be deaf to steeple bells, but in the
quiet night we hear. It is wise to seek both stillness and
privacy.

Prayer should be offered in *an accustomed place*. We
are creatures of place and habit, and worthy habits
fashion worthy life. Anything we learn returns more
easily in the place where we learned it. If we should
master Chinese in China, come home to speak our own
tongue, and then return to China, the very setting would
be our cue for the recovery of the foreign words, even
before we heard people speak. Rousseau "wrote" best
when walking, Sheridan composed best at night with a
profusion of lights, and Vacano for his creative work
sought the "hubbub of peasant life near an old mill."[8]
In each instance the environment was accustomed.
There was no distraction of newness. The place not only
suggested the task, but held in store the encouragement
of past experience. These facts pertain also to a familiar
place of prayer. That setting gives prompting and remembrance. A kneeling bench may be found helpful,
with a few treasured books of devotion: Thomas à
Kempis' *Imitation of Christ,* Pascal's *Pensées,* Amiel's
Journal Intime, the *Theologica Germanica;* or more
modern books such as John Baillie's *A Diary of Private
Prayer;* and always a Bible. Protestants might well
adopt a Roman Catholic practice, and pray privately in
church. Infinity has its center everywhere, and men can
find God in any place, even in the roar of traffic; but
the habit of prayer is best established in a quiet and
accustomed place.

II

When shall we pray? At any time: God is not bound
by occasions and seasons, and prayer is spontaneous
like any friendship. But, for us, there is value in allotted
and customary periods of prayer. Three times during
the day have especial purpose. One is in the morning.
"Well begun is half done," but, "Things bad begun
make strong themselves by ill."[9] The first moments of
the day are an arena in which the revived worries or
joys of yesterday, the responsible tasks of the coming
hours, desires and hopes and fears, compete for our
reinvigorated thought. Those moments are crucial. They
often determine the day: they may make it an autopsy
of past failures, an overleaping ambition, or an anxiety.
There is great gain in pausing to realize that the day is a
unity: a kindly Providence each night draws a line on
one day soiled and marred, and each morning grants a
new day fresh from time's loom. There is much greater
gain in setting the tone and standard for the day by
quiet prayer. After that worship the day will not be a
distraction or a jumble: it will have integration like a
poem or a picture. We shall be saved from the drab
doom of "practical" people to whom "everything matters except everything." This prayer before or after
breakfast may wisely be brief: the day's labor summons
us. For the same reason it may wisely have a set form,
to be changed only when its reality is threatened by
rote. Dr. George S. Stewart, whose book *The Lower
Levels of Prayer* is outstandingly helpful, suggests a
five-minute sequence of morning prayer. It provides an
act of adoration, a thanksgiving and dedication, an intercession, an avowal of faith, and the Lord's Prayer, as
follows:

*Now blessed be the God of Israel, who only doeth won-
drous things. And blessed be His Holy Name for ever: and
let the whole earth be filled with His glory. Amen, and
Amen.*
Almighty God, my King and Saviour, I offer Thee my

thanks for the night's rest and for all the hope of this new day, looking to Thee for Thy blessing on its work and its rest. I offer to Thee now my thoughts and my words, my actions and my resting, my temptations and any suffering that may come, that Thou mayest use them for any purpose of Thy Holy Will. I seek that this day be wholly Thine. By the Grace of Jesus Christ. Amen.

O God, the giver of all love, who hast given me the blessings of friendship, I thank Thee for all my friends. I commit into Thy loving care . . . . all other friends unnamed, and those whom I shall meet in the course of this day. May the Grace of the Lord Jesus Christ, Thy love, O God, and the Communion of Thy Holy Spirit, be with them all. Amen.

I believe in God the Father Almighty, Maker of Heaven and earth, and in Jesus Christ His only son, our Lord. . . . . I believe in the Holy Ghost, the holy catholic Church, the communion of saints, the forgiveness of sins, the resurrection of the body and the life everlasting. Amen.

Our Father, which art in Heaven, hallowed be Thy name. Thy Kingdom come, Thy will be done, in earth as it is in heaven. Give us this day our daily bread. And forgive us our debts as we forgive our debtors. And lead us not in to temptation, but deliver us from evil: For Thine is the kingdom, the power, and the glory, for ever. Amen.[10]

Dr. Walter Russell Bowie, in his book of prayer, *Lift Up Your Hearts*, offers two morning meditations for private prayer. One is as follows:

Our Father, who art in heaven,
   Help me to believe this day that there is power to lift me up which is stronger than all the things that hold me down.
Hallowed be thy Name.
   Help me to be sensitive to what is beautiful, and responsive to what is good, so that day by day I may grow more sure of the holiness of life in which I want to trust.
Thy kingdom come.
   Help me to be quick to see, and ready to encourage, whatever brings the better meaning of God into that which otherwise might be the common round of the uninspired day.

Thy will be done, On earth as it is in heaven.

Help me to believe that the ideals of the spirit are not a far-off dream, but a power to command my loyalty and direct my life here on our real earth.

Give us this day our daily bread.

Open the way for me to earn an honest living without anxiety; but let me never forget the needs of others, and make me want only that benefit for myself which will also be their gain.

And forgive us our trespasses, As we forgive those who trespass against us.

Make me patient and sympathetic with the shortcomings of others, especially of those I love; and keep me sternly watchful only of my own. Let me never grow hard with the unconscious cruelty of those who measure themselves by mean standards, and so think they have excelled. Keep my eyes lifted to the highest, so that I may be humbled; and seeing the failures of others be forgiving, because I know how much there is of which I need to be forgiven.

And lead us not into temptation, But deliver us from evil.

Let me not go carelessly this day within the reach of any evil I cannot resist, but if in the path of duty I must go where temptation is, give me strength of spirit to meet it without fear.

For thine is the kingdom, and the power, and the glory for ever and ever. Amen.

And so in my heart may I carry the knowledge that thy greatness is above me and around me, and that thy grace through Jesus Christ my Master is sufficient for all my needs. *Amen.*[11]

The day is "well begun" in such prayer. The pilgrim then walks secretly armed and cheered.

The second time for daily prayer is determined, not by the clock, but by the day's happenings. That is to say, our waking hours should be punctuated by ejaculatory prayers. The word *jacula* means spear. These prayers are thrown spears of resolve or thanksgiving or trust. The sense of gratitude for the sight of ocean, for great music, or for a friend's loyalty should become an instant prayer: "My Father, I thank thee for this bless-

ing, from whom cometh every good and perfect gift."
Sympathy for a neighbor when news comes of his misfortune should find expression in a prayer: "Do Thou
defend him as he walks through shadow. Show me what
I can do to help. May his pain not be wasted, but lead
him to light." A journey should prompt a prayer for
journeying mercies. Each new task, each sudden responsibility, should have its undelayed dedication: "I
am able unto all things through Christ who makes me
strong."[12] Success and failure, joy and sorrow, are thus
made consecrate. There have been people, among them
the Celts and the Scandinavians, who had brief forms of
prayers for each task of the day. The bread-baking, the
feeding of the cattle, the lamplighting, each had its reverent ritual. It was a gracious custom. Even the scanty
records of the Gospels show clearly that Jesus prayed at
every juncture of his ministry. Ejaculatory prayers
should be part of the day's order of prayer. Added
treasure is given by a few moments of noonday prayer
in church.

But the most solving time to pray is at night. A wise
mother offers her counsel and comfort when day is
done, and sends her children to sleep with her blessing:
so God deals tenderly and wisely with His children of
earth. Facts gather to underscore the peculiarly creative
grace of evening prayer: the day's clamor is done, and
there is chance for meditation; the sunset glory is an
open gate of vision; fading light gives retrospection; and
the encroaching dark, in which we must lie unconscious,
reminds us of our helplessness. There is a further fact
which has incalculable issues: the nightly prayer lays
under fee our hours of sleep. We say, "I'd better sleep
on it before making a decision." The name which we
cannot remember when we go to bed is on our lips of
itself when we awake. Why? Because the mind is not
inactive during sleep: its subconscious processes continue, carrying on the business—especially the urgent
business or the last business—that has engaged the
waking thought. Paul was a good psychologist when he
advised, "Let not the sun go down upon your wrath."[13]
Anger churning in the mind at nightfall churns on dur-

ing sleep: the next morning is turned sour. By the same token the night prayer works radiantly in our nature while we sleep: the subconscious becomes prayer's ally, doubling prayer's power. While we rest we gain a deeper rest: God visits us by a secret stair. Problems are solved and questions answered, ready for our waking. Perhaps a better translation of "he giveth his beloved sleep" is, "he giveth unto his beloved *in their sleep.*" [14] At any rate that blessing *is* given through evening worship. What form should be impressed on this creative center of prayer? We now seek answer.

III

Evening prayer begins, not in a clamant asking, but in *a silent self-preparation.* We should not rush into the Presence, with a jostling crowd of fears, sins, and desires, like a mob breaking through a chancel door on pretense of worship. The church of nightly devotion should be entered through the vestibule in an orderly quietness. The psychologist speaks of "relaxation." Sometimes, when we are too tired to sleep, we realize that all our muscles are tense. Then we persusade each limb in turn to forgo its straining. So with the mind: we must calm each hungry desire—the psychologist advises—each vexing remorse, each bitter grudge or clamorous resolve. It is good counsel—if we can follow it. But can we? Man's self-tinkering has never been successful. The "relaxation" commended by psychology comes best as a by-product of a mind focused on God. This concentration is under no rule of thumb. Christian prayer will call upon Christ in reverent imagination. Almost any word of his is sufficient prompting: "I am the light of the world." [15] We say to ourselves. "His light fills the world. It fills this room. His light pains a sickened eye. But it heals, guides, illumines. It cheers, as daybreak after the night watch. 'God is light, and in him is no darkness at all.' " [16] Thus we meditate. Then, in specific act of devotion, we say: "Before this God, in all His holy love, in all His wisdom and delivering grace, I now kneel." Clearly the reading of a few verses from the Gospels is often the best prelude to our nightly prayer. In any event, the prelude of prayer is this preparation of ourself and realization of God: "I have set the Lord always before me." [17] Jesus entered prayer through that vestibule: we can see him quietly realizing the Presence: "Our Father which art in heaven, Hallowed be thy name." [18] Sometimes the prayer may go no further: it may remain in adoration. Perhaps that is the explanation of the prayer of St. Francis, which the eavesdropper heard him repeat all night: "My God and my All." The focusing of the mind on God is the proper beginning of prayer.

The next step is an *act of faith,* on which Jesus laid constant stress: "All things whatsoever ye shall ask in prayer, believing, ye shall receive."[19] The word "believing" is there a radiantly qualifying word: true prayer believes that God is like Christ, and asks what may be asked "in his Name and Nature." Therefore, in this initial silence of prayer we say to ourselves that whatever we ask in the "nature of Christ" is ours, granted only our earnestness in prayer and life. Sometimes this act of faith is an instant freedom: we know through Christ that God does not wish us to live in carking fear or unforgiven sin; and our prayer then is not in an importunity, but a joyous acceptance of a promised grace. Sometimes faith waits with confidence on fuller light: "If it is God's will for me to help So-and-so, or to discharge such-and-such a task, I can do it." Sometimes faith moves in the dark, believing in the ultimate good of untoward circumstance:

> Out of my stony griefs
> Bethel I'll raise.[20]

But always prayer is prefaced by an act of faith. We take counsel with our certitudes, not with our doubts and fears: "For he that cometh to God must believe that he is, and that he is a rewarder of them that diligently seek him."[21]

IV

For the prayer itself there is no fixed order, but both a primary impulse and the experience of praying men show that the first stage may be _thanksgiving._ A lecturer to a group of businessmen displayed a sheet of white paper on which was one blot. He asked what they saw. All answered, "A blot." They overlooked the white expanse, and saw only the blot. The test was unfair: it invited the wrong answer. Nevertheless, there is an ingratitude in human nature by which we notice the black disfigurement and forget the widespread mercy. We need deliberately to call to mind the joys of our journey. Perhaps we should try to write down the blessings of one day. We might begin: we could never end: there are not pens or paper enough in all the world. The attempt would remind us of our "vast treasure of content." Therefore the prayer of thanksgiving should be quite specific: "I thank thee for _this_ friendship, _this_ threat overpassed, _this_ signal grace." "For all thy mercies" is a proper phrase for a general collect, but not for a private gratitude. If we are thankful "for everything," we may end by being thankful for nothing. The thanksgiving should also probe deep, asking, "What are life's _abiding_ mercies?" Thus gratitude would be saved from earthiness and circumstance, and rooted in Life beyond life. "Count your many blessings," says the old hymn, "and it will surprise you what the Lord hath done."[22] This prayer should end in glad and solemn resolve: "Lord, seal this gratitude upon my face, my words, my generous concern for my neighbors, my every outward thought and act."

Prayer may next become _confession._ A rebound of nature hints that this is a wise order: "God has been passing kind, and I have given Him selfishness for love." True confession is neither self-excoriation—"To be merciless with anyone, even ourselves, is no virtue"[23]—nor casual evasion. Overconscientiousness becomes morbid: underconscientiousness becomes indifference and decay. Confession to those we have

wronged is sometimes, not always, wise: there are circumstances in which such confession would spread and
aggravate the hurt. But confession to God, whom we
have more deeply wronged, is always wise: He has understanding and love. Our sin is sin against the Living
Order, and we have neither inward peace nor inward
power until we have offered prayers of penitence. Confession, like thanksgiving, should be specific. It should
not be ruthless, but it should not excuse: it should set
hooks into the facts. "I confess *this* sharp judgment, *this*
jealousy, *this* cowardice, *this* bondage of dark habit, *this*
part in the world's evil." Contrition is not easy work: it
is surgery. But, like surgery, it is not an end in itself:
the wise prayer of confession always leads to an acceptance of God's pardon. Lancelot made confession, perhaps dealing too harshly with himself:

> Happier are those that welter in their sin,
> Swine in the mud, that cannot see for slime,
> Slime of the ditch: but in me lived a sin
> So strange, of such a kind, that all of pure,
> Noble, and knightly in me twined and clung
> Round that one sin, until the wholesome flower
> And poisonous grew together, each as each,
> Not to be pluck'd asunder.

But King Arthur, the type of Christ, granted him absolution and hope:

> Nay—but thou errest, Lancelot: never yet
> Could all of true and noble in knight and man
> Twine round one sin, whatever it might be,
> With such a closeness, but apart there grew,
> Save that he were the swine thou spakest of,
> Some root of knighthood and pure nobleness;
> Whereto see thou, that it may bear its flower.[24]

God does not wish us to remember, save as admonition
and reminder of our dependence, anything He is willing
to forget. It might be wise to rise from kneeling at this
point in the prayer as token of our acceptance of God's
pardon, our sure faith in His absolution, and our new

Would standing be helpful for soul action?

freedom in His grace. That standing erect might also symbolize both our resolve to make wise restoration insofar as we have power to mend our blunders, and our sincere renunciation of our sins. Confession is incomplete without that resolve. Our will, however feeble it may be, must descend squarely on the side of a new life. Otherwise even our penitence may become a self-deceit and an abuse of God's goodness. But true confession is a very cleansing of the soul.

Then may follow a prayer of *intercession,* without which the most earnest prayer might sink into selfishness. *The Lord's Prayer* in almost every phrase keeps us mindful of our neighbors: *"Our* Father." . . . *"our* daily bread." . . . *"our* trespasses." Private intercession should be specific. "We humbly beseech Thee for all sorts and conditions of men,"[25] is an appropriate phrase in a collect—which, as the very word indicates, draws all worshipers into one act of devotion, and provides a form into which each worshiper may pour his secret prayer—but it is out of place in individual petition. Genuine love sees faces, not a mass: the good shepherd "calleth his own sheep by name."[26] Intercession is more than specific: it is pondered: it requires us to bear on our heart the burden of those for whom we pray. Whose name should come first? Perhaps the name of our enemies. The injunction of Jesus is plain: "Pray for them which despitefully use you."[27] He told us that worship is vain if we are embittered; that we would be wise to leave our gift before the altar, go to make peace with our neighbor, and then worship. Only then can we truly worship. So the first intercession is: "Bless So-and-so whom I foolishly regard as foe. Bless So-and-so whom I have wronged. Keep them in Thy favor. Banish our bitterness." Intercession names also the leaders of mankind in statecraft, medicine, learning, art, and religion; the needy of the world; our comrades in work and play, and our loved ones. A sense of responsibility may prompt us to prepare a chart of intercession, so that night by night we may enter earnestly into the need of the world, and not forget nor fail anyone who closely depends upon our prayers. So true intercession is spe-

cific and pondered. It is also daring: it carries on its
heart-entreaty the crisis of the world. Like thanksgiving,
it is not complete without our vow. Sincere prayer-in-
love is never in vain.

The fourth order in our prayer may be *petition*. It
comes last, not because it is most important, but because it needs the safeguard of earlier prayer. We
should not fear to lift our earthly needs before Eternal
Eyes, for we are held in Eternal Love; but we should
fear the encroachment of a selfish mind. Petition is defended against that threat if first we give thanks, confess
our sins, and pray for our neighbors. Then the petition
may have free course. Sometimes, in sorrow, dread, or
helplessness, it will be a crisis cry of creaturehood—a
beating on Heaven's door with bruised knuckles in the
dark. Sometimes it will be friendship-talk with God
about the affairs of everyday. Surely both prayers would
be approved by Christ: his disciples cried in their extremity, "Save, Lord"; and day by day they spoke with
him about the besetments, enigmas, and joys of the
journey. To try to thwart the prayer of petition is to
deny human nature. The New Testament has better wisdom: "Be overanxious for nothing; but in everything by
prayer and supplication with thanksgiving let your requests be made known unto God."[28] Yet petition
should grow in grace so as to "covet earnestly the best
gifts"; and it should always acknowledge that our sight
is dim and that our purposes are mixed in motive. It
should always conclude with, "Nevertheless not my will,
but thine, be done."[29]

The intervals of these four prayers should be filled by
meditation. After thanksgiving we should contemplate
God's abounding goodness, and await His word concerning His own gifts. After confession we should adore
the pardoning Love made known in Christ, and listen
for His guidance. After intercession we should pause to
try to see the whole world's need as Christ saw it from
his cross. After petition we should wait again to meditate upon the Will. Prayer is listening as well as speaking, receiving as well as asking; and its deepest mood is
friendship held in reverence. So the nightly prayer

should end as it begins—in adoration. The best conclusion is, "In the name of Jesus Christ: Amen." For in the name or nature of Jesus is our best understanding of God, and the best corrective of our blundering prayers. The word "Amen" is not idle: it means "So let it be." It is our resolve to live faithfully in the direction of our prayers, and our act of faith in God's power. It is the proper ending to our evening prayer.

V

Certain practical questions remain, and merit an answer. *Should private prayer be spoken or silent?* There is no binding rule, but there are certain guiding facts. Silence is the proper language of awe and adoration. The abyss of the night sky and the heartbreak of the Cross are literally beyond words: the tongue is helpless. So the beginning and ending of private prayer are an instinctive stillness. Silence is the language also of contemplation and receptiveness: we cannot hear if we always speak. So the intervals of meditation just described may all be silent. But silence has its dangers, especially in the waywardness of thought; and speech has its virtues. Any teacher knows that a lesson spoken is clearer than a lesson merely pondered. Words fashion our prayers to a spear point, and give them an action thrust. "Take with you words, and turn to the Lord."[30] Words clarify thought, focus desire, and translate resolves into deeds. Therefore our prayers of thanksgiving, confession, intercession, and petition may wisely be spoken *aloud*. The words need not be wrought and polished. They may rush in intolerable craving, halt in ignorance, or break in sorrow. God regards the heart, not the word. Yes, in ordinary times, we are helped if we try to give clear, simple, and sincere expression to our prayer. By that effort the prayer itself becomes clear, simple, and sincere.

How shall we find time to pray? The very question shows the disproportion of our life. "First things" are not "first." Three hundredth things, the make of an automobile, the fashion of a coiffure, are now first; and "first things" have dropped out of sight. St. Ignatius required of initiates in his order an initial thirty days of silence. Luther habitually prayed for three hours each day. Jesus often prayed all night, and said that "men ought always to pray, and not to grow weary in praying."[31] If prayer is friendship with God, that friendship should rule all our time. Work or play should wait on prayer, not prayer on work or play. But since our age is frenzied, since with all the time gained from time-saving devices we have ever less time to live, this fact is worth stress: prayer saves time, and the saving is genuine. When a man prays, his thought is proportioned and clear: evil memories are purged to save him from distraction, and he can meet responsibility with confidence. Another man may lack concentration, fill time with lost motion, and delay or blunder in decisions; but the praying man is in tune with life. It is no accident that Paul could be prodigious and versatile in labor, as tent-maker, friend, traveler, administrator, preacher, writer, theologian: he was much in prayer. His nature was like a cathedral: many an arch and aisle, many a carving and picture, many a chapel, many a peal of bells, but all brought to focus and purpose in an altar. Prayer saves time. We should not offer God the shreds and tatters of our day. But, if events crowd and responsibilities summon, prayer's brevity can be atoned in prayer's sincerity. Five minutes in the morning, arrow flights of prayer during the day, and fifteen minutes at night do not seem too large a demand for life's highest Friendship. That time spent in prayer can conquer time.

There is a sharper question. *How can we overcome an arid mind in private prayer?* The mind's periods of dryness are hard to explain. Any artist knows times when his imagination is like the dust and darkness of a forsaken church, and other times when it is like a church with banners hung, organ music rolling through high arches, and candles burning bright on every altar. The children of Israel wandered forty years in a desert before they reached their Promised Land. The wanderings were not loss: they taught Israel to trust God's leadings, purged them of a slave mind, and welded them

into nationhood. In their history we can trace the reason
for desert and disappointment: "O give thanks unto the
Lord . . . . to him which led his people through the
wilderness: for his mercy endureth for ever."[32] A realization that the arid stretches have a purpose will help us
to journey through them in resolute faith. We must walk
through darkness in memory of the light, and in confidence that light will return. There is some drudgery in
every high art: in music there are weary hours of practice. The drudgery is not only the test of courage and
patience, and therefore a bestowal of manhood, but it is
promise of mastery. Prayer has its drudgery: if we
shrink from the discipline we shall never gain the joy.
In any art the period of irksomeness yields finally to an
"opening," and the "openings" multiply to become freedom. When the mind is dry we should still persist in
prayer, offering God the dryness in lack of better gift—
telling Him about our journey of dust until he gives
springs in the desert.

*How can we overcome a wandering and moody
mind?* Dr. George S. Stewart suggests wisely that waywardness in prayer would be conquered if our prayers
were more adventurous, and if expectantly we traced
their answer.[33] Jesus challenged men to daring prayer:
he bade them "remove mountains" by their faith. He
himself marked God's way in the world, and gave
thanks for answers to prayer. Even more searchingly
Dr. Stewart suggests that failure in prayer's disciplines
may reflect a failure in life's disciplines, and that therefore moody distraction may itself reveal the prayer we
most need to offer. If baleful humors come of secret
unworthiness, the "line" of our prayer is clear: we must
bring our secret sins into the light of God's countenance. Then prayer itself is the road of victory. Not every dark mood, of course, comes of unworthiness. The
saints also have been overtaken by "the black night of
the soul." Our wrestling is not against "flesh and blood"
only, but against the "darkness of this world"; not only
against the ebb and flow of human moods, but against
the sudden unseen antagonism of unaccountable depres-
sions. But we must endure the balefulness as we endure

the drudgery. If there is nothing else we can do, we can
tell God about the evil mood, making it our strange oblation to Him who gives His treasure for our need.
There will come other hours so radiant that they atone
for every untoward cloud:

> Ah, did you once see Shelley plain,
>   And did he stop and speak to you?
> And did you speak to him again?
>   How strange it seems, and new! . . . .
>
> I crossed a moor, with a name of its own
>   And a use in the world no doubt,
> Yet a hand's-breadth of it shines alone
>   'Mid the blank miles round about:
>
> For there I picked up on the heather,
>   And there I put inside my breast
> A molted feather, an eagle-feather!
>   Well, I forget the rest.[34]

In the very midst of prayer's barrenness, or when prayer
is vexed by dark moods, the man on his knees may suddenly see Jesus plain. Then he can well "forget the
rest."

These counsels are only a rough map: they cannot
photograph each individual journey. They are hints, not
dictates. Each traveler in this land must find his own
way. Yet what we have written may show him that he
does not lack signposts for guidance or friends for
cheer. His best confidence, as he goes pilgrim-clad on
these uplands of life, is that God looks on the intention
of the heart, and overlooks the blundering and the
blindness. Moses once heard a shepherd praying, "O
God, show me where Thou art, that I may become Thy
servant. I will clean Thy shoes, and comb Thy hair, and
sew Thy clothes, and fetch Thee milk." Moses rebuked
him: "God is a Spirit, and needs not such gross minis-
trations. . . . ." Thereupon the shepherd rent his
clothes in dismay, and fled to the desert. Then Moses

heard a voice from Heaven, "O Moses, wherefore have you driven away my servant? . . . . I regard not the words that are spoken, but the heart that offers them."[35] The shepherd in his desert of dismay was met by ministering angels.

"I regard not the words that are spoken, but the heart that offers them."

CHAPTER XIX

A WAY OF CORPORATE PRAYER

FRIENDS AND CRITICS tell the wane of public worship. The news is old: every generation prints that premature death notice. A magazine article on the decrepitude of organized religion is a sure stimulant for declining circulation. But the church, like a famous monarch, is a "most unconscionable time a-dying." Some wiser magazine writer may one day infer that the Church does not die, but has a secret of renewal; and that genuine religion, being a judgment on the world, must often be a minority faith. The striking fact is not the wane of public worship but its steady glow. People do not come to church, or stay away, because of the preaching. They think that is the focus. But the real purpose, in clear or vague intention, is to pray. Theaters spend a fortune on advertising, make frequent change in program, and resort to a thousand sensational tricks to persuade people to be amused. Church advertising is puerile, and, even if it were skillful and worthy, might be a doubtful blessing. Church sensationalism is only repellent, like a gentlewoman rouged for evening devotions. The real church, with a few great hymns, a few great prayers, some preaching good or bad, and no shallow expedients, draws folk generation after generation, not to be amused, but to be judged and blessed. What draws them? What draws the compass needle of all ships? There is a Mystery and a Magnetism: "For where two or three are gathered together in my name, there am I in the midst of them."[1]

But organized religion may take no complacent com-

305

fort. Neglect of worship is not all due to a stiff-necked world: the church is lazy and foresworn. It fails most where it should be most vital—in private and corporate prayer. Church machinery is well oiled, and the wheels spin busily, even though they are not always geared to genuine service. Church friendliness is not neglected: there are many who "leave the word of God, and serve tables."[2] Educational ventures generate much heat, and some light. The sermons are faithfully prepared, and are effective, at least to the extent that they provoke discussion among the congregation. But the prayers—are they the fruit of labor and prayer? Corporate worship—is it a hearty act, deeply understood in reverence? How healthy is the prayer meeting? If the minister had to choose between prayer and sermon, he might better forget the sermon. Critics of the church are blind to the worst sin. This sin: the prayers are dismissed as "preliminaries"!

I

We shall now try to give some guidance in corporate prayer. The field is vast, and human nature is varied in its needs: our attempt must be only an elementary primer. Those who do not need it may ignore it. Others may find some "first aid." Our purpose is not a study of liturgies or a history of Christian worship, but some simple instruction in corporate prayer for the average man and the average church.

The family girds the individual, and knits society. What of *family prayer?* The family altar is broken. Round its fragments gather our modern failures and yearnings. The home itself is under threat. It is beset by the glare and congestion of urban life, the demands of factory civilization, the cult of gadgets, the distraction of raucous pleasures, and the tense restlessness of the times. Add poverty and war, as we must, and the odds are desperate. Meanwhile psychiatric records show that many psychoses and breakdowns are due to failure in the home. This man received a needless shock in infancy; that woman was a spoiled "only child"; this man was thwarted by the lovelessness of quarreling parents; that woman was bruised in nature by a jealous mother; this man was made introvert because his parents played favorites among their children; that woman received no wise counsel, and adolescence became a fear. The instances are legion and pathetic. Any compassionate psychiatrist, doctor, or minister wishes he had a world-megaphone to cry, "Look to the home!" Other failures gaze curiously or wistfully at the broken family altar. For instance, the attempt of the home to transfer responsibility to school, welfare groups, and church seems already doomed. These other comradeships are allies, even essential allies, but not proxies. The instinct of parenthood, with its issuing love, ensures the home; and while home endures the best nurture of children will be within its walls. Despite the clamant world, children spend much of their time at home. They spend there the determinative periods of morning and night. Life situations rise naturally there, and educators are agreed that creative teaching is through life situations. Even the church is no substitute: its one Sunday-school hour, however godly, can hardly compete with thirty godless hours at home. Unless religion in the church is reinforced by home religion, both home and church are sore bestead. Meanwhile, marriage as an end in itself is a path that ends in sand. If it is fleshly indulgence, it turns to nausea or boredom. If it is worldly convenience, it crumbles like clay. It is not an end in itself. It has a wider biological purpose—the continuance of the race. It has a wider character purpose—to carry parents and children towards what the philosophers call "ideal ends." What ends? Marriage and the home in their modern failure cry aloud for the meaning and support of some ultimate Sanction. If the broken altar were restored it might repel the modern threat and mend the modern failure.

We are fond of saying, in an unexamined platitude, that children are the hope of the race. We forget that the guidance of children is still entrusted to adults. There would be real hope if children and parents together would daily pray. The practical difficulties can be overcome. If the early morning is inconvenient because school and work summon different members at different hours, the evening meal may be the right time. Good books are available. One church printed a list of books for home religion—a list which met the interest of various age groups—and mailed it to every home in the parish. That same church holds frequent courses for parents in the use of the suggested material. In one home, in wintertime, the mother or father reads the evening prayer with each child in turn—a plan which yields in summer to morning family devotions. In these each member in turn takes charge. The family is seated while scripture is read, and kneels for the prayer and Lord's Prayer. This is a typical devotion, read perhaps by the youngest member of the family:

THE EXAMPLE OF JESUS
John 15: 9-12

It was because Jesus kept so close to God in all his thoughts that he had so much of love and wisdom and happiness to share with others. If we obey his teachings and follow his example, we shall truly share his strength and feel his love and find our happiness complete.

> I have loved you as the Father has loved me. You must retain my love. If you keep my commands you will retain my love, just as I have observed the Father's commands and retain his love. I have told you all this so that you may have the happiness I have had, and your happiness may be complete. The command that I give you is to love one another just as I have loved you.

Let us pray: Once more a new day lies before us, Our Father. As we go out among our fellows in our work and play, touching the hands and lives of all about us, make us, we pray thee, friends of all the world. Grant that we may look all men in the face with the eyes of brotherly love. If anyone needs us, make us glad to give our help, and may we be happy that we have it in us to be helpful to our fellow men. In Jesus' name, we pray together, Our Father, who art in heaven. . . . [3]

If some member has the gift of free prayer to gather in petition the family need and acknowledge the family joy, there is added blessing. This family act, with grace at meals, may seem small; but as it grows into habit its issues are wide and radiant. It is the tiny filament by which Electricity comes in warmth, light, and power. It is a fountain, too long choked, by which the barrenness of our world might break in beauty. Let the reader ask how family prayers might affect the threats and failures of our time.

II

What has become of *group prayer?* The Christian enterprise began, not in an organization, but in the group prayer of Jesus and his disciples. The Church originated at Pentecost in an "upper room" where the followers of Jesus "continued with one accord in prayer and supplication."[4] Every revival of religion has been heralded and generated by prayer groups. The world outreach of American Protestantism started from the now famous hayrick prayer meeting of a group of students. This sequence of group prayer and faith's renewal seems to be a causal bond. The new world for which we yearn will not arrive without the prayers of friendship groups.

Not only the public good, but friendship itself, needs this prime endeavor. Friendship lives both in affinities and tensions. If friends were altogether different, there could be no friendship, only alienation. If they were wholly alike, there could be no friendship, only identity. Friends must be "like" in meshing enthusiasms, and "unlike" in differences which make the meshing firm. Two friends are words and music, not replicas of the words or replicas of the music. If the likeness is on low ground of some earthy hankering, the friendship is both debasing and under threat: the tensions soon break it. If the common cause is high, a love of nature or a common battle for clean politics, the friendship is enlightening and strong: the tensions then are not menace but enrichment. Is any friendship sure? William S. Gilbert and Arthur S. Sullivan were destined friends: the libret-

tos of one and the music of the other matched like color
and form. Yet they quarreled. Then neither was creative in labor. The one surety of friendship is the highest
common cause, the friendship of each with God, for
that is the one unbreakable bond. A common love of
music, mathematics, social service, or theology is not
enough: such friends may still ruinously quarrel. But
they cannot sincerely pray together—and quarrel. At
Pentecost the differences were absorbed in light, yet remained in love: "The multitude . . . . were confounded, because that every man heard them speak in
his own language."[5] The barrier even of language and
race now was overpassed! Both the public good and
friendship's own joy are pendant on group prayer.

The discussion groups which characterize our time
are a good augury. They spell new earnestness and resolve. They withstand slogans, and leaven mass movements. But they will evaporate in sound or break in tension, like random organ notes, unless they are caught
and fused in Music. Wisdom does not come by pooling
ignorances, or joining viewpoints, but by baptizing honest differences in higher Light. Here, in rough, is the
pattern for discussion groups: a common altruistic
task—as in the Quaker work camps—with hard manual
labor, common play, the friction of friendly minds in
honest inquiry, *and,* as *sine qua non,* individual and
group prayer. Where there is divergence in faith silent
prayer should have wide place, with litanies or collects
in which all may unite. Where minds are akin in Christian conviction, prayer may be through Bible reading,
silence, unison or responsive prayers, bidding prayers,
and the free audible prayer of individuals. The writer
could testify to the solving light of one such group
prayer. There were college professors, businessmen,
state officials, and ministers in the friendship circle.
They had spent two days thinking and talking about the
world's dire need. One member finally drew all minds
when he asked the bishop present to administer the Sacrament. Perhaps the bishop broke his canon law. His
name therefore shall be secret, in surety that God loved
him for the "sin." Late at night we went to a little

church—men different in faiths even about the Sacrament, but one in yearning over the world's anguish. There we ourselves lit the candles. There kneeling in the choir stalls we received from the bishop's hand the bread and wine of the Eternal Sacrifice.

III

There are *public occasions* which call for corporate prayer. Paramount are the family crises of joy or sadness—*baptisms, weddings, funerals*. Then the togetherness of human nature prompts us to ask other families to share and consecrate our gladness or grief. These services are sometimes held at home—a practice which has the merit of making the home temporarily a chapel. But probably they could better be held in church. We depend on our setting. A home has many associations, whereas a church by architecture and memory suggests prayer. Joseph and Mary took the child Jesus to the Temple.[6]

In some communions the prayer at *Infant Baptism* is in fixed form. Where that rule holds, the prayer should be read over with the parents before the service, and printed on the baptismal certificate as a memento. Free prayer also has a rightful place. There are particular circumstances which dictate particular prayers. The child may have been adopted, or may be the recompense of many childless years, or joy and sorrow may have come to make strange light and shadow in the home, or the mother may have recovered from critical sickness at childbirth. Prayer is friendship with God. Friendship is not merely a generalized mood: every event is its occasion. Free prayer gives chance for the acknowledgment of God in the instances and occasions of His coming. But, whether prayer be free or formal, our nature is thwarted in its deepest movement if the mystery of birth is not confessed and celebrated before Creative Love:

Eternal Father, of whom the whole family in heaven and earth is named, we acknowledge Thee in the mystery of birth. Thou hast chosen us, even in our unworthiness, for the ongoing of life in the earth; and given us the trust and joy of children. Only by Thy help may the trust be kept and the joy fulfilled. Lead us now, by that same mercy which restored the mother to strength, and blessed us in a living gift. Keep us faithful to the vows this day made. Be Thou the constant Guest in our home. Give us the "word in season," the better word of good example, and the best word of Thine own spirit. Carry this child in Thine arms, Thou Good Shepherd of the Lambs. May he grow in grace as he grows in body and mind, and become a praise in the earth. Hold in Thy care all families and all children in all lands. Make us one family, for his sake who came to earth a little child, even Jesus Christ our Lord. *Amen.*

The prayers at the *Marriage Service* are formal in almost every communion. This is wise, for the marriage service has a ceremonial aspect. Besides, the printed prayers in nearly all the well-known service books are worthy both in language and spirit. Recent revisions, like that in *The Book of Common Prayer,* have banished anachronisms and given new grace to old treasure. The minister should read the whole service with bride and groom before the wedding day. He should not make Christian vows a social convenience or an empty form. At the service proper the prayers should be read reverently, not hurriedly or by rote. The Lord's Prayer should be the united audible petition of the congregation. It is appropriate for the bride and groom to kneel for the benediction, which might well include the age-old prayer: "The Lord bless thee, and keep thee: the Lord make his face shine upon thee, and be gracious unto thee: the Lord lift up his countenance upon thee, and give thee peace."[7]

At the *Funeral Service* prayer is the only language of the soul. The sermon is not in place: long exhortations or interpretations do not belong in epic tragedy. "Personal remarks" may be accordant, when they are the grateful, poignant, yet restrained expressions of personal grief and love, such as Tennyson might—or might not—have uttered at a funeral service for Arthur Hallam; but in many instances, perhaps in most, such "remarks" border on feeble impertinence. Our little twitterings of comment and eulogy are almost a sacrilege in face of death's silent majesty. Prayer is our only word: "Out of the depths have I cried unto thee, O Lord."[8] Great scripture is in place, for great scripture is the warp and woof of prayer: the twenty-third psalm, the fourteenth chapter of John's Gospel, and the "I am persuaded" of the eighth chapter of Romans are an inevitable language. Music is in place, but it should be worthy music—like the slow movement from Beethoven's *Seventh Symphony,* or a hymn of triumphant faith such as

> For all the saints, who from their labors rest,
> Who Thee by faith before the world confessed,
> Thy name, O Jesus, be forever blessed.
> Alleluia![9]

The music and the scripture must be in the deepest mood of prayer, for at death prayer is the only word:

Eternal Father, before whose face the generations rise and pass away, in Thy will is our peace. In life and death we acknowledge Thee. In joy and grief we confess Thee to be good.

God of Ages, who hast made our days few and swift on earth, our strength fails like grass. Yet Thou dost know our frame: Thou rememberest that we are dust. Lift us above the fret of time and ventures scarce begun into enduring Light.

God of all souls, before whom stand the living and the dead, we give Thee hearty thanks for all Thy servants who, having finished their course in faith, do now rest from their labors. Thou hast taken, but Thou didst give—in their devotion, daily cheer, and deeper faith. We give thanks, though in tears, for gifts beyond price. We make our vow: help us to keep the gift unsullied. We dare to pray for our dear and sacred dead. Cancel the hurt we may have done by hasty word or unkind deed. Hold them in Thy perpetual light, from grace to grace, from strength to strength.

Father of our Lord Jesus Christ and our Father, whose grace became incarnate for us men and our salvation, we bless Thee for the promise that in Thy house are many

homes. Thou hast sealed the Gospel of Christ by the white-
ness of his life, the mercy of his cross, and the living word
of his resurrection. Help us now to believe our soul's surmise rather than our eyes and hands. Yea, help us to forget
ourselves in his obedience.

God of all comfort and Father of all mercies, who dost
afflict for a little time and gather again in everlasting love,
we pray Thy peace for those who mourn. Speak Thou the
word we cannot speak. Make perfect Thy strength in weakness. Beset them in their sorrow and in their hope, and lay
Thy hand upon them. Show them that victory waits on
courage, and insight on accepted pain. As they sow in tears
may they reap in joy.

Lord of grace and God of glory, who art high and lifted
up, yet near to our need, we know not how to pray. Answer
our best desires; yea, fulfill Thy best desire for us. Teach
us by death some worthier way of life. Forsake not the
work of Thine own hands. Let Thy mercy be upon us, as
our trust in Thee. O Lord, in Thee have we trusted. Let us
never be confounded. In Jesus' Name. *Amen.*

The inclusion of a prayer for the dead calls for comment. Protestantism has suffered because, in proper recoil from arbitrary theories of purgatory, it has erased
from prayer the memory and mention of the "communion of saints." The claims of spiritualism are often not
spiritual, but earthbound. It would be strange if loved
ones gone should communicate with friends on earth
through mediums previously unknown. Even were the
claims proved, we might well hesitate to ask "those on
before" to talk to us by sound and sense—in terms of
this world's life. But we believe there is an open way
between the worlds: they are both in God's keeping. We
believe in communion—through the better language of
love and prayer, which both worlds speak and understand. Therefore we pray, privately and corporately, for
the dead. Their world is hidden; and prayer therefore
gropes. But the groping is in light, not in darkness. The
language is baffled, but radiant. Such prayer penetrates
another world, fulfills our love, comforts our sadness,
and is worthy of him in whom our faith dwells. We believe that with such prayer God is pleased. The prayers

above printed are broken hints of what prayer should be
in the solemn celebration of death. But their sequence
and content may give some guidance. This is the sequence: a prayer of acknowledgment and acceptance, a
confession of need, a prayer of gratitude, a prayer for
comfort, and a prayer of new commitment to God. By
such prayer the harshness of death is melted, and

> a trumpet sounds
> From the hid battlements of Eternity;
> Those shaken mists a space unsettle,[10]

and sorrow dares ask,

> "Is my gloom, after all,
> Shade of His hand, outstretched caressingly?"[10]

True prayer at the crises of our life, in birth and marriage and death, would consecrate the whole journey.
Each crisis would be an "opening," and the stretches in
between would be filled with light.

IV

There are *public occasions in the wider family, in the
community, and in the state,* which call for corporate
prayer. Our sectarian divisions are calamitous, not
mainly because of creedal bickering or foolish overlap,
though these are deplorable, but because they prevent
the united celebration of our common life in prayer. A
church should be dedicated by the petitions and vows of
the whole community in words like those of Solomon at
the consecration of the ancient Temple.[11] A new home
should be dedicated, with neighbors joining in the litany; and an alert church will provide for its people an
appropriate service. A school, a factory, or a symphony
hall ought likewise to be made consecrate. But how in
our unhappy strife? In one American city the nurses,
three thousand strong, attend an annual church service,
there to renew the pledge of their calling. Suppose there
were such a service for teachers, railroad clerks, doc-

tors, mailmen, and bankers. Suppose that mayors and
senators were dedicated to their task in prayer. The
doctrine of separation of church and state never meant,
and can never mean, the dichotomy of life into secular
and sacred. The age-old frictions of the doctrine prove
that fact. Our founding fathers, mindful of the tyrannies
they had fled, intended a wise separation of function.
But they never doubted that both functions were religious in nature, or that both should find fulfillment in
Faith.

Suppose every man of honorable and needed endeavor were "set apart" by prayer. In the days of the
trade guilds the carpenters adopted as their motto, "I
am the door."[12] By their deliberate intent the two small
upper panels and the two larger lower panels of a door
form a raised cross. Most of us go in and out unwittingly by that sign! But our divisions, cutting across
lines of work and neighborhood, almost forbid the
united consecration of our trades and skills. Nevertheless, there are communities where such services might
be held, with the indirect and added blessing of greater
religious unity. Suppose every school and college were
rooted in prayer. The chapter "Prayer, Imagination,
and Thought" has its own word concerning education—
a word which is underlined by the modern impasse of
knowledge. To teach facts without meanings is worse
than teaching notes without music. To cultivate the
mind without purpose, so that it yields no sustenance, is
worse than intensive farming that yields no food. Either
education must become dedicate to a genuine faith or
religion will be compelled—by public chaos and its own
integrity—to provide a reverent education. Suppose social service workers were ordained. Their task is implic-
itly religious: they honor some "needs-must" of compassion in themselves, and they see in every human
being an intrinsic worth. By this implicit religion their
venture lives. But religion cannot remain merely implicit. Unless the faith is made explicit, social service
may travel for a time on the religious momentum given
by an earlier generation, and then die. Suppose labor
union meetings and bank directors' meetings were

opened and closed in silent and spoken prayer. The notion sounds incredible? Actually it is essential. A labor union cannot endure without a deeper creed than wages and hours, and banks which see only dollars are doomed.

Happily there are occasions when at least a partial truce is called on our sectarian strife—at Christmas, Watchnight, Memorial Day, and Thanksgiving Day. The latter especially is a national festival. It is like the harvest festivals of Europe, but with ampler bounds of praise. On that day prayer is harvest seed:

Eternal Father, *Most High, Omnipotent, Good Lord: Thine be the praise, the glory, the honor, and all benediction.*[13] Thou openest Thine hand, and satisfiest the desire of every living thing. We bless and praise Thy holy Name.

Praise be to Thee, O Lord, for the beauty and bounty of earth, for our health of body and mind, for the human faithfulness which undergirds our days, for friendship's light, and the solace of our homes.

Praise be to Thee, O Lord, for peace and freedom, and grace of worship. Not of our deserving is this gift, and not for our selfishness or pride. Freely we have received: freely would we give. Lay on us Thy vows that nationhood and toil may be bonds of brotherhood—lest joy become ashes, and our vast treasure of content fade like a flower!

Praise be to Thee, O Lord, for an inner world—for books, music, pictures, and the land of vision! Yea, praise for our sorrows and pain if these have driven us to Thy side in prayer, or to our brothers' side in sympathy. If in our blindness we cannot thank Thee for all things, help us to thank Thee *in* all things.

Praise be to Thee for Jesus Christ, whom to know is truth, whom to love is life! Keep us in his forgiveness, and the fellowship of his sufferings, and the power of his resurrection.

Eternal Father, who art the Giver of every good and perfect gift, help us to set the mark of praise on the street and home, on shop and school and church. And may that mind be in us which was also in Christ Jesus, who, though he was rich, for our sakes became poor, that we through his poverty might be rich. *Blessed are they who are found in Thy most holy will.* In his Name we pray. *Amen.*

The school and the Senate, the mill and the home, the hospital and the church should all be consecrate—by corporate prayer. Prayer is the light without which cities are vain and homes decay.

V

The decline of the *church prayer meeting* is a more disturbing symptom of ill health than the alleged decline in church attendance or even than sectarian strife. Neglect of public worship may be due rather to the world's blindness than to the Church's ebbing zeal; and sectarian strife, however unseemly, may be a sign of life. But disregard of prayer among the faithful, that inner group in any church who are the golden heart of the grain, is unmistakable sign for alarm. The cause was not single. There was an outer assault: scientific secularism swept the prayer meeting like a duststorm. But there was also inner weakness: the prayer meeting itself became stereotyped and casual. Phrases were repeated *ad nauseam.* There were some who came to coddle their souls. But the cure for abuse is not disuse. The church cannot redeem a tragic world without the vitality of corporate prayer. On that score Christian history gives invincible testimony. One prime question confronts those who love the church: how shall the prayer meeting be revived? There must be a greater rectitude in daily life before corporate prayer can flourish. An employee cheating his employer, or an employer victimizing his employees, cannot pray except in pretense or resolve on amendment. Prayer is killed by pretense, or by continually postponed amendment. There must be greater fervor in private prayer before corporate prayer can flourish: the body is more than its members, but it depends on their separate health. Yet these two dearths might be overcome by the prayer meeting—that inner fellowship in which lowly souls delight, and God Himself draws near—if some revitalizing wind should blow upon its "valley of dry bones."[14] Revival must begin through one man, presumably through the minister of the church, but perhaps in some layman in whom the flame of prayer still burns. He must pray for the renewal of corporate prayer. Then, acting in faith upon his prayer, he must gather round him one or two like-minded folk. Numbers do not matter. The prayer meeting might find new impetus if the minister should say from the pulpit: "Please do not come from church loyalty or for the minister's encouragement. The loyalty and encouragement are good. But this is a *prayer* meeting. This is a powerhouse: spectators may be only in the way: they may even get hurt. So come only if you believe in corporate prayer or would like to believe. Numbers do not matter." That realism might be far more effective than complaints and pleadings.

Then the leader must *lead*. He must give the prayer meeting due form, but defend it from stereotypy. There is more than one channel through which the zeal of corporate prayer may flow. Here are some means which have been tried, tested, and measurably proved. Let the leader present each week for six weeks a good book about prayer (such as E. Herman's *Creative Prayer*,[15] Harry Emerson Fosdick's *The Meaning of Prayer*,[16] and George S. Stewart's *The Lower Levels of Prayer*),[17] and a good book of prayers (such as John Baillie's *A Diary of Private Prayer*[18] or Russell Bowie's *Lift Up Your Hearts*);[19] and let him briefly describe each book to urge that it be read. Then let him read appropriate prayers from one of the books of prayer, allowing intervals for silent prayer. Or let the leader use "bidding prayers":[20] "We pray now for our country. Think about its needs. Try to see it as Christ might see it from his cross. Then pray in one spoken sentence your prayer for your country, and we will pray with you." He must gently curb discursive prayers, remembering that the conversion of Wilfred Grenfell began when he heard Dwight L. Moody say, "The rest of us will sing a hymn while that brother finishes his prayer." Or let the leader

propose a period of completely silent prayer: the Quaker
witness cannot be gainsaid, and should be laid under fee
by the whole church. Or let him prepare in multigraph a
series of fine litanies—a Litany of Adoration, a Litany of
Thanksgiving, a Litany of Confession, a Litany of Intercession—in which the group may join in responsive prayer. Many books of services, such as John Hunter's *Devotional Services*,[21] or the Presbyterian *Common Worship*,[22]
offer just such treasure. Or let the leader use the liturgical prayers of other religious communions, and thus
confirm the essential unity of the Church. Or, if a good
organ and a competent organist are available and the
prayer meeting is held in the church, let the group *read*
silently the words of some great prayer hymn while the
organist gives the music of each verse its proper expression. The hymns should be strong, not sticky; and they
should be hymns of the commonwealth as well as of
private devotion—such hymns as "Spirit of God, Descend upon My Heart"[23] and "O God of Earth and
Altar."[24]

These suggestions are not exhaustive, but only hints
for variations on a fine theme. The prayer meeting
should usually be held within strict limits of time: a
thirty-minute period is not too brief. There are psychological limits to our power of concentration, and for
many people the demands of life are pressing. A wise
leader will keep faith with these plain facts. The hour of
day should be convenient or challenging: Wednesday
evening is not sacrosanct; Tuesday afternoon at five or
Thursday morning at eight might be a better hour.
Meanwhile the leader of the prayer meeting may tell
himself with joy that he is a "keeper of the springs." In
his care is the fountainhead of the river which turns all
wheels and fertilizes all fields.

VI

The stronghold of corporate prayer is the *Sunday
Service of Worship*. The world proposes that the Fourth
Commandment is "just another man-made law," and
assumes no need to "remember the sabbath day, to

keep it holy."[25] The proposal is unproved. If it were
granted, it would still be unsound, for the Fourth Commandment was in human nature before it was graven on
Moses' tables of stone. Physical health requires one
day's rest in seven. Mental health demands some sanctuary, even though it be only a sanctuary of mood, from
the "lust of the flesh and the lust of the eyes and the
vainglory of life." If the week-end habit should starve
the Sabbath, we would soon institute another Sabbath
on Wednesday—or see our world darken. The ever-
present magazine article on "Why I Do Not Go to
Church" usually betrays the littleness and ignorance of
the writer more than it demonstrates those same faults
in the Church. But if the latter demonstration were
made, as it could be made, the magazine writer would
be obligated by his own truth to help to revitalize the
Church; for apparently men must worship. Then how
may the corporate prayer of Sunday worship be rekindled? The magazine article need not dismay us, but
there is enough truth in its customary nonsense to give
pause to those who love the Church.

We are tempted to discuss church architecture, but
must refrain, except to recall that common prayer requires its helpful setting—those symbols which focus
the scattered self, unite worshipers in one adoration,
and give memorial to past experience of God. Preaching
also tempts comment, but it is beyond our present survey. Even the order of service must not distract us save
as it touches corporate prayer. That order should not
open abruptly: worship, like the church itself, has its
vestibule of reverent approach. There should be a call
to worship followed by the invocation and a hymn of
praise. An alternative sequence is the processional
hymn of praise, followed by the call to worship and the
invocation. Then may come the prayer of confession
and absolution. Man's instinctive sense of unworthiness
when in the Presence demands for penitence this early
place. The rhythm of worship, in its systole and dias-
tole, also demands it. The next act may be the responsive reading. This has obvious value; too often people
make the minister their proxy: corporate worship is a

corporate act. Then may come the "Gloria," and the prayer of thanksgiving. Then the treasure of the scripture reading. The Bible is *the* Book. It enshrines the genius of Old Testament insight and the sole glory of the New Testament Christ; and in our age, when men deem it wisdom to devour the "latest book" and neglect *the* Book, there is more need that the Bible be read in public worship—and be well read, with careful choice of passages, and with understanding mind. The Bible, moreover, gives true content to prayer. After the scripture may come music. But it should be good music worthily rendered, just as the sanctuary should be good architecture well built. The word "anthem" derives from *antiphon:* it was originally an antiphonal hymn of praise. It should still be an act of worship—not a sentimental orgy, nor display, nor even rendition, but an oblation. After the music may come the prayers, the offering, and the doxology or a hymn. After the doxology may come the sermon. That should be followed by a hymn—if only that the congregation may *ex*press what worship has *im*pressed. The final act is the benediction, which in the Early Church had great weight and sacredness. This order is not inflexible. Interest in worship requires that it should vary. But its main flow and rhythm have been validated by the experience of praying men.

Corporate prayer is the heart of corporate worship. Ritual is not central; for, however necessary and vital, it is still ritual. Scripture is not central; for, however indispensable and radiant, it is still scripture—that which is written, the record not the experience, the very word but not the Presence. Preaching is not central; for preaching, however inevitable and kindling, is still preaching—the *heralding,* not the very Lord. Friedrich Heiler has rightly written: "Not speech *about* God but speech *to* God, not the preaching of the revelation of God, but direct intercourse with God is, strictly speaking, the worship of God."[26] When the rite is made central, prayer may become an incantation. When the Book is made central, prayer may become an appendage of scribal interpretations. When preaching is made central, prayer, as in even Zwingli's order of public worship, may become only an introduction and conclusion to the sermon. The heart of religion is in prayer—the uplifting of human hands, the speaking of human lips, the expecting waiting of human silence—in direct communion with the Eternal. Prayer must go *through* the rite, scripture, symbolism, and sermon, as light through a window.

Then with what burden and awe the minister should *prepare* the prayers for public worship! Therein is the grievous failure, not to say disgrace, of Protestantism. "Brother So-and-so will lead us in prayer"; whereupon Brother So-and-so, in too many instances, offers God a slipshodness and a jumble, sometimes almost a brash irreverence, and has the temerity to call it prayer. Where public prayer is undisciplined, corporate public worship decays. There is a necessary preparation both of the pray-er and the prayer. What are its steps? The minister and congregation should explore the wealth of prayers, "free" and liturgical, offered through the years. Wisdom was not born with us. There are collects of St. Chrysostom which are the perfect bloom of devotion. They cannot be touched without being spoiled. They can only be prayed, in gratitude for men who pray for us better than we pray for ourselves. Furthermore, prayers should spring from prior inquiry. What *are* the blessings for which we should praise God? What *are* the sins which should find corporate confession? What *are* the conflicts and sorrows that should be upborne in corporate intercession? As that last question is asked the compassionate minister will see the faces of his people and the tragic need of the world until intercession then and there interrupts his ponderings.

Then the minister must plan and write prayers as rigorously as sermons. The language should be wrought. God may be pleased with a clumsy prayer, but not when the clumsiness comes of sloth or a casual mind. The wording should not be "modern," despite the glib plea of the modern mind. Assuredly it should not be scientific or psychological. Every endeavor has right to its own idiom, providing the idiom is not a prison which the initiate cannot escape and the stranger cannot unlock. Religion is entitled to its own vocabulary—on the same terms. The idiom should be modern only in the sense that it does not rehearse ancient theological strife or outmoded ideas, or use coinage whose image and superscription is worn smooth. Otherwise prayer language should not be ancient or modern, but movingly human and plainly reverent—the language of a devotional poem. There such words as "reaction," "blitzkrieg," "moratorium" would be forbidden; but words that glow in common speech would find welcome. Trite phrases—"Lord, bless all those we come in contact with"—and explosive phrases—"Lord, split our souls"—would be taboo; but quickening phrases, to give the mind its picture and the will its resolve, would be sought as treasure.

The planning of a prayer should be deliberate and clearly drawn. Later, in public utterance, the prayer may break its bounds to "take heaven by storm," but only if the bounds have first been set. How can petition or intercession be real unless it is specific and ordered? Prayer has its rapture like great music. Bach's *Toccata and Fugue in E Minor* breaks into a torrent of suns and stars. But the torrent has its reservoir, its gates opened and closed, and its appointed river bed. True rapture always knows prior disciplines.

Can prayer guidance be more detailed? Only as guidance, not as bondage. The *invocation,* as the word implies, is a *call.* As such it should be brief. Its *indirect* result is to gather the congregation, diverse in mood and life, into one worship. Its *direct* purpose is to open the door to God without whose coming all worship is vain. The invocation should be general and accustomed, in language and in content; for the congregation is diverse, and needs a recognized sign. This collect is almost archetypal:

Almighty God, unto whom all hearts are open, all desires known, and from whom no secrets are hid; cleanse the thoughts of our hearts by the inspiration of thy Holy Spirit, that we may perfectly love thee, and worthily magnify thy holy Name; through Jesus Christ our Lord. *Amen;*

or this other well-known collect, from St. Chrysostom, which is equally appropriate for the opening as for the close of worship:

Almighty God, who hast given us grace at this time with one accord to make our common supplications unto thee; and dost promise that when two or three are gathered together in thy Name thou wilt grant their requests; Fulfill now, O Lord, the desires and petitions of thy servants, as may be most expedient for them; granting us in this world knowledge of thy truth, and in the world to come life everlasting. *Amen.*

These two are a pattern for prayer. They are addressed to God—as Jesus taught. They do not lapse from that reverence to address the congregation. After the divine Name, they meditate on some divine attribute ("unto whom all hearts are open"), then make simple petition, then offer proof of the sincerity of the petition ("that we may perfectly love thee"), and end with an ascription in the name of Christ. The language is universal, as witness such words as "all." It prunes away adjectives, and stresses verbs. These prayers have beauty, rigor, and holiness.

The "long prayer" is condemned by the very name—which also hints at remedy. The prayer should *not* be long. The ordinary laws regarding attention cannot be violated: while the minister continues his tedious harangue, the mind of his congregation will wander across the world and into other worlds, and may not return during the rest of the service. Dr. Willard L. Sperry in a fine book on worship has reminded us that Edwards Park of Andover, when he could not remember a name, would say, "I cannot remember it now, but I shall think of it during the long prayer next Sunday."[27] If the prayer of thanksgiving, the prayer of confession, the prayer of intercession, the prayer of petition, and the prayer of adoration are offered in one time-period in the service—a plan which is unwise—they should not be "The Long Prayer" but "The Prayers." Each should be brief; each should begin with an address to God and end with an ascription to Christ; and the congregation should be encouraged to respond to each with a sincere "Amen." That congregational sharing might be confirmed if "The Prayers" began with an antiphon. The following antiphon was used in both the Eastern and Western Churches, and should not be the monopoly of any one communion:

Minister: The Lord be with you.
People: And with thy spirit.
Minister: Lift up your hearts.
People: We lift them up unto the Lord.
Minister: Let us give thanks unto the Lord.
People: It is meet and right so to do.

By that act minister and people become "one body," disposed to prayer. The prayers might wisely be spaced, as in the order of worship already suggested. The prayer of thanksgiving might be printed, so as to permit the congregation to offer it in united voice. Even then the prayers of intercession and petition should be broken into brief prayers. Whatever the order, prayer should not expose itself to the title "The Long Prayer." "The Long Prayer" should become "The Prayers."

The old issue between "free prayer" and formal prayer need not distract us. Experience and common sense alike suggest that both have their place in public worship. The *collect* does collect people: its necessarily general language covers individual need, and yet provides a communal tie. Besides, it links the worshiping generations, joining each congregation with the communion of saints. It is vindicated by time's test and present blessing. But so is free prayer. When formal prayer becomes a dry routine, people turn to free prayer: when free prayer becomes slipshod or merely contemporaneous, people turn to formal prayer. Each has its function, and each should be held in realism and reverence. As for free prayer, human need is specific. So prayer should be specific— the expression of personality in the midst of present life. Any true comradeship, human or divine, grapples with the moment and the occasion.

Free prayer lays on the leader added burdens. The language should not be merely his language, but that also of all his neighbors; and it should befit a man confronting God. Private emotion should not obtrude. The leader should speak within the feeling-tone of the group—with undertones of reverence. The very voice, though always natural, should be measured—the instinctive voice of one who speaks for men to God. "The Prayers" may have both links of formal prayer, such as the fine collects in which *The Book of Common Prayer* is passing rich, and links of free prayer. The following may give some broken hint of "The Prayers at Evening Service":

Eternal Father, to whom darkness and light are both alike, lighten our darkness, and call us home to Thy grace, for his sake, even Jesus Christ our Lord. *Amen.*

God of Life, who hast loved us into life, Thy shepherding care guides and sustains us. Our wisdom does not rule the chances and changes of the world. Thou hast nourished us with bread of fields, bread of friendship, bread of Providence, and the living Bread of Christ. How can we praise Thee as we ought? We would be thankful in prayer and deed and inmost spirit; through Jesus Christ our Lord. *Amen.*

God of Pardon, with whom there is forgiveness that Thou mayest be feared, we confess our sins. We confess their sinfulness: we know the right and do the wrong. We confess their folly: the joy we sought has turned to ashes. We confess their cruelty: our wrong inflicts on Thee and men a deeper wrong. Often we live as if Jesus had never lived. This darkness we bring to Thee. Create in us a clean heart, O Lord, and renew a right spirit within us. Restore unto us the joy of Thy salvation, through Jesus Christ our Lord. *Amen.*

God of the Common Good, who hast bound all in one bundle of life, we confess the brotherhood. We plead our neighbor's need. For the nations we pray: give peace in our time. For the workers of the world we pray: gird them and us that none may lack bread or comradeship, since Thou hast given enough for all. For the sorrowing and the sick we pray: make their shadow the secret way of Thy coming.

For our friends and loved ones: befriend them in Thine own befriending. Remember in Thy mercy those whom we forget. Gather all needy folk within the healing of Thy wings. Teach us to bear one another's burdens, that we may fulfill the law of Christ; for his sake. *Amen.*

God of Grace and God of Glory, great Thou art and greatly to be praised. Kind art Thou and deeply to be loved. We adore Thee, before whom angels veil their faces. Thou art Life and Light. Thou art Journey and Home. We bow before Thee asking nothing, save that our life may be Thy flame. Glory be to Thee, O Lord most high! Through Jesus Christ our Lord. *Amen.*

The minister might wisely pause after each prayer to give chance for silent prayer. Or he might pause in the midst of certain prayers: "We confess our sins, which now we name in silence" . . . . "We pray for our friends whom now we name before Thee in silence." The service may also include a spoken prayer after the offertory. Or there may be offertory scripture sentences—"Freely ye have received, freely give"—with the doxology sung by the whole congregation as the offering is presented. Another brief collect should follow the sermon. All these suggestions are only roughly drawn. But even if they were only roughly heeded, worship would have a more vital impact and a more lasting glow.

VII

The climax of Christian corporate prayer is in the celebration of the Sacrament. That was the burning heart of worship in the Early Church. It seems to have the fire of Eternity. Neither theological strife, nor attempts to make it magic, nor seasons of ebbing zeal, nor the world's despisings have quenched its altar flame. The journeying generations are blessed by its light and warmth. How simple it is—a child may understand its tokens of bread and wine—yet how unfathomable its mystery! How lowly—bread and wine were on every poorest table—yet how awe-filled and alone! How

Children & communion

comradely—it was the Sabbath meal in the Early Church—yet how sharp in individual challenge and redemption! How rich in symbolism—as wheat is sown in darkness, lives again to be cut by the reaper, is ground between millstones, and thus becomes man's nourishment, so is the sacrificial love of Christ; as the grapes are trodden in the winepress, so is his bruised body and outpoured blood—how rich in symbolism, yet how tangibly real! How stored with history—it has been the benediction of vast cathedral and lonely bedside, the solace of Covenanter and priest—yet how instant in a Presence! Its varied treasures shine in its titles. It is a *Eucharist*—a Thanksgiving. It is a *Sacrament*—the Memorial of the Passion of Christ. It is an *Oblation* (the "Offering")—the dedication of all life for his sake. It is *Communion*—the confession of our oneness with all mankind and with God. It is the *Real Presence*—Christ "made known in the breaking of bread." It is the *Lord's Supper*—spiritual food of grace and power. Different churches gave different meanings to these titles, which are but names for "the Nameless of a thousand names." But because the churches are members of one Church, all acknowledge in each title the token of a deep experience. These names[28] may grant us the order and content of the sacramental prayer. The liturgies of the Sacrament, with which the Christian years have enriched us, are for a testimony.

In the Early Church congregational participation was a marked feature of the prayers at the Sacrament. The *Didache,* in its ceremonial instructions for the Eucharist, gives the following litany:

Leader: We thank thee, our Father, for the holy vine of thy servant David, which thou hast made known to us through thy Son Jesus.

Congregation: To thee be glory for ever and ever!

Leader: We thank thee, our Father, for the life and knowledge which thou hast revealed to us through thy Son Jesus!

Congregation: To thee be the glory for ever and ever!

Leader: As this broken bread was strewed on the
                   mountains and being collected became
                   one, so let thy Church be brought together
                   from the ends of the earth into thy king-
                   dom!

Congregation: For thine is the glory, and the power,
                   through Jesus Christ, for ever and ever.

Such guidance is still wisdom. An alert church might
also print for its people, especially for new communicants, some simple instruction to aid the silent prayer in
which the bread and wine are taken. Today in the Eastern and Western liturgies there is first the "Liturgy of
the Catechumens," and then the "Liturgy of the Faithful"—an order which continues a practice of the Early
Church. One Protestant church, on the day when its
young communicants were received into the church and
"took first communion," printed the following guidance:

· PRAYING AT THE COMMUNION SERVICE

When we receive the Bread and Wine of the Sacrament,
what should occupy our thoughts and prayers? The answer
depends on individual need, but there are some thoughts
and prayers in which we are one:

Our Lord Jesus Christ—God's gift of love and power
through him to all mankind.
The Church—its steady witness in Christ's spirit; and our
own witness through the Church by prayer, gift, and
service.
Our Failures—of low aim, ignoble deed, and wasted opportunities; our forgetting that all people belong to God's
family; and our share in such social wrongs as race intolerance, economic strife, and war.
Our Comrades—those we have hurt and those who have
hurt us; our family, friends, employers, servants; the sad
and the suffering, known and unknown; missionaries,
ministers, peacemakers, and the host of those by whom
our days are guided; and the world-wide comradeship of
Christ.

Our Need of strength and joy for daily living in Christ's name.

Such thoughts and prayers should be ours as we receive the Sacrament. Then by faith we shall receive also the power of Christ, and the calmness of the dedicated life.

The same church follows his order of the Celebration of the Sacrament: Scripture Sentences of Invitation to the Table, Eucharistic Hymn, The Words of the Institution, The Prayer at the Sacrament, The distribution of Bread and Wine, Scripture Sentences of the New Hope, Concluding Collect, Final Hymn, and Benediction.

The prayer at the Sacrament should be wrought in disciplined thought and ardent prayer. An anthology of church prayers, such as Morgan Phelps Noyes's *Prayers for Services,*[29] and the steadily improving books of worship provided by the various communions, not only give guidance but also indicate rich sources. The following is written to hint a course, a mood, and a content:

Almighty God, uncreated Light and Love, we bless and magnify Thy holy Name. All things come of Thee. Earth and heaven are of Thy will. All souls are Thine. Worthy art Thou to receive all glory and praise!

Gracious Father, we thank Thee more especially for Jesus Christ our Lord, whose life is our example, whose death is our redemption, and whose rising is the first fruits of our immortality.

Giver of all good, help us now to give ourselves to Thee, our bodies and souls, a living sacrifice, which is our reasonable service.

Father of the whole family in heaven and earth, purge us of bitterness and deliver us from hate. We would be joined with the need of the whole world. We would be joined with the bright company of heaven. May Thy will be done in earth as it is in heaven until there is "one fold and one Shepherd."

Lord God Incarnate, we remember Christ according to his word: his lowly way, his truth which does not pass though heaven and earth be shaken, his trust in our blind and wayward nature, his courage unto death, his love unto

Sacrifice. The remembrance of him quickens into a Presence. May he be made known to us in the breaking of bread.

Thou who art Bread and Wine, we would feed on Thee in the hunger and thirst of our sorrow and pain, our want and weariness, our folly and sin, our yearnings and hope. Renew our life, Thou Food Celestial.

Therefore with angels and archangels we laud and magnify Thy holy Name, evermore praising Thee and saying, Holy, Holy, Holy, Lord God of Hosts. Heaven and earth are full of Thy glory. Glory be to Thee, O Lord most high. *Amen.*

This prayer follows the sixfold meaning of the Sacrament as shown in its worthiest titles. The conclusion is the "Sanctus" with which the early liturgies ended the prayer of thanksgiving. It can well be the conclusion of the whole prayer. Precisely because the Sacrament has been made the central act of worship, it has become the very "means of grace." Men have forgotten themselves in this supreme adoration of God, to discover unawares that God has remembered them. The legends of the Holy Grail grew round a core of living truth and fact. The truth and fact still hold, and many a lowly celebrant can claim with Galahad that "never yet hath . . . ."

> This Holy Thing failed from my side, nor come
> Cover'd, but moving with me night and day,
> Fainter by day, but always in the night
> Blood-red, and sliding down the blacken'd marsh
> Blood-red, and on the naked mountain top
> Blood-red, and in the sleeping mere below
> Blood-red. And in the strength of this I rode
> Shattering all evil customs everywhere.[30]

Still today the Sacrament moves across the world to make life sacramental, and lives within the heart as "the heart's true food."

This survey of corporate prayer is cursory, and the instruction is poor. But poor instruction may induce the reader to seek a better guidance. The state of the churches leaves sincere men ill at ease. The world looks at the clothing and finds it ragged; the faithful look at the heart and find it cold. Ragged clothing might be no misfortune if the heart were warm. The heart of the Church is prayer. We need a specialized ministry: only thus can the church meet a diversified need. We need new unity: a torn world finds little hope in a divided Church. We need an earnest and intelligent grappling with the task of religious education, since merely secular education must fail and may become a snare. We need a rebirth of pastoral care, which now might be girded with new psychiatric understandings and skills. We need a new river of prophetic preaching to cleanse our Augean stables—with purer flow than the rivers of Hercules. The needs of the Church are many and urgent. But they might all be met by the leaven of genuine corporate prayer. Only in God's light can the Church see light; only in His grace can the Church be redeemed—or redeem.

CHAPTER XX

PRAYER AND THE NEW WORLD

HIS PICTURE WAS on a magazine cover—the wounded soldier kneeling on a prayer bench in the church aisle. We could see round about him the whole congregation at prayer with faces equally intent. What were they praying? Perhaps what men are everywhere saying—that it is now or never, that we must build a better world quickly or see decency engulfed, that our crisis is beyond the wisdom and broken goodness of man, and that we have no refuge save in God:

> Our God, our Help in ages past,
>   Our Hope for years to come,
> Our Shelter from the stormy blast,
>   And our eternal Home.[1]

Perhaps that was the prayer. But what can *they* do, the kneeling folk? The skeptic says, "They waste breath." The aggressor says, "They waste time and strength, and invite destruction." The scientific materialist says, "They waste intelligence: it is a universe of fixed laws." Yet—that eagerness of face, that intensity of spirit! Perhaps the kneeling folk are now in a Deeper Economy which holds man's plans and pother as the universe holds our little earth. Perhaps they are now allied with the Spirit which is "in the mind of man, and rolls through all things." What can *they* do?

I

To propose that they can divert God from His holy purpose would profane God and degrade man. To affirm that they can summon instant external change to meet every blind desire would merit Longfellow's sharp comment: "What discord should we bring into the universe if our prayers were all answered! Then *we* should govern the world, and not God. And do you think we should govern it better? It gives me only pain when I hear the long, wearisome petitions of men asking for they know not what."[2] Even so, Longfellow's rebuke is not an echo of heaven. Not every human prayer is "asking for they know not what"; and there is a measure in which we *must* govern the world, or God himself becomes Dictator. Democracy, in its long and costly evolution, its distortions and false freedoms, its excesses and renewals, is the upspringing of faith in man's birthright under God. Chemically man is worth about a dollar in carbohydrates, unless we raise the price because he is an ingenious chemical process. But aesthetically man has links with Ultimate Beauty; intellectually, with Ultimate Truth; morally, with Ultimate Goodness; and prayerfully, with Ultimate Spirit. The adjective "Ultimate" is not a begging of the question: the scientist *does* know final Truth, however vaguely, or he could not know that his present science is only partial. He does not create this Sanction of Truth, for he cannot create himself: the Sanction creates him. Thus democracy is not a political form: it is a spiritual faith. "All men *are* created equal," not in the shallow sense of equal health or equal intelligence quotient, but in the deep sense that every man has his direct commission from the Sky. That is why a man's house must be free from "unreasonable searches and seizures." That is why all business must be suspended to release one child from a landslide, or all medical resource lavished on one "drunk" taken from the gutter. Each man has his intrinsic worth, his "secret orders," his intimate dealings with Eternity. This worth vanishes unless we *do* govern our

world—measurably and under God. Unless man has
some power over events, not alone by deed but by
prayer, his birthright as a man is lost and his freehold
usurped. Longfellow's comment is half blind. Children
do not "govern it better" than their parents, but as free
beings and for their growth they must be given *some*
chance to govern.

The welfare of the race turns on events—events
rightly interpreted and eliciting our right response.
Prayer within the guiding friendship and parenthood of
God *has some power over events.* Our world is not a
realm of fixed law: it is a realm of spontaneity and surprise within a faithfulness. Look out of a window: why
does that tree catch just those lights and shadows in the
play of sun and wind? Why does *that* man appear at
that corner at *that* moment? The fluidity of "natural"
happening and human thought are as marked a feature
of the universe, and apparently as characteristic a trait,
as what we have been pleased to call "law." Science can
arrive at general laws only by emptying the world of its
particular events, and the world refuses to be emptied.
Science draws its basic patterns by getting rid of happenings, but things still happen. The innocent-looking
phrase "it came to pass" still hides the deepest myster-
ies. It is almost unbelievable that we could have been
blinded to that fact. But we have been blinded. In the
name of science we have accepted fables more unreal
than *The Arabian Nights.* What governs events? Not
"law": law is a vacant scheme which we have made by
eliminating events. Then what—or Who? In the novel
Ararat[3] Elgin Groseclose grapples with that question.
Why were such and such men saved in the Armenian
massacre? Why should an unforseen delay deliver them
from the pursuer? Why should an army officer, who
otherwise might have killed them, weaken in a surge of
"unaccountable" memory? Why should a thunderclap
divert a surgeon from drugging a man before execution,
and thus permit the man's escape? Why should the river
flood at precisely that juncture to work deliverance?
And why should many die without rescue? These are
the real questions. The schemata of science by compari-

son are easy work. Obviously there are regularities: we could not live in a topsy-turvydom. But they are not the living nerve of our adventure: the nerve is the newness of inward impelling and outward event. The wonder of music is not in the keyboard, or even in the laws of music, but in the magic of woven sound. God's answers to prayer come through the music played on the keyboard according to music's laws. The answers come through the Faithfulness which sometimes seems friendly and sometimes stern, and through the music which sometimes gainsays and sometimes grants our petitions.

The praying man turns the event—not always, not often, but sometimes. If he turned it always Longfellow would be right: we would govern—unto chaos. But if he turned it never, man would be a slave and God would be Coercion.

> God answers sharp and sudden on some prayers,
> And thrusts the things we have prayed for in our face,
> A gauntlet with a gift in 't.[4]

Moreover, the man's eyes and ears are more alert as he prays: events have a new meaning to win from him a new response. Then he says, "I just go about my business, but I find doors opening, things happening, help given, opportunities given, which have a direct connection with my prayers, and I accept these as the answer from God."[5] Or another says, "As I wait with a willing spirit, ideas colored by my prayer come into my mind, which seems to be made sensitive by the approach of God. I accept these as the response of God."[5] By prayer men are in tune with God, both in the play of events and in the play of thought. Mary Queen of Scots said she feared the prayers of John Knox more than all the armies in Europe. That is a word for our time. The blows which Luther struck were not those of his hammer as he nailed his theses to the church door at Wittenberg, but those he struck by prayer: "In his prayer closet," says a historian, "the Reformation was born." The history of the Church gives evidence that

men have worked "miracles" by prayer—miracles
which are not arbitrary rendings of a faithfulness, but
events in a Faithfulness occurring in such wise that
men, looking at the event, feeling its impact, and remembering their prayer, have said, "This is the doing of
God!" The exclamation is just as valid as the scientist's,
"This is truth!"

II

Longfellow's comment, though it fails in justice to
man's birthright of personality, nevertheless carries a
sharp warning. If prayer had no deeper gift than some
measure of event-power, it would be no blessing. There
are deeper gifts. For epochal instance, _prayer brings
men into contact and communion with a Purpose above
events and humanity._ Amid the fatal relativisms of our
time, prayer gives a point of ultimate reference.

The relativisms and their deadliness are not far to
seek. John Galsworthy in _Loyalties_ shows how earthly
fealties inevitably conflict. The army captain stole
money from a wealthy Jew, who was his fellow guest at
a house party, and gave the money to an Italian girl to
purchase her silence on the eve of his marriage. Then
the ravelment began. The Jew, bitter at being "black-
balled" at a London club, brought suit. So the Jew and
the Gentile were each loyal to his race. The army set
meanwhile was loyal to Dancy; the Italian tried to
"hush up" the incident because he was loyal to his
daughter; Dancy was—too late—loyal to his wife; the
wife was loyal to her husband; the attorneys refused the
case because they were loyal to "the standards of the
firm"—until the threads of human relationship were almost hopelessly snarled. "Criss-cross," said an onlooker
in acid comment, "criss-cross, we all cut each other's
throats from the best of motives." The dramatist offers
no solving word—perhaps because he had none, perhaps
because he is a dramatist. Here is the fact which points
the answer: the acid comment was palpably untrue: _no_
character acted from "the best of motives."[6] Every
character acted from the _second-best_ of motives, and

that was the rub! Human loyalties of race, nation, class, profession, and even of home "cut one another's throats"—from the second-best of motives—unless men learn to worship an overarching, all-controlling Loyalty. No human devotion is safe except within the higher Fealty, and earth is chaotic without a Purpose above the earth. Thus Jesus said, the urgency of the issue giving a deliberately overkeen edge to his words: "If any man come to me, and hate not his father, and mother, and wife, and children, ... he cannot be my disciple."[7]

The chaos spreads in our time. Is our scientific skill merely for our comfort? We would become spiritually diabetic, and comfort soon palls! Is science for mutual slaughter? We would invite extinction! Then for our self-glorying? We wither like grass!

> Imperious Caesar, dead and turn'd to clay,
> Might stop a hole to keep the wind away.[8]

Some modern cynic has added:

> The great god Ra whose shrine once covered acres
> Is filler now for crossword puzzle makers.[9]

The same questions could be asked of education, art, marriage, or any human quest; and would meet the same answer. These purposes are so puny, even though we live and die for them, that one sight of stars turns them to folly. In any event, if *our* purpose is at odds with the Purpose of the world which brought us to birth, our purpose cannot stand. Astounding that we should live for the means, and never inquire for the end! Doubly astounding that we should assume that unworthy means can hold their own poison and never infect any end! "Now is the judgment of this world!"

Men and nations, labor unions and churches and employers' associations, may make their individual clocks, but not their individual time: they must take their time from the Sky, or turn life into confusion. Prayer gives celestial time. Sailors may make their own journeyings, but not their own map: they may not paint their own

horizons on the cabin ceiling: they must obey the stars
and a magnetism-out-of-sight, or the ocean lanes become shambles. Prayer gives the guidance of stars. Men
may choose their architecture, but not their own rules of
construction: they must build by an "invisible vertical,"
or the house will fall. Prayer is the "invisible Vertical."
Prayer gives us the master light for all our seeing, the
"chord of nature" for all our music. The facade of Bath
Abbey shows two ladders on which men are climbing
up and up—to Christ. Is *that* the End, and this world
only a ladder? We would then not care too much about
this world, except to strengthen its rungs that men may
climb.

III

Even *this* gift of prayer, the revealing of a Purpose, is
vain without a deeper gift. *Can prayer change human
nature until it is in tune with the Purpose?* If not, the
best event will be perverted. Ambitious old men of Italy
saw in Galileo's "tube" only a new advantage in war.
Unworthy men will try to use even their prayers. Peer
Gynt boasted on his yacht that he took religion only
intermittently:

> And, as one needs in days of trial
> Some certainty to place one's trust in,
> I took religion imtermittently.
> That way it goes more smoothly down.
> One should not read to swallow all,
> But rather see what one has use for.[10]

Then he found himself left on the beach, a castaway,
and prayed after his own fashion:

It is I, Peer Gynt! Oh, our Lord, give but heed!
Hold thy hand o'er me, Father; or else I must perish!
Make them back the machine! Make them lower the gig!
   Stop the robbers! Make something go wrong with the
   rigging!
Hear me! Let other folks' business lie over!
The world can take care of itself for the time![11]

Then, amazed and indignant that his prayer is not answered according to demand, he exclaimed:

> I'm blessed if he hears me! He's deaf as his wont is!
> Here's a nice thing! A God that is bankrupt of help!
> Hist; I've abandoned the nigger-plantation!
> And missionaries I've exported to Asia!
> Surely one good turn should be worth another!
> Oh, help me on board![11]

Prayer is not that debasing selfishness. It is the supreme act of worship, by which the stagnant pool unawares invites the cleansing River. Prayer opens life to the Eternal goodness. If men try to use prayer, turning it into a Tammany system of favors and spoils, their only help is still in prayer—their own poor prayer breaking in undreamed-of light or the interceding prayers of nobler men.

Steadfastly we refuse to ask *how* bad people are made good. Thrashing a bad man may improve him, if—if he believes that his folly merits the thrashing, and that the thrasher acts in wisdom and love. It is a big "if"! Yet, lacking fulfillment of the "if," the thrashing may make the bad man more stubborn. Therein we find new evidence of the folly of war. Does a defeated nation ever believe she merited defeat, and that the victor strove in wisdom of love? Wars issue only in worse wars, unless genuinely creative forces enter to mend destruction. *Men become good only by contagion of goodness.* Goodness cannot be compelled or even taught: it is caught. If it is taught, it is taught only by those from whom it can be caught. Sometimes even the contagion of daily goodness fails to cure badness: the Pharisees scoffed at Jesus, and killed him. Then goodness must become sacrificial. Then goodness suffering unto death, rather than be anything else but good, is the only cure of badness. Paul was converted by the face of the martyr Stephen praying for his murderers. The real question therefore is: How is goodness kept regnant and radiant in good folk? And the real answer seems to be: only by renewal from the source of Goodness—by the

friendship called prayer. We recover from the poisons
of fatigue by flinging ourselves on the earth, or on a bed
on the earth—by surrendering in utter helplessness,
even in unconsciousness, to the whole scheme of things.
We find healing from a disease only through nature's
healing: again our cure is in utter dependence on the
whole order of life. These are parables of a deeper cure.
In the last resort there is nothing to do but pray—to
cast our weariness upon a vast Strength, to expose our
sickness to a healing Light, to bring our badness to the
redemptive contagion of sacrificial Goodness. Prayer
saves our human nature from itself: it opens a window
in a room filled with monoxide fumes. How we need a
genuine revival of faith! All such revivals have begun,
not in any artificial whipping up of enthusiasm, but in
the intensity of private and group prayer. The new pentecost will come as the first Pentecost came—through a
little company of people, committed to Jesus, who wait
in prayer for the baptism of the Eternal Spirit.

IV

These are the claims we have made for prayer: it
turns the event within the measure of our freehold under God; it enthrones Ultimate Purpose not merely by
postulate but in Comradeship; and it renews personality
at the springs of primal Goodness. There is another bestowal without which even these gifts might still spell
poverty. *Prayer cancels our homelessness.* A profound
nostalgia afflicts our age. We rarely confess it, but its
symptoms we cannot hide. These are the signs: masses
of mankind making violence a refuge from their fears,
feeling no bond with one another because they acknowledge no bond with God; cities grotesque in flaunted
wealth and abject poverty, garish in architecture and
obtrusive in greed, their streets cacophonous with
crowds; the clamant dissonance of our music and the
worse discords of our order of toil; the lurid pleasures
in which we seek a momentary respite from our secret
desolation; the appalling epidemic of nervous ills. These
are the signs of a pathetic and terrifying loneliness. We

have no "hills of home"—only the emptiness and endlessness of cosmic space. We have no hereafter—only a little trouble of breath. We have no values—only notoriety and a cynical "yeah?" Mankind has always suffered a homesickness of the soul:

> For men are homesick in their homes,
>   And strangers under the sun;
> And they lay their heads in a foreign land
>   Whenever the day is done.[12]

Always we have been "strangers and pilgrims in the earth." The conversation between Rebecca and George in *Our Town* is eloquent of our loneliness and longing. Rebecca tells George of a letter:

Rebecca: It said: Jane Crofut; the Crofut Farm; Grover's Corners; Sutton County; New Hampshire; United States of America.

George: What's funny about that?

Rebecca: But listen, it's not finished: the United States of America; Continent of North America; Western Hemisphere; the Earth; the Solar System; the Universe; the Mind of God—that's what it said on the envelope.

George: What do you know!

Rebecca: And the postman brought it just the same.[13]

Always that loneliness, to which the new astronomy has added a dismay. But in other ages the yearning was endurable; for then men by faith and prayer caught glimpses of a homeland, and were sure that at death they would live at home. Their paradox of loneliness and at-homeness had a certain smart of tension which gave tang to life. But now mankind no longer accepts orthodoxy—which the Church has often made angular and narrow—and can find no hope or nourishment in the nihilism of natural law. Behind our wars is the loss of ultimate Sanction: the wars will not end until the

Sanction is recovered. Behind our weariness, which is not disproved but only underscored by our insistence that we are "having such a good time," is the loss of Horizons: the play will be boring until there is some background of mountains and sky. Behind our restlessness and nervous breakdown is a fear we dare not face—the fear that there *is* no Home, and that we are only driven fugitives of time and dust: the fear will vex us until we find God!

These ills are not cured by pulpit exhortation or psychiatric tinkering, still less by the glittering toys of electricity and steel with which we try to comfort our misgivings, and least of all by naturalistic science. They are cured by prayer, however blind and poor, as a man overcomes weariness by flinging himself helplessly on the bosom of the earth. "We dream alone," wrote Amiel, "we suffer alone, we die alone, we inhabit the last resting-place alone. But there is nothing to prevent us from opening our solitude to God. And so what was an austere monologue becomes dialogue."[14] He wrote truth, for though we suffer together we still suffer alone. "Dialogue" is the faulty word: he should have written "the welcome of Home." Prayer transcends our bickering dogmatisms even more than the science of the future must transcend its sterile cult of law. In prayer, the flinging of our life on God in faith, is the overcoming of our deep nostalgia.

To live worthily we must have rapport with the strange play of event, the intermeshing of personal lives, which science almost overlooks. What *is* the meaning of events? Which happenings shall we seize, and which ignore? Can *our* hands also be given to the weaving? There is no answer until we are in communion with the Weaver! What *is* the purpose of life? Does this planet exist merely as a splinter from the cosmic grinding? Is it created only that it may become extinct, or is it a ladder by which we may climb nearer Christ? There is no answer until we know the Creator! How *can* badness in people, our rampant nationalisms, commercial greeds, and individual perversity, be made good? There is no answer until we drink at primal Springs of Goodness!

How shall the nostalgia of the soul, the terrifying loneliness of the earth, be cured? There is no answer until we
see Home, and hear in distance its welcoming voice!
There can be no new earth without prayer.

In a kindling book about prayer, E. Herman has reminded us of the story of "The Nun of Lyons."[15] She
was dancing at a fashionable ball. None was gayer or
lovelier: her marriage to the most eligible man of her
set was due within a week. Suddenly, in the midst of a
minuet, she saw the vision of the world dying—for lack
of prayer. She could almost hear the world's gasping, as
a drowning man gasps for air. The dance now seemed
macabre, a dance of death. In the corner a priest, smiling and satisfied, discussed the eligibles with a match-
making mother: even the Church did not know that the
world was dying—for want of prayer. As instant as a
leaping altar flame, she vowed her life to ceaseless intercession, and none could dissuade her. She founded a
contemplative order of prayer—lest the world should
die. Was she quite wrong? Was she wrong at all? Or is
our world saved by those who keep the windows open
on another World? Some spiritual watcher of our planet
may have seen our lights extinguished in recent years—
one light for every prayer scorned or forgotten. Will he
soon see lights rekindled, one by one, until the planet is
full of light? A certain pastor, who lives where simple
faith is shadowed by dark persecution, was asked to tell
the secret of his calm endurance. "When the house is
dark," he answered, "I do not try to sweep away darkness with a broom: I light a candle." Prayer is more
than a lighted candle: it is the contagion of health. It is
the pulse of Life.

Chapter I

"THIS GREAT ROUNDABOUT, THE WORLD"

1. *Psychology: Briefer Course,* Henry Holt & Co., 1892, p. 192.
2. Thomas Hobbes, *Leviathan* (1651 ed.), Part I, Chap. 13.
3. *Le problème de la prière,* 2nd ed., Librairie Félix Alcan, Paris, 1932, p. 2. (Trans. mine.)
4. "Instans Tyrannus."
5. Francis Thompson, "Health and Holiness."
6. The Macmillan Co. 1936.
7. Shakespeare, *Twelfth Night,* V, i, 385.
8. Harper & Bros., 1935, Chap. VI, esp. pp. 215, 222.
9. Edwin G. Conklin, retiring president, A.A.A.S. in a speech at America's Annual Parliament of Science, Indianapolis, December 27, 1937; reported in *New York Times,* December 28, 1937.
10. Leo C. Roster, "Men Like War," *Harper's Magazine,* July, 1935; reprinted in *Reader's Digest,* August, 1935.
11. James Thomson, *The Seasons,* "Autumn," 1. 233.
12. Psalm 100:3.
13. Alfred Tennyson, *Harold,* III, ii.
14. Matthew Arnold, "Dover Beach."
15. William Cowper, "The Jackdaw."
16. Alfred A. Knopf, 1927, p. 98.
17. *Ibid.,* p. 99.
18. Rev. Henry Francis Lyte, 1847.
19. Shakespeare, *Hamlet,* I, i, 158.

Chapter II

JESUS AND PRAYER

1. "The Modernist's Quest for God," *Atlantic Monthly*, February, 1926; quoted by William Adams Brown, *The Life of Prayer in a World of Science*, Charles Scribner's Sons, 1928, p. 11.
2. "Thy Kingdom Come," *Yale Review*, XXIV (1935), 430-31.
3. For a fuller discussion, see Chap. III, pp. 43 ff.
4. See Alexander Martin, *The Finality of Jesus for Faith*, Charles Scribner's Sons, 1933, p. 63.
5. Maurice Goguel, *The Life of Jesus*, trans. by Olive Wyon, The Macmillan Co., 1933, p. 580. Used by permission.
6. *Ibid.*, pp. 584-85. (Italics mine.) Used by permission.
7. Luke 11:19.
8. Matthew 16:4.
9. Luke 11:1.
10. Friedrich Heiler, *Prayer*, trans. by Samuel McComb, Oxford University Press, 1932, p. xix.
11. *Ibid.*, p. 292.
12. Matthew 26:39.
13. Matthew 14:23.
14. William Ellery Leonard, Viking Press, 1928.
15. Witter Bynner, "The Poet."
16. Rex Boundy, "A Virile Christ."
17. Matthew 7:7; Luke 11:9; Matthew 17:20; Mark 11:24. See Chaps. IV, X.
19. Mark 11:22.
20. Luke 18:9-14.
21. Luke 18:1-8; 11:5-13.
22. See Chap. V.
23. It is an unfortunate confusion that one part of the Christian Church uses the word "debts" and the other part "trespasses." The original Greek seems to be a little nearer our word "debts," but the difference is slight. Inasmuch as more people use "trespasses" it would seem wise for the whole Church to agree on that word.

24. Our approval of this particular translation by Dr. Torrey need not commit us to his theory that the Gospels were originally written in Aramaic. The weight of present evidence seems to be against the theory.

25. Matthew 17:21; Mark 9:29.

26. Matthew 5:44; Luke 6:28.

27. Luke 22:42.

28. Trans. by R. Farquharson Sharp, IV, xii.

29. *Modern Painters*, VIII, i, 7 f.

30. I John 4:7.

31. John 17:2.

Chapter III

SOME DEFECTIVE THEORIES OF PRAYER

1. Alfred Tennyson, *In Memoriam*, cxxiv.

2. Quoted by Heiler, *op. cit.*, p. 63.

3. The Macmillan Co., 1926, I, 27.

4. *The Everlasting Man*, Dodd, Mead & Co., 1925, pp. 7-23.

5. Mario Puglisi, *Prayer*, trans. by Bernard M. Allen, The Macmillan Co., 1929, p. 88.

6. *Ibid.*, p. 90.

7. George A. Coe, *The Psychology of Religion*, University of Chicago Press, 1917, p. 25n.

8. *The Meaning of God in Human Experience*, Yale University Press, 1928, pp. 49, 50. Used by permission.

9. *The Idea of the Holy*, trans. by Harvey, Oxford University Press, 1923.

10. *Elementary Forms of the Religious Life*, trans. by J. W. Swain, The Macmillan Co., 1912, p. 206.

11. See William E. Hocking, *Human Nature and Its Remaking*, Yale University Press, 1932, esp. pp. 235 ff.

12. Exodus 20:17.

13. James Russell Lowell, "The Present Crisis."

14. Matthew 5:21, 27, 33, 38, 43.

15. *Antigone*, trans. by E. H. Plumptre.

16. Luke 23:40.

17. For a fuller discussion and argument see, for instance, Bronislaw Malinowski, "Magic, Science and Reli-

gion," in *Science, Religion and Reality*, ed. by Joseph Needham, The Macmillan Co., 1925.

18. Matthew 10:26.
19. Psalm 139:23.
20. *The Spirit*, ed. by B. H. Streeter, The Macmillan Co., 1919, pp. 110 f.
21. An interesting recent testimony is given by Richard Cabot and Russell Dicks, *The Art of Ministering to the Sick*, The Macmillan Co., 1936.
22. *The Christian Fact and Modern Doubt*, Charles Scribner's Sons, 1935, esp. Chaps. II, III.
23. See esp. Chaps. V, VI.
24. Luke 23:34.
25. *The Riddle of the World*, Round Table Press, 1938, pp. 127-28.
26. Luke 6:12.

Chapter IV

JESUS' ASSUMPTIONS IN PRAYER

1. Mark 1:15; Matthew 28:19; 9:38; John 7:17.
2. Luke 11:2.
3. John 5:17; 16:23.
4. Tennyson, *In Memoriam*, xcvi.
5. Tennyson, "Vastness."
6. Acts 2:6.
7. John 10:3.
8. Edward FitzGerald, *The Rubáiyát of Omar Khayyám*.
9. A liberty taken with two lines of the famous speech in Shakespeare, *Macbeth*, V, v, 19, 21.
10. Clarence Darrow in the Loeb trial, the record of which can, I believe, be found in the files of the Chicago Criminal Court.
11. Philippians 4:13.
12. Matthew 22:25-32; Mark 12:20-27; Luke 20:29-38.
13. See e.g., *Science and the Modern World*, The Macmillan Co., 1926, Chap. XI, esp. pp. 256 ff.
14. See *Methods of Private Religious Living*, The Macmillan Co., 1929, pp. 46 ff.
15. For a fuller description see Heiler, *op. cit.*, pp. 96 ff.
16. Acts 17:28.

17. Quoted by W. Macneile Dixon, *The Human Situation*, Longmans, Green & Co., 1937, p. 276.

18. See Douglas Clyde Macintosh, *Theology as an Empirical Science*, The Macmillan Co., 1919, pp. 92-98.

19. Francis Thompson, "The Kingdom of God." Used by permission of Dodd, Mead & Co.

20. *Op. cit.*, p. 100.

21. *Ibid.*, pp. 100-1.

22. Genesis 1:10, etc.

23. Shakespeare, *Hamlet*, V, ii, 10.

24. I Corinthians 13:12. The tense of the Greek verb justifies the suggested translation.

25. Psalm 32:8.

26. *The Meaning of God in Human Experience*, p. 284. Used by permission of Yale University Press.

27. Herbert H. Farmer, *The World and God*, Harper & Bros., 1936, pp. 23 ff.

28. Isaiah 55:8, 9.

29. Matthew 24:35; Mark 13:31; Luke 21:33.

30. See Chap. VI.

31. Esther 4:14.

32. Galatians 4:4; Ephesians 1:10.

33. John Milton, *Paradise Lost*, V, 574.

34. Edward Young, *Night Thoughts*, Night V, 1. 176.

35. See W. A. Brown, *op. cit.*, pp. 125 ff.

36. See Chap. X.

37. Hebrews 11:6.

38. *The Meaning of God in Human Experience*, pp. 146-47. Used by permission of Yale University Press.

Chapter V

THE PROBLEM OF PETITIONARY PRAYER

1. Richard Chevenix Trench, "Prayer." (Italics mine.)

2. See esp. Chaps. I, VIII, IX.

3. *Prayer in Christian Theology*, Morehouse Publishing Co., 1927, pp. 5, 7.

4. In Sidney Strong, ed., *We Believe in Prayer*, Coward-McCann, Inc., 1930, p. 187.

5. *Op. cit.*, pp. 241-42.

6. *The Soul's Sincere Desire*, Harper & Bros., 1925, and others of his books.

7. *Op. cit.*, p. 129.

8. Roy Wallace Thomas, *We Pray Thee, Lord*, Abingdon-Cokesbury Press 1937, p. 53. Used by permission.

9. Quoted by Heiler, *op. cit.*, p. 89.

10. Luke 9:24.

11. Thomas, *op. cit.*, p. 41.

12. Edna St. Vincent Millay, "God's World," in *Renascence and Other Poems*, Harper & Bros. Copyright 1917 by Edna St. Vincent Millay. Used by permission.

13. Charles Wesley, "Jesus, Lover of My Soul," 1740.

14. See also pp. 43 ff.

15. Strong, ed., *op. cit.*, p. 95.

16. Matthew 8:25.

17. John 1:14.

18. Quoted by S. H. Mellone, "Prayer and Experience," in *The Power of Prayer*, ed. by W. P. Patterson and David Russell, The Macmillan Co., 1920, p. 87.

19. I am indebted for this suggestion to Thomas, *op. cit.*, p. 47. Quoted from Mark Twain, *The Adventurers of Huckleberry Finn*.

20. Tennyson, *In Memoriam*, vi.

21. John 14:14; 15:7. (Italics mine.)

22. E.G., Mark 11:23, 24, and parallel passages.

23. *The Life of Trust*, Thomas Y. Crowell Co., 1898.

24. Quoted by Mellone, *op. cit.*, p. 101.

25. Quoted by Heiler, *op. cit.*, 278.

26. *Ibid.*, p. 279.

27. Strong, ed., *op. cit.*, p. 114.

28. Psalm 34:6.

29. Young, *Night Thoughts*, Night VIII, 1, 721.

30. Isaiah 63:9.

31. Romans 11:33.

32. *Op. cit.*, p. 283n.

Chapter VI

PETITIONARY PRAYER AND NATURAL LAW

1. "Saul," xvii.

2. William Blake, "The Grey Monk," st. 10.

3. Quoted by W. R. Sorley, *Moral Values and the Idea of God,* The Macmillan Co., 1921, p. 248.
4. Francis Thompson, "The Hound of Heaven." Used by permission of Dodd, Mead & Co.
5. See Chap. V, p. 81.
6. Karl R. Stolz, *The Psychology of Prayer,* Abingdon Press, 1923, p. 153.
7. A. & C. Boni, 1927.
8. *Op. cit.,* p. 517. (Trans. mine.)
9. E.g., Mellone, *op. cit.*
10. "God's World," in *Renascence and Other Poems,* Harper & Bros. Copyright, 1917, by Edna St. Vincent Millay. Used by permission.
11. Percy Bysshe Shelley, "Adonais," st. 52.
12. See Chap. IV.
13. Matthew 7:11.
14. For a similar discussion, slightly different in approach, see Farmer, *op. cit.,* esp. Chaps. VII, IX, X.
15. Quoted by Puglisi, *op. cit.,* p. 6. Puglisi himself would rule out petitionary prayer.
16. *Op. cit.,* pp. 520-21.
17. Elizabeth Barrett Browning, *Aurora Leigh,* II, 952 ff.
18. E.g., *The Soul's Sincere Desire.*

Chapter VII

THE PROBLEM OF INTERCESSORY PRAYER

1. Thomas, *op. cit.,* pp. 25-32.
2. *Op. cit.,* e.g., p. 329.
3. "De Profundis," Greeting I, ll. 1ff.
4. Robert Frost, "Mending Wall," from *North of Boston,* Henry Holt & Co., 1915. Used by permission.
5. *Sonnets from the Portuguese,* xliii.
6. *Alcestis,* trans. by A. S. Way, ll. 163 ff.
7. Quoted by Heiler, *op. cit.,* p. 80.
8. *Ibid.,* p. 291.
9. Exodus 32:32.
10. Quoted by Puglisi, *op. cit.,* pp. 201ff.
11. See Strong, ed., *op. cit.,* p. 46.
12. I Corinthians 12:12; Ephesians 4:25.
13. *Op. cit.,* p. 196.

14. Luke 22:32.
15. Matthew 19:13.
16. John 11:42.
17. Matthew 5:44; Luke 6:28.
18. Matthew 9:38; Luke 10:2.
19. John 17:20.
20. E.g., Ephesians 3:14-21.
21. Frederic W. H. Myers, *Saint Paul,* The Macmillan Co., 1928, p. 44. Used by permission.
22. George S. Stewart, *The Lower Levels of Prayer,* Abingdon-Cokesbury Press, 1940, pp. 91-92. Used by permission.
23. Psalm 118:23.
24. *Op. cit.,* pp. 137 f.
25. Edwin F. Dakin, *Mrs. Eddy,* Charles Scribner's Sons, 1929. See Index.
26. William Wordsworth, "The Solitary Reaper."
27. John Masefield, "The Widow in the Bye Street," in *Poems,* the Macmillan Co., 1923. Used by permission.
28. Romans 11:34, 36.
29. *Robert Burns and Mrs. Dunlop,* ed. by William Wallace, Dodd, Mead & Co., 1898, I, 192.
30. John 17:19.
31. Quoted by E. Herman, *Creative Prayer,* Doran, 1921, p. 186.
32. Strong, ed., *op. cit.,* p. 53.
33. *Ibid.,* p. 158.
34. *Ibid.,* p. 68.
35. "Saul," xvii, xviii.
36. In *Collected Poems,* The Macmillan Co., 1924. Used by permission.

Chapter VIII

THE BOUNDS AND BOUNDLESSNESS OF PRAYER

1. Reynal & Hitchcock, 1937. See esp. p. 403. We are not necessarily commending the book. It is interesting and valuable as a psychological study of the evolution of a skeptic, and as a footnote on the harm done

by a narrow conservatism in religion, but decidedly overrated as a contribution to religious thinking.

2. There is a similar comment in George Canning, *New Morality*.

3. Matthew 17:20; Mark 11:23; Luke 17:6.

4. Reported by F. O. Beck, *The American Journal of Religous Psychology and Education*, II, 118; quoted by Stolz, *op. cit.*, p. 158.

5. Psalm 36:6.

6. Matthew 12:39; 16:4.

7. Matthew 24:20; Mark 13:18.

8. *Op cit.*, p. 397.

9. By Antoine de Saint Exupéry, Reynal & Hitchcock, 1939, pp. 20, 55.

10. Psalm 104:23.

11. Shakespeare, *As You Like It*, II, vii, 142.

12. William Blake, "Auguries of Innocence."

13. *Op. cit.*, p. 211. Used by permission of The Macmillan Co., publishers.

14. Henry Wadsworth Longfellow, "The Village Blacksmith."

15. John 5:17.

16. Thomas Carlyle, *Past and Present*, III, xi.

17. Constant C. Vigil, *El Erial*, trans. by F. Testena, 1924; quoted by Puglisi, *op. cit.*, p. 212.

18. Matthew 22:37; Mark 12:30; Luke 10:27.

19. "Morte d'Arthur."

20. Second Inaugural Address, March 4, 1865.

21. A letter by Chester Warner, "Are Peace Prayers Too Late?" *The Christian Century*, September 20, 1939.

22. Luke 23:42, 43.

23. II Corinthians 6:1.

24. John 14:13. (Italics mine.)

25. Luke 22:42.

26. John 4:34.

27. FitzGerald, *The Rubáiyát of Omar Khayyám*.

28. Psalm 19:12.

29. Rev. Robin Adair, formerly of New Zealand, more recently resident in New York City.

30. II Corinthians 12:9.

Chapter IX

PRAYER AND OUR WANDERING ATTENTION

1. See Chap. V, note 1.
2. Matthew 6:27; Luke 12:25.
3. Ecclesiastes 9:2.
4. Matthew 14:2.
5. See Chap. VI for a fuller discussion of the defects of science as a world-view.
6. I Corinthians 2:13, 14.
7. *Psychology, an Elementary Textbook*, trans. and ed. by Max Meyer, D. C. Heath and Co., 1908, p. 9.
8. See Walter B. Pillsbury, *Attention*, George Allen & Unwin, London, 1908, p. 1.
9. "Happy Thought," in *A Child's Garden of Verses*.
10. J. G. Morris, *Quaint Sayings and Doings of Luther*, United Lutheran Publishing House, 1912, p. 131; quoted by Stolz, *op. cit.*, p. 52.
11. Gardner Murphy, *General Psychology*, Harper & Bros., 1933, pp. 221 ff.
12. Matthew 6:6.
13. Mentioned by Murphy, *op. cit.*, p. 318.
14. *Belief Unbound*, Yale University Press, 1930, p. 7; quoted by John Baillie, *And the Life Everlasting*, Charles Scribner's Sons, 1933, p. 192.
15. Philippians 3:13, 14.
16. Pillsbury, *loc. cit.*
17. *Journals of Søren Kierkegaard*, trans. and ed. by Alexander Dru, Oxford University Press, 1938, p. 36. Used by permission.
18. See Edward S. Robinson, *Man as Psychology Sees Him*, The Macmillan Co., 1934, esp. pp. 116, 117.
19. These rules are set forth in straightforward fashion by Murphy, *op. cit.*, pp. 214 ff., 226, 306.
20. See Chap. X for a discussion of the nature and meaning of faith.
21. II Corinthians 5:14.
22. In this teaching Alexander F. Shand has been pioneer, e.g., *The Foundations of Character*, The Macmillan Co., 1914.

23. Alfred Tennyson, *Idylls of the King*, "Lancelot and Elaine," 11. 871 f.

24. Matthew 22:37; Mark 12:30; Luke 10:27.

25. Psychologists disagree concerning this list of factors: e.g., John B. Watson, *Behavior, an Introduction to Comparative Psychology*, Henry Holt & Co., 1914; Edward L. Thorndike, *Animal Intelligence*, The Macmillan Co., 1911.

26. *The Principles of Psychology*, Henry Holt & Co., 1890, I, 120 ff.

27. Romans 7:19.

28. For a helpful chapter on this issue and a helpful book on the whole issue of the practice of prayer, see Stewart, *op. cit.*, esp. pp. 47-61.

29. Shakespeare, *Richard the Second*, I, iii, 294.

30. Romans 7:19, 24, 25.

31. Philippians 4:7-9.

Chapter X

PRAYER, SUGGESTION, AND FAITH

1. A paper, "The Faith That Heals," quoted in Harvey Cushing, *Life of Sir William Osler*, Clarendon Press, Oxford, 1925, II, 222.

2. Matthew 9:28.

3. E.G., Matthew 9:22.

4. Luke 18:8.

5. II Timothy 4:7.

6. G. K. Chesterton, "The House of Christmas," *Collected Poems*, Dodd, Mead & Co., 1939. Used by permission.

7. Oliver Wendell Holmes, "The Chambered Nautilus."

8. *Lalla Rookh*, "The Veiled Prophet of Khorassan," Part II.

9. Hebrews 11:1.

10. Hebrews 11:8, 10.

11. Hebrews 11:24, 25.

12. *The Excursion*, IV, 1925.

13. *The Little White Bird*, Chap. IX.

14. Job 23:3.

15. See Chap. IV, pp. 58 ff., for fuller discussion of these signs whereby we apprehend God as personal.
16. Hebrews 12:2.
17. *Op. cit.*, p. 43.
18. Luke 12:57.
19. *Modern Man in Search of a Soul*, trans. by W. S. Dell and Cary F. Baynes, Harcourt, Brace & Co., 1933, p. 224.
20. G. P. Putnam's Sons, 1939, pp. 451 f. Used by permission.
21. *Paracelsus*, I, 830-832.
22. George Santayana, "O World, Thou Choosest Not the Better Part!" Used by permission of Charles Scribner's Sons.
23. Mark 9:24; John 9:38.
24. Acts 10.
25. By Dale Carnegie, Simon and Schuster, 1936.
26. Psalm 23:3.
27. Revelation 22:4.
28. *The Subconscious,* Houghton Mifflin Co., 1906, p. 99.
29. Alfred Tennyson, *Enoch Arden.*
30. Psalm 100:3.
31. Sidney Lanier, "A Ballad of Trees and the Master," 1880.
32. Alfred Tennyson, "The Higher Pantheism."
33. Franz Werfel, *Embezzled Heaven,* Viking Press, 1940, p. 73.
34. James 2:20.

Chapter XI

PRAYER, INSTINCT, AND MOTIVE

1. See the James-Lange theory of emotion, William James, *Principles of Psychology,* Henry Holt & Co., 1890, II, 449-53.
2. *Human Nature and Its Remaking,* pp. 72 ff. For further examples the reader should consult William McDougall, *Social Psychology,* Methuen & Co., 1908; a list of man's instincts will be found on pp. 43-76.
3. Jeremiah 17:9.

 4. Luke 24:29.
 5. *Pastoral Psychology*, rev. ed., Abingdon-Cokesbury Press, 1940, pp. 130 ff.
 6. *Psychology and Morals*, Robert McBride & Co., 1933, pp. 25-54.
 7. Milton, *Paradise Lost*, II, 112. This is adopting a sentence in which Aristophanes criticizes the philosophy of Socrates.
 8. *Why Not Try God?* H. C. Kinsey & Co., 1934.
 9. John 2:25.
10. Matthew 5:21, 22.
11. Luke 12:13, 15.
12. Luke 5:8.
13. Luke 23:28.
14. Psalm 36:9.
15. By Zsolt de Harsanyi, trans. by Paul Tabor, G. P. Putnam's Sons, 1939, pp., 254-56.
16. *Human Nature and Its Remaking*, p. 37.
17. *Op. cit.*, pp. 35-38.
18. Edward Sandford Martin, "Mixed," *A Little Brother of the Rich and Other Verse*, Charles Scribner's Sons, 1895. Used by permission.
19. *Op. cit.*, p. 81.
20. Romans 7:19, 24.
21. William Wordsworth, "Expostulation and Reply."
22. Hebrews 11:27.
23. Ernest Raymond, *In the Steps of St. Francis*, H. C. Kinsey & Co., 1939, pp. 105 ff.
24. *Ibid.*, pp. 321 ff.
25. Matthew Arnold, "East London."
26. Psalm 139:23, 24.

Chapter XII

PRAYER, MEMORY, AND THE SUBCONSCIOUS

 1. *Thoughts on Life and Death*, Harper & Bros., 1937, pp. 65, 71.
 2. *Confessions*, X, 15.
 3. "Intimations of Immortality," st. 5.
 4. E.g., Murphy, *op. cit.*, pp. 299-374.
 5. This phrase comes almost certainly from a novel by A.

S. M. Hutchison, though I have not been able to trace it.

6. Repressed evil memory is discussed more fully in Chap. XIV.

7. Illustration from John B. Watson, "The Psychology of Wish Fulfillment," *Scientific Monthly*, III, 481; quoted by E. S. and F. R. Robinson, *Readings in General Psychology*, University of Chicago Press, 1923, p. 704.

8. *The Freudian Wish and Its Place in Ethics*, Henry Holt & Co., 1915, p. 23.

9. *The Integration of the Personality*, trans. by Stanley Dell, Farrar and Rinehart, 1939, p. 13.

10. *Op. cit.*, p. 199.

11. *Op. cit.*, p. 17.

12. Psalm 27:1.

13. Matthew 4:4, 7, 10, and parallel passages.

14. Psalm 145:2.

15. John 14:2, with one word properly changed.

16. I John 4:18.

17. Stolz, *The Psychology of Prayer*, p. 98.

18. Quoted by Robinson, *op. cit.*, p. 125.

19. Psalm 62:5.

20. For fuller discussion of this question see Chap. XIII.

21. *Pastoral Psychology*, p. 135.

22. *Op. cit.*, p. 16.

23. *Thoughts on Life and Death*, p. 80.

24. Psalm 27:1.

25. Psalm 51:6.

Chapter XIII

PRAYER, IMAGINATON, AND THOUGHT

1. *Paradise Lost*, I, 17-26.

2. "Essay on Shelley."

3. "Epistle to Mrs. Scott."

4. John Masefield, "Waste," in *Poems*, The Macmillan Co., 1923. Used by permission.

5. John Masefield, "The Seekers," *ibid*. Used by permission.

6. Philippians 3:10.

7. Romans 7:24. (Change in wording is mine.)
8. Alfred Tennyson, "Locksley Hall," 1. 76.
9. See esp. Chap. IV.
10. See the experiments of Oswald Külpe, as reported by Robinson, *op. cit.*, pp. 134 ff.
11. Harald Höffding, *Outlines of Psychology,* trans. by Mary E. Lowndes, The Macmillan Co., 1891, pp. 172 ff.
12. These contentions are amplified by Hocking, *Human Nature and Its Remaking,* pp. 41 ff., 105 ff.
13. Herbert Sydney Langfeld, "Concerning the Image," *Psychological Review,* XXIII (1916), 180-82; reported in Robinson and Robinson, *op. cit.*, p. 508.
14. *How We Think,* D. C. Heath & Co., 1909, esp. pp. 68 ff.
15. Rev. Samuel Johnson, "Father, in Thy Mysterious Presence Kneeling," 1846.
16. Judges 13:2-25.
17. Similar instances are given by Stolz, *The Psychology of Prayer,* pp. 116-23.
18. Edward S. Robinson, *Practical Psychology,* The Macmillan Co., 1926, pp. 311, 312; Robinson and Robinson, *op. cit.*, pp. 470-71.
19. Quoted from two letters to his patron, Mr. Butts, written April 25, 1803, and July 6, 1803; Alexander Gilchrist, *Life of William Blake,* II, 192, 194.
20. *Man as Psychology Sees Him*, p. 126.
21. William Wordsworth, "Elegiac Stanzas, Suggested by a Picture of Peele Castle, in a Storm, Painted by Sir George Beaumont."
22. Matthew 26:39.
23. Matthew 26:46.

Chapter XIV

PRAYER AND CONSCIENCE

1. January 29, 1940, p. 5.
2. Columbia University Press, 1920, p. 202; quoted by Hocking, *Human Nature and Its Remaking,* p. 114.
3. *Ibid.*, p. 118.
4. Shakespeare, *Hamlet,* III, iii, 52-65.

5. *Op. cit.*, p. 48.
6. *Human Nature and Its Remaking*, p. 123.
7. *Ibid.*, p. 122.
8. Psalm 139:1.
9. Clifford E. Barbour, *Sin and the New Psychology*, Abingdon, 1930, p. 107.
10. Isaiah 1:5,6.
11. Exodus 20:17.
12. Luke 12:2.
13. Psalm 25:7; 51:2.
14. *Op. cit.*, pp. 210 ff.
15. Phrases quoted from Psalm 139.
16. "The Widow in the Bye Street," in *Poems*, The Macmillan Co., 1923. Used by permission.
17. Margaret Widdemer, "Barter," in *Collected Poems*. Copyright, 1928, by Harcourt, Brace & Co. Used by permission.
18. Augustus M. Toplady, "Rock of Ages," 1776.
19. Galatians 2:20.

Chapter XV

PERSONALITY AND PRAYER'S MOODS

1. Shakespeare, *Hamlet*, III, i, 63.
2. Charles Dickens, *A Christmas Carol*.
3. *The Letters of Katherine Mansfield*, ed. by J. Middleton Murry, Alfred A. Knopf, 1929, II, 389 (a letter written in 1921); quoted by Henry Sloane Coffin, *What Men Are Asking*, Cokesbury, 1933, p. 26.
4. Browning, "Saul," ix.
5. Job 38:7.
6. Psalm 118:1,8; Matthew 26:30; Mark 14:26.
7. "Biography," in *Poems*, The Macmillan Co., 1923. Used by permission.
8. Ecclesiasticus 39:2.
9. I John 4:18.
10. Shakespeare, *Macbeth*, IV, iii, 209.
11. Deuteronomy 33:27.
12. I John 4:18.
13. *Op. cit.*, p. 292. (Trans. mine.)
14. *Ibid.*, p. 9. (Trans. mine.)

15. E.g., the one to the Emperor Theodosius demanding
    that the synagogues should not be restored to the
    Jews.
16. Shakespeare, *Henry the Eighth*, III, ii, 443.
17. Job 42:10.
18. I John 4:16.
19. *La Sagesse et la Destinée*, Paris, 1908, pp. 212-13;
    quoted in Ménégoz, *op. cit.*, 531-32: (Trans. mine.)
20. The classic studies in mysticism are still probably Wil-
    liam R. Inge, *Christian Mysticism*, London, 1899;
    Evelyn Underhill, *Mysticism*, Methuen & Co., Lon-
    don, 1912.
21. Luke 22:42, and parallel passages.
22. Matthew 26:39.
23. II Samuel 23:16,17; I Chronicles 11:18,19.

Chapter XVI

PERSONALITY AND PRAYER'S FORMS

1. Psalm 141:2.
2. John Donne, "An Anatomie of the World."
3. Romans 1:20.
4. *Paradise Lost*, V, 574-76.
5. *Op. cit.*, pp. 74, 76, 88. Used by permission of The
   Macmillan Co. publishers.
6. Exodus 20:4,5.
7. II Kings 18:4.
8. Micah 6:8.
9. Matthew 23:25.
10. "The Idol," in *Immanence*, E. P. Dutton & Co., 1912,
    p. 30. Used by permission.
11. *Defensio pro populo*.
12. *Idylls of the King*, "Balin and Balan."
13. II Kings 5:17, 18.
14. John Masefield, "Biography," in *Poems*, The Macmil-
    lan Co., 1923 Used by permission.
15. Sabine Baring-Gould, 1865.
16. Puglisi, *op. cit.*, pp. 79 ff.
17. James Russell Lowell, "The Present Crisis."
18. Tennyson, "Morte d'Arthur," 1. 408.

19. Matthew 14:23, and similar passages; also Mark 11:19.
20. Matthew 19:15; Mark 6:5; Luke 4:40.
21. Matthew 3:15.
22. See Chap. XIX.
23. *Vision and Authority*, rev. ed., Harper & Bros., 1929, Chap. IX.
24. II Corinthians 3:6.

Chapter XVII

PERSONALITY AND CORPORATE PRAYER

1. Revelation 12:12.
2. Proverbs 14:10.
3. Luke 15:6.
4. Choruses from "The Rock," *Collected Poems*, Harcourt, Brace & Co., p. 188.
5. William L. Shirer, *Berlin Diary*, Alfred A. Knopf, 1941, pp. 17 ff, has a fascinating account of a Hitler demonstration with its deliberate employment of music and pageantry to whip up fanatic zeal.
6. William Wordsworth, "Lines Composed a Few Miles Above Tintern Abbey," 1. 52.
7. See Chap. III.
8. E.g., Fritz Kunkel and Roy E. Dickerson, *How Character Develops*, Charles Scribner's Sons, 1940, to which book this chapter is much indebted.
9. *Ibid.*, pp. 26-27. Used by permission.
10. *Action*, Chatto and Windus, London, 1928, pp. 1 ff.
11. Genesis 1:11.
12. Heiler, *op. cit.*, p. 321.
13. Bernard of Cluny, twelfth century, trans. by J. M. Neale.
14. Shakespeare, *Measure for Measure*, V, i, 12.
15. Nina Feodorov, *The Family*, Little, Brown & Co., 1940.
16. Rev. Godfrey Thring, "O God of Mercy, God of Might," 1877.
17. Matthew 18:20.
18. Mark 11:17.
19. Matthew 6:20; Luke 12:33.

Chapter XVIII

A WAY OF PRIVATE PRAYER

1. Luke 11:1.
2. Matthew 6:9.
3. Romans 8:16.
4. This illustration comes from John Oman, *Vision and Authority,* Harper & Bros., 1929, pp. 48 ff.
5. Matthew 6:6: (A.R.V.)
6. Mark 1:35.
7. Psalm 46:10.
8. Bergstrom, *American Journal of Psychology,* VI, 267; mentioned by Edward S. Robinson, "The Sources of Original Thought," in Robinson and Robinson, *op. cit.,* p. 473.
9. Shakespeare, *Macbeth,* III, ii, 55.
10. Pp. 143-44. Used by permission of Abingdon-Cokesbury Press.
11. The Macmillan Co., 1939, p. 3. Used by permission.
12. The correct translation of Philippians 4:13.
13. Ephesians 4:26.
14. Psalms 127:2.
15. John 8:12.
16. I John 1:5.
17. Psalm 16:8.
18. Matthew 6:9.
19. Matthew 21:22.
20. Sarah F. Adams, "Nearer, My God, to Thee," 1841.
21. Hebrews 11:6.
22. Johnson Oatman, Jr., "Count Your Blessings."
23. Stewart, *op. cit.,* p. 97.
24. Alfred Tennyson, *Idylls of the King,* "The Holy Grail."
25. *The Book of Common Prayer,* Order of Morning Prayer.
26. John 10:3.
27. Matthew 5:44; Luke 6:28.
28. Philippians 4:6. (Change mine.)
29. Luke 22:42.
30. Hosea 14:2.
31. Luke 18:1. (Trans. mine.)

32. Psalm 136:1,16.
33. *Op. cit.*, pp. 53, 55.
34. Robert Browning, "Memorabilia."
35. Masnavi I Ma'navi, *The Spiritual Couplets of Jalálu-'D-Din Rúmí*, trans. and abridged by E. H. Whinefield, Trübner & Co., London, 1887, II, vii, 82.

Chapter XIX

A WAY OF CORPORATE PRAYER

1. Matthew 18:20.
2. Acts 6:2.
3. Robbins W. Barstow, *Getting Acquainted with God*, The Macmillan Co., 1928, pp. 80-81. The prayer is adapted from a morning prayer in Walter Rauschenbusch, *Prayers of the Social Awakening*, The Pilgrim Press, 1925. Used by permission.
4. Acts 1:14.
5. Acts 2:6.
6. Luke 2:27.
7. Numbers 6:24-26.
8. Psalm 130:1.
9. William W. S. Howe, 1864.
10. Francis Thompson, "The Hound of Heaven." Used by permission of Dodd, Mead & Co.
11. I Kings 8:27-30.
12. John 10:9.
13. The sentences in italics are from St. Francis, "The Canticle of the Sun," which also suggested the form of the prayer. There is a phrase from Psalm 145:16 in the first paragraph, from Philippians 3:10 in the fifth paragraph, and from James 1:17 and II Corinthians 8:9 in the sixth paragraph.
14. Ezekiel 37:1-14.
15. Doran, 1921.
16. Association Press, 1916.
17. Abingdon-Cokesbury Press, 1939.
18. Charles Scribner's Sons, 1939.
19. The Macmillan Co., 1939.
20. This form, sometimes called guided prayer, is old. See

The Book of Common Prayer, in the section entitled "Prayers and Thanksgivings."

21. J. M. Dent & Sons, 1924.
22. Presbyterian Board of Christian Education, 1932.
23. George Croly, 1854.
24. Gilbert K. Chesterton.
25. Exodus 20:8.
26. *Op. cit.,* p. 307.
27. *Reality in Worship,* The Macmillan Co., 1925, p. 324.
28. See Evelyn Underhill, *Worship,* Harper & Bros., 1937, esp. pp. 120-62.
29. Charles Scribner's Sons, 1934.
30. Tennyson, *Idylls of the King,* "The Holy Grail."

Chapter XX

PRAYER AND THE NEW WORLD

1. Isaac Watts, 1719.
2. *Final Memorials of Henry Wadsworth Longfellow,* ed. by Samuel Longfellow, Ticknor & Co., 1887, p. 382.
3. Carrick and Evans, Inc., 1940.
4. Elizabeth Barrett Browning, *Aurora Leigh,* II, 952.
5. Stewart, *op. cit.,* p. 162.
6. Charles Scribner's Sons, 1922, II, ii.
7. Luke 14:26.
8. Shakespeare, *Hamlet,* V, i, 236.
9. This is from memory. I can only crave the indulgence of the unknown author.
10. Henrik Ibsen, *Peer Gynt,* trans. by William and Charles Arthur, Charles Scribner's Sons, 1911, IV, i. Used by permission.
11. *Ibid.,* IV, ii. Used by permission.
12. Gilbert K. Chesterton, "The House of Christmas," *Collected Poems,* Dodd, Mead & Co., 1939. Used by permission.
13. By Thornton Wilder. Copyright, 1938, by Coward-McCann, Inc., publishers. Used by permission.
14. Henri Frédéric Amiel, *Journal Intime,* trans. by Mrs. Humphrey Ward, Brentano's, 1928, p. 388.
15. *Creative Prayer,* Doran, 1921, p. 15 ff.

INDEX